W9-CCA-575

PRAISE FOR
THE SOUL'S CODE
BY JAMES HILLMAN

THE SOUL'S CODE

THE
SOUL'S
CODE

IN SEARCH OF
CHARACTER
AND CALLING

JAMES HILLMAN

WARNER BOOKS

A Time Warner Company

Warner Books Edition
Copyright © 1996 by James Hillman
All rights reserved.

This Warner Books edition is published by arrangement with Random House, New York, NY

Warner Books, Inc., 1271 Avenue of the Americas, New York, NY 10020
Visit our Web site at
http://warnerbooks.com

 A Time Warner Company

Printed in the United States of America

First Warner Books Printing: October 1997

10 9 8 7 6 5 4 3 2 1

Library of Congress Cataloging-in-Publication Data

Hillman, James.
    The soul's code : in search of character and calling / James Hillman.
        p.   cm.
    Originally published: New York : Random House, 1996.
    Includes bibliographical references and index.
    ISBN 0-446-67371-4
    1. Individuality. 2. Individuality in children. 3. Fate and fatalism. 4. Gifted persons. I. Title
[BF697.H46 1997]
150—dc21   97-8702
                                                CIP

Cover design by Andy Carpenter
Cover photo by Marc Tauss

For four daimones:
Baby Joo, Cookie, Mutz, and Boizie

EPIGRAPHS IN LIEU
OF A PREFACE

. . . genius can be bounded in a nutshell and yet embrace the whole fullness of life.

—Thomas Mann

If life has a base that it stands upon . . . then my [life] without a doubt stands upon this memory. It is of lying half asleep, half awake, in bed in the nursery of St. Ives. It is of hearing the waves . . . breaking, one, two, one, two, behind a yellow blind. It is of hearing the blind draw its little acorn across the floor as the wind blew the blind out. It is of lying and hearing . . . and feeling, it is almost impossible that I should be here . . .

—Virginia Woolf, "A Sketch of the Past"

Coming into this particular body, and being born of these particular parents, and in such a place, and in general what we call external circumstances. That all happenings form a unity and are spun together is signified by the Fates [*Moirai*].

—Plotinus, II.3.15

Moira? the finished shape of our fate, the line drawn round it. It is the task the gods allot us, and the share of glory they allow; the limits we must not pass; and our appointed end. Moira is all these.

—Mary Renault, *The King Must Die*

When all the souls had chosen their lives, they went before Lachesis. And she sent with each, as the guardian of his life and the fulfiller of his choice, the daimon that he had chosen, and this divinity led the soul first to Clotho, under her hand and her turning of the spindle to ratify the destiny of his lot and choice, and after contact with her, the daimon again led the soul to the spinning of Atropos to make the web of its destiny irreversible, and then without a backward look it passed beneath the throne of Necessity.

 —Plato, *Republic* X, 620e

In the final analysis, we count for something only because of the essential we embody, and if we do not embody that, life is wasted.

 —C. G. Jung

Of course, you can argue with the proposition that all we are is . . . genes and environment. You can insist that there's . . . something *more*. But if you try to visualize the form this something would take, or articulate it clearly, you'll find the task impossible, for any force that is not in the genes or the environment is outside of physical reality as we perceive it. It's beyond scientific discourse. . . . This doesn't mean it doesn't exist.

 —Robert Wright, *The Moral Animal*

Meaning is invisible, but the invisible is not contradictory of the visible: the visible itself has an invisible inner framework, and the in-visible is the secret counterpart of the visible.

 —M. Merleau-Ponty, *Working Notes*

Neither in environment nor in heredity can I find the exact instrument that fashioned me, the anonymous roller that passed upon my life a certain intricate watermark whose unique design becomes visible when the lamp of art is made to shine through life's foolscap.

 —Vladimir Nabokov, *Speak, Memory*

Scientists have been unable to discover many profound principles that relate the action of mothers, fathers, or siblings to psychological characteristics in the child.

—Jerome Kagan, *The Nature of the Child*

The so-called traumatic experience is not an accident, but the opportunity for which the child has been patiently waiting—had it not occurred, it would have found another, equally trivial—in order to find a necessity and direction for its existence, in order that its life may become a serious matter.

—W. H. Auden

One always learns one's mystery at the price of one's innocence.

—Robertson Davies, *Fifth Business*

Because they have so little, children must rely on imagination rather than experience.

—Eleanor Roosevelt, *You Learn by Living*

There is neither beginning nor end to the imagination but it delights in its own seasons reversing the usual order at will.

—William Carlos Williams, *Kora in Hell*

It was Karl Marx, I think, who once proposed that evolution be studied in reverse, with an eye firmly fixed on the evolved species while glancing backward for hints.

—Jerome Bruner, *In Search of Mind*

I don't develop; I am.

—Pablo Picasso

Even before reason there is the inward movement which reaches out towards its own.

—Plotinus, III.4.6

In every artist's development the germ of the later work is always found in the earlier. The nucleus around which the artist's intellect builds his work is himself . . . and this changes little from birth to death.

The only real influence I've ever had was myself.

—Edward Hopper

Adolescents sense a secret, unique greatness in themselves that seeks expression. They gesture toward the heart when trying to express any of this, a significant clue to the whole affair.

—Joseph Chilton Pearce, *Evolutions End*

I wish that you know all that I think about Genius and the Heart.

—John Keats, *Letters*

Is that what they call a vocation, what you do with joy as if you had fire in your heart, the devil in your body?

—Josephine Baker

A method that fits the small work but not the great has obviously started at the wrong end. . . . It seems to be a lesson of history that the commonplace may be understood as a reduction of the exceptional, but the exceptional cannot be understood by amplifying the commonplace. Both logically and causally the exceptional is crucial because it introduces (however strange it may sound) the more comprehensive category.

—Edgar Wind, "An Observation on Method"

CONTENTS

Epigraphs in Lieu of a Preface ix

1. In a Nutshell: The Acorn Theory
   and the Redemption of Psychology 3

2. Growing Down 41

3. The Parental Fallacy 63

4. Back to the Invisibles 92

5. *"Esse* Is *Percipi"*: To Be Is to Be Perceived 113

6. Neither Nature nor Nurture—Something Else . . 128

7. Penny Dreadfuls and Pure Fantasy 155

8. Disguise 172

9. Fate 191

10. The Bad Seed 214

11. Mediocrity 249

Coda: A Note on Methodology 275

Notes 287

Bibliography 307

Index 321

THE SOUL'S CODE

— 🜨 —

CHAPTER 1

IN A NUTSHELL:
THE ACORN THEORY
AND THE REDEMPTION
OF PSYCHOLOGY

There is more in a human life than our theories of it allow. Sooner or later something seems to call us onto a particular path. You may remember this "something" as a signal moment in childhood when an urge out of nowhere, a fascination, a peculiar turn of events struck like an annunciation: This is what I must do, this is what I've got to have. This is who I am.

This book is about that call.

If not this vivid or sure, the call may have been more like gentle pushings in the stream in which you drifted unknowingly to a particular spot on the bank. Looking back, you sense that fate had a hand in it.

This book is about that sense of fate.

These kinds of annunciations and recollections determine biography as strongly as memories of abusive horror; but these more enigmatic moments tend to be shelved. Our theories favor traumas setting us the task of working them through. Despite early injury and all the slings and arrows of outrageous fortune, we bear from the start the image of a definite individual character with some enduring traits.

This book is about that power of character.

Because the "traumatic" view of early years so controls psychological theory of personality and its development, the focus of our rememberings and the language of our personal storytelling have already been infiltrated by the toxins of these theories. Our lives may be determined less by our childhood than by the way we have learned to imagine our childhoods. We are, this book shall maintain, less damaged by the traumas of childhood than by the traumatic way we remember childhood as a time of unnecessary and externally caused calamities that wrongly shaped us.

So this book wants to repair some of that damage by showing what else was there, is there, in your nature. It wants to resurrect the unaccountable twists that turned your boat around in the eddies and shallows of meaninglessness, bringing you back to feelings of destiny. For that is what is lost in so many lives, and what must be recovered: a sense of personal calling, that there is a reason I am alive.

Not the reason to live; not the meaning of life in general or a philosophy of religious faith—this book does not pretend to provide such answers. But it does speak to the feelings that there is a reason my unique person is here and that there are things I must attend to beyond the daily round and that give the daily round its reason, feelings that the world somehow wants me to be here, that I am answerable to an innate image, which I am filling out in my biography.

That innate image is also the subject of this book, as it is the subject of every biography—and we will encounter many biographies throughout these pages. The biography question haunts our Western subjectivity, as its immersion in therapies of self show. Everyone in therapy, or affected by therapeutic reflection even as diluted by the tears of TV-talk, is in search of an adequate biography: How do I put together into a coherent image the pieces of my life? How do I find the basic plot of my story?

To uncover the innate image we must set aside the psychological frames that are usually used, and mostly used up. They do not reveal enough. They trim a life to fit the frame: developmental growth, step by step, from infancy, through troubled youth, to midlife crisis and aging, to death. Plodding your way through an already planned map, you are on an itinerary that tells you where you have been before you get there, or like an averaged statistic foretold by an actuary in an insurance company. The course of your life has been described in the future perfect tense. Or, if not the predictable highway, then the offbeat "journey," accumulating and shedding incidents without pattern, itemizing events for a résumé organized only by chronology: This came after That. Such a life is a narrative without plot, its focus on a more and more boring central figure, "me," wandering in the desert of dried-out "experiences."

I believe we have been robbed of our true biography— that destiny written into the acorn—and we go to therapy to recover it. That innate image can't be found, however, until we have a psychological theory that grants primary psychological reality to the call of fate. Otherwise your identity continues to be that of a sociological consumer determined by random statistics, and the unacknowledged daimon's urgings appear as eccentricities, compacted with angry resentments and overwhelming longings. Repression, the key to personality structure in all therapy schools, is not of the past but of the acorn and the past mistakes we have made in our relation with it.

We dull our lives by the way we conceive them. We have stopped imagining them with any sort of romance, any fictional flair. So, this book also picks up the romantic theme, daring to envision biography in terms of very large ideas such as beauty, mystery, and myth. In keeping with the romantic challenge, this book also risks the inspiration of big words,

such as "vision" and "calling," privileging them over small re-
ductions. We do not want to belittle what we do not understand. Even when, in a later chapter, we do look carefully at
genetic explanations, we find mystery and myth there, too.

At the outset we need to make clear that today's main paradigm for understanding a human life, the interplay of genetics
and environment, omits something essential—the particularity
you feel to be you. By accepting the idea that I am the effect of
a subtle buffeting between hereditary and societal forces, I reduce myself to a result. The more my life is accounted for by
what already occurred in my chromosomes, by what my parents did or didn't do, and by my early years now long past, the
more my biography is the story of a victim. I am living a plot
written by my genetic code, ancestral heredity, traumatic occasions, parental unconsciousness, societal accidents.

This book wants to lift the pall of victim mentality from
which individual people cannot recover until the theoretical
paradigms that give rise to that mentality have been seen
through and set aside. We are victims primarily of theories
before they are put into practice. The current American
identity as victim is the tail side of the coin whose head
brightly displays the opposite identity: the heroic self-made
"man," carving out destiny alone and with unflagging will.
Victim is flip side of hero. More deeply, however, we are victims of academic, scientistic, and even therapeutic psychology, whose paradigms do not sufficiently account for or
engage with, and therefore ignore, the sense of calling, that
essential mystery at the heart of each human life.

In a nutshell, then, this book is about calling, about fate,
about character, about innate image. Together they make up
the "acorn theory," which holds that each person bears a
uniqueness that asks to be lived and that is already present before it can be lived.

"Before it can be lived" raises doubts about another principal paradigm: time. And time, that takes survey of all the world,
must have a stop. It, too, must be set aside; otherwise the before

always determines the after, and you remain chained to past causes upon which you can have no effect. So this book devotes more of its time to the timeless, attempting to read a life backward as much as forward.

Reading life backward enables you to see how early obsessions are the sketchy preformation of behaviors now. Sometimes the peaks of early years are never surpassed. Reading backward means that growth is less the key biographical term than form, and that development only makes sense when it reveals a facet of the original image. Of course a human life advances from day to day, and regresses, and we do see different faculties develop and watch them wither. Still, the innate image of your fate holds all in the copresence of today, yesterday, and tomorrow. Your person is not a process or a development. You *are* that essential image that develops, if it does. As Picasso said, "I don't develop; I am."

For this is the nature of an image, any image. It's all there at once. When you look at a face before you, at a scene out your window or a painting on the wall, you see a whole gestalt. All the parts present themselves simultaneously. One bit does not cause another bit or precede it in time. It doesn't matter whether the painter put the reddish blotches in last or first, the gray streaks as afterthoughts or as originating structure or whether they are leftover lines from a prior image on that piece of canvas: What you see is exactly what you get, all at once. And the face, too; its complexion and features form a single expression, a singular image, given all at once. So, too, the image in the acorn. You are born with a character; it is given; a gift, as the old stories say, from the guardians upon your birth.

———

This book sets out on a new course based on an old idea. Each person enters the world called. The idea comes from Plato, his Myth of Er at the end of his most well-known work, the *Republic*. I can put the idea in a nutshell.

The soul of each of us is given a unique daimon before we are born, and it has selected an image or pattern that we live on earth. This soul-companion, the daimon, guides us here; in the process of arrival, however, we forget all that took place and believe we come empty into this world. The daimon remembers what is in your image and belongs to your pattern, and therefore your daimon is the carrier of your destiny.

As explained by the greatest of later Platonists, Plotinus (A.D. 205–270), we elected the body, the parents, the place, and the circumstances that suited the soul and that, as the myth says, belong to its necessity. This suggests that the circumstances, including my body and my parents whom I may curse, are my soul's own choice—and I do not understand this because I have forgotten.

So that we do not forget, Plato tells the myth and, in the very last passage, says that by preserving the myth we may better preserve ourselves and prosper. In other words, the myth has a redemptive psychological function, and a psychology derived from it can inspire a life founded on it.

The myth leads also to practical moves. The most practical is to entertain the ideas implied by the myth in viewing your biography—ideas of calling, of soul, of daimon, of fate, of necessity, all of which will be explored in the pages that follow. Then, the myth implies, we must attend very carefully to childhood to catch early glimpses of the daimon in action, to grasp its intentions and not block its way. The rest of the practical implications swiftly unfold: (a) Recognize the call as a prime fact of human existence; (b) align life with it; (c) find the common sense to realize that accidents, including the heartache and the natural shocks the flesh is heir to, belong to the pattern of the image, are necessary to it, and help fulfill it.

A calling may be postponed, avoided, intermittently missed. It may also possess you completely. Whatever; eventually it will out. It makes its claim. The daimon does not go away.

For centuries we have searched for the right term for this "call." The Romans named it your *genius;* the Greeks, your *daimon;* and the Christians your guardian angel. The Romantics, like Keats, said the call came from the heart, and Michelangelo's intuitive eye saw an image in the heart of the person he was sculpting. The Neoplatonists referred to an imaginal body, the *ochema,* that carried you like a vehicle.[1] It was your personal bearer or support. For some it is Lady Luck or Fortuna; for others a genie or jinn, a bad seed or evil genius. In Egypt, it might have been the *ka,* or the *ba* with whom you could converse. Among the people we refer to as Eskimos and others who follow shamanistic practices, it is your spirit, your free-soul, your animal-soul, your breath-soul.

Over a century ago, the Victorian scholar of religions and cultures E. B. Tylor (1832–1917) reported that "primitives" (as nonindustrial peoples were then called) conceived that which we name "soul" to be a "thin insubstantial human image, in its nature a sort of vapour, film, or shadow . . . mostly palpable and invisible, yet also manifesting physical power."[2] A later ethnological reporter, Åke Hultkrantz, whose special field is the Amerindians, says that soul "originates in an image" and is "conceived in the form of an image."[3] Plato in his Myth of Er uses a similar word, *paradeigma,* a basic form encompassing your entire destiny. Though this accompanying image shadowing your life is the bearer of fate and fortune, it is not a moral instructor or to be confused with conscience.

The Roman *genius* was not a moralist. It "knew everything about the individual's future and controlled his fate," yet "this deity held no moral sanction over the individual; he [*sic*] was merely an agent of personal luck or fortune. One might ask without opprobrium to have evil or selfish desires fulfilled by his Genius."[4] In Rome, in West Africa, in Haiti you could well ask your daimon (whatever it might be called) to harm enemies, spoil their luck, or aid in manipulations and seductions. This "evil" aspect of the daimon we also shall explore in a later chapter ("The Bad Seed").

The concept of this individualized soul-image has a long, complicated history; its appearance in cultures is diverse and widespread and the names for it are legion. Only our contemporary psychology and psychiatry omit it from their textbooks. The study and therapy of the psyche in our society ignore this factor, which other cultures regard as the kernel of character and the repository of individual fate. The core subject of psychology, psyche or soul, doesn't get into the books supposedly dedicated to its study and care.

I will be using many of the terms for this acorn—image, character, fate, genius, calling, daimon, soul, destiny—rather interchangeably, preferring one or another depending on the context. This looser mode follows the style of other, often older cultures, which have a better sense of this enigmatic force in human life than does our contemporary psychology, which tends to narrow understanding of complex phenomena to single-meaning definitions. We should not be afraid of these big nouns; they are not hollow. They have merely been deserted and need rehabilitation.

These many words and names do not tell us *what* "it" is, but they do confirm *that* it is. They also point to its mysteriousness. We cannot know what exactly we are referring to because its nature remains shadowy, revealing itself mainly in hints, intuitions, whispers, and the sudden urges and oddities that disturb your life and that we continue to call symptoms.

Consider this event. Amateur Night at the Harlem Opera House. A skinny, awkward sixteen-year-old goes fearfully onstage. She is announced to the crowd: "The next contestant is a young lady named Ella Fitzgerald. . . . Miss Fitzgerald here is gonna dance for us. . . . Hold it, hold it. Now what's your problem, honey? . . . Correction, folks. Miss Fitzgerald has changed her mind. She's not gonna dance, she's gonna sing . . ."

Ella Fitzgerald gave three encores and won first prize. However, "she had meant to dance."[5]

Was it chance that suddenly changed her mind? Did a singing gene suddenly kick in? Or might that moment have been an annunciation, calling Ella Fitzgerald to her particular fate?

Despite psychology's reluctance to let individual fate into its field, psychology does admit that we each have our own makeup, that each of us is definitely, even defiantly, a unique individual. But when it comes to accounting for the spark of uniqueness and the call that keeps us to it, psychology too is stumped. Its analytical methods break down the puzzle of the individual into factors and traits of personality, into types, complexes, and temperaments, attempting to track the secret of individuality to substrata of brain matter and selfish genes. More strict schools of psychology kick the question right out of the lab, packing it off to parapsychology for the study of paranormal "callings," or to research stations in the distant colonies of magic, religion, and madness. At its most bold, and most barren, psychology accounts for the uniqueness of each by a hypothesis of random statistical chance.

This book refuses to leave to the lab of psychology that sense of individuality at the core of "me." Nor will it accept that my strange and precious human life is the result of statistical chance. Please note, however, that these refusals do not therefore bury our heads in the folds of a church. The call to an individual destiny is not an issue between faithless science and unscientific faith. Individuality remains an issue for psychology—a psychology that holds in mind its prefix, "psyche," and its premise, soul, so that its mind can espouse its faith without institutional Religion and practice its careful observation of phenomena without institutionalized Science. The acorn theory moves nimbly down the middle between those two old contesting dogmas, barking at each other through the ages and which Western thought fondly keeps as pets.

———

The acorn theory proposes and I will bring evidence for the claim that you and I and every single person is born with a defining image. Individuality resides in a formal cause—to use old philosophical language going back to Aristotle. We each embody our own idea, in the language of Plato and Plotinus. And this form, this idea, this image does not tolerate too much straying. The theory also attributes to this innate image an angelic or daimonic intention, as if it were a spark of consciousness; and, moreover, holds that it has our interest at heart because it chose us for its reasons.

That the daimon has your interest at heart may be the part of the theory particularly hard to accept. That the heart has its reasons, yes; that there is an unconscious with its own intentions; that fate plays a hand in how things turn out—all this is acceptable, even conventional.

But why is it so difficult to imagine that I am cared about, that something takes an interest in what I do, that I am perhaps protected, maybe even kept alive not altogether by my own will and doing? Why do I prefer insurance to the invisible guarantees of existence? For it sure is easy to die. A split second of inattention and the best-laid plans of a strong ego spill out on the sidewalk. Something saves me every day from falling down the stairs, tripping at the curb, being blindsided. How is it possible to race down the highway, tape deck singing, thoughts far away, and stay alive? What is this "immune system" that watches over my days, my food sprinkled with viruses, toxins, bacteria? Even my eyebrows crawl with mites, like little birds on a rhino's back. We name what preserves us instinct, self-preservation, sixth sense, subliminal awareness (each of which, too, is invisible yet present). Once upon a time what took such good care of me was a guardian spirit, and I damn well knew how to pay it appropriate attention.

Despite this invisible caring, we prefer to imagine ourselves thrown naked into the world, utterly vulnerable and fundamentally alone. It is easier to accept the story of heroic self-made development than the story that you may well be loved by this guiding providence, that you are needed for what you bring, and that you are sometimes fortuitously helped by it in situations of distress. May I state this as a bare and familiar fact without quoting a guru, witnessing for Christ, or claiming the miracle of recovery? Why not keep within psychology proper what once was called providence—being invisibly watched and watched over?

Children present the best evidence for a psychology of providence. Here I mean more than providential miracles, those amazing tales of children falling from high ledges without harm, buried under earthquake debris and surviving. Rather, I am referring to the humdrum miracles when the mark of character appears. All of a sudden and out of nowhere a child shows who she is, what he must do.

These impulsions of destiny frequently are stifled by dysfunctional perceptions and unreceptive surroundings, so that calling appears in the myriad symptoms of difficult, self-destructive, accident-prone, "hyper" children—all words invented by adults in defense of their misunderstanding. The acorn theory offers an entirely fresh way of regarding childhood disorders, less in terms of causes than of calls and less in terms of past influences than of intuitive revelations.

In regard to children and their psychology, I want the scales of habit (and the masked hatred within the habit) to fall from our eyes. I want us to envision that what children go through has to do with finding a place in the world for their specific calling. They are trying to live two lives at once, the one they were born with and the one of the place and among the people they were born into. The entire image of a destiny is packed into a tiny acorn, the seed of a huge oak on small shoulders. And its call rings loud and persistent and is as demanding as any scolding voice from the surroundings. The call shows in the tantrums and obstinacies, in the shyness and retreats, that seem to set the child against our world but that may be protections of the world it comes with and comes from.

This book champions children. It provides a theoretical foundation for understanding their lives, a foundation that draws its own foundations from myths, from philosophy, from other cultures, and from imagination. It seeks to make sense of children's dysfunctions before taking these disorders by their literal labels and sending the child off for therapy.

Without a theory that backs the child from its very beginning and without a mythology that connects each child to something before its beginning, a child enters the world as a bare product—accidental or planned, but without its own authenticity. Its disturbances can have no authenticity either, since the child does not enter the world for its own reasons, with its own project and guided by its own genius.

The acorn theory provides a psychology of childhood. It affirms the child's inherent uniqueness and destiny, which means first of all that the clinical data of dysfunction belong in some way to that uniqueness and destiny. Psychopathologies are as authentic as the child itself, not secondary, contingent. Given with the child, even given to the child, the clinical data are part of its gift. This means that each child is a gifted child, filled with data of all sorts, gifts peculiar to that child which show themselves in peculiar ways, often maladaptive and causing pain. So this book is about children, offering a way to regard them differently, to enter their imaginations, and to discover in their pathologies what their daimon might be indicating and what their destiny might want.

CALLINGS

Two stories of children: the first of a significant English philosopher, R. G. Collingwood (1889–1943); the second of a brilliant Spanish bullfighter, Manolete (1917–1947). The first shows how the daimon breaks suddenly into a young life; the second exhibits the disguises and tortuous concealments the daimon sometimes uses:

> My father had plenty of books, and . . . one day when I was eight years old curiosity moved me to take down a little black book lettered on its spine "Kant's Theory of Ethics." . . . as I began reading it, my small form wedged between the bookcase and the table, I was attacked by a

strange succession of emotions. First came an intense excitement. I felt that things of the highest importance were
being said about matters of the utmost urgency: things
which at all costs I must understand. Then, with a wave of
indignation, came the discovery that I could not understand them. Disgraceful to confess, here was a book
whose words were English and whose sentences were
grammatical, but whose meaning baffled me. Then, third
and last, came the strangest emotion of all. I felt that the
contents of this book, although I could not understand it,
were somehow my business: a matter personal to myself,
or rather to some future self of my own. . . . there was no
desire in it; I did not, in any natural sense of the word,
"want" to master the Kantian ethics when I should be old
enough; but I felt as if a veil had been lifted and my destiny revealed.

There came upon me by degrees, after this, a sense of
being burdened with a task whose nature I could not define except by saying, "I must think." What I was to think
about I did not know; and when, obeying this command,
I fell silent and absent-minded.[6]

The philosopher who thought out major works in meta-
physics, aesthetics, religion, and history was already called and
beginning to practice "philosophizing" as an eight-year-old.
His father provided the books and access to them, but the
daimon chose that father, and its "curiosity" reached for that
book.

As a child, Manolete did not seem in any way to be a
prospective bullfighter. The man who changed old styles and
renewed the ideals of the corrida was a timid and fearful boy.

Delicate and sickly, having almost died of pneumonia
when he was two, little Manuel was interested only in
painting and reading. He stayed so much indoors and clung
so tightly to his mother's apron strings that his sisters and
other children used to tease him. Around his hometown,

he was known as "a thin, melancholy boy who wandered around the streets after school lost in thought. He rarely joined other boys' games of soccer or playing at bullfighting." This all changed "when he was about eleven, and nothing else mattered much except the bulls."[7]

Radical transformation! At his first corrida, Manolete, hardly out of short pants, stands his ground without moving a foot—and does in fact suffer a groin wound, which he regards diffidently, refusing to be helped home to Mother, so as to return with the comrades with whom he came.

Clearly heroism is constellated. A myth of the hero calls from within his acorn.

Was a dim knowledge of the call there all along? Then of course little boy Manolete was afraid and clung to his mother. (Were her "apron strings" a metaphor, or was he already using her apron, her skirt, as a cape?) Of course he kept away from torero games in the street, taking shelter in the kitchen. How could this nine-year-old boy stand up to his destiny? In his acorn were thousand-pound black bulls with razor-sharpened horns thundering toward him, among them Islero, the one that gored him through groin and belly and gave him death at age thirty and the largest funeral ever witnessed in Spain?

Collingwood and Manolete exhibit a basic fact: The frail competencies of a child are not equal to the demands of the daimon. Children are inherently ahead of themselves, even if they are given low grades and left back. One way for the child is to race ahead, as in the famous cases of Mozart and other "infant prodigies" who benefit from good guidance. Another way is to shrink back and hold the daimon at bay, as did Manolete in his mother's kitchen.

The "wave of indignation" that assaulted Collingwood belonged with his inadequacy; he was not up to Kant, who was his "business, a matter personal to myself." One part of him was too untutored to read the meanings of the text; another part was not an eight-year-old child, never was a child.

Two similar examples also show the distinction between the ability of the child and the needs of the genius. First, the pioneering geneticist Barbara McClintock; second, the renowned violinist Yehudi Menuhin.

McClintock received a Nobel Prize for her research, which required the solitary thinking and handwork in the lab that gave her the deepest pleasure. She reports that "at the age of five I asked for a set of tools. [My father] did not get me the tools that you get for an adult; he got tools that would fit in my hands. . . . they were not the tools I wanted. I wanted *real* tools, not tools for children."[8]

Menuhin also wanted what his hands could not hold. Before Yehudi was four he frequently heard the concertmaster (first violinist) Louis Persinger break into a solo passage as little Yehudi sat with his parents up in the gallery of the Curran Theatre. "During one such performance I asked my parents if I might have a violin for my fourth birthday and Louis Persinger to teach me to play it." His wish was granted, it seems, when he was given by a family friend a toy violin made of metal with metal strings. "I burst into sobs, threw it on the ground and would have nothing more to do with it."[9]

Because the genius is not bound by age, by size, or by education or training, each child is too big for its britches and has eyes bigger than its stomach. It will be narcissistic, demanding excessive attention, and it will be accused of childish omnipotence fantasies, such as asking for instruments it cannot handle. What is the source of this omnipotence, if not the grandeur of the vision accompanying the soul into the world? The Romantics understood this inherent grandiosity of the child. How did they put it: "trailing clouds of glory as we come"?

Barbara's hands could not heft a heavy hammer, nor could Yehudi's arms extend and fingers articulate enough for a full-sized violin, but the vision was full-sized to match the music in his mind. He had to have what he wanted because "I did know, instinctively, that to play was to be."[10]

Let us consider that little Yehudi's daimon refused to be treated as a child, despite the fact that the boy himself was only four. The daimon threw the fit, demanding the real thing, for playing the violin is not playing with a toy. The daimon does not want to be treated as a child; it is not a child, and not an inner child either—in fact, it may be intensely intolerant of this mixture, this incarceration inside the body of an unaccomplished child, this identification of its complete vision with an incomplete human being. Rebellious *intolerance,* as the example of Yehudi Menuhin shows, is a primary characteristic of acorn behavior.

When we look at the childhood of the French writer Colette, we find that she, too, was fascinated by the instruments of her craft. Unlike Menuhin's fate, which pounced like a tiger, hers, more like a French cat on the windowsill, watched and waited, deviating her own necessity to write by observing her father's attempts. More like Manolete, she drew back—in self-protection?

As Colette herself says, her resistance to writing guarded her from beginning too soon, as if her daimon did not want her to start before she was able to receive its gift, but rather to read and read, to live and learn, to sense and smell and feel. Writing and the torture of it would afflict her life, and bless it, soon enough, but first she had to absorb the sensuous stuff that would enter the compositions. This stuff refers not only to the perceived events that entered her sensuous memory, but the very palpable stuff of writing as a physical craft. For although she abjured words, she craved the materials of her calling:

> A pad of virgin blotting paper; an ebony ruler; one, two, four, six pencils, sharpened with a penknife and all of different colors; pens with medium nibs and fine nibs, pens with enormously broad nibs, drawing pens no thicker than a blackbird's quill; sealing wax, red, green and violet; a hand blotter, a bottle of liquid glue, not to mention slabs

of transparent amber-colored stuff known as "mouth glue"; the minute remains of a spahi's cloak reduced to the dimensions of a pen wiper with scalloped edges; a big inkpot flanked by a small inkpot, both in bronze, and a lacquer bowl filled with a golden powder to dry the wet page; another bowl containing sealing wafers of all colors (I used to eat the white ones); to right and left of the table, reams of paper, cream-laid, ruled, watermarked.

Menuhin knew exactly what he wanted: to play the violin; Colette knew just as surely what she did not want: to write. Although in her sixth year and well able to read, she "refused to learn to write."

No, I would not write, I did not want to write. When one can read, can penetrate the enchanted realm of books, why write? . . . in my youth I never, *never* wanted to write. No, I did not get up secretly in the night to scribble poems on the cover of a shoebox! No, I never flung inspired words to the West wind or to the moonlight! No, I never made good marks in composition between the ages of twelve and fifteen. For I felt, and felt it each day more intensely, that I was made exactly for *not* writing. . . . I was the only one of my kind, the only creature sent into the world for the purpose of not writing.[11]

I want to recapitulate what we have learned so far about how destiny affects childhood. In Collingwood, an unexpected annunciation; in Manolete and Colette, an inhibition causing them to retreat. As well, we saw in McClintock, Menuhin, and Colette an obsessional desire for the tools that make realization possible. And we saw the discrepancy between child and daimon. Mainly we learned that the call comes in curious ways and differently from person to person. There is no overall pattern, but only the particular pattern in each case.

However, any reader with a keen Freudian nose will have detected one common factor: all these fathers—Collingwood's, McClintock's, Menuhin's, Colette's!—as if what the father might facilitate accounts for the child's call. This "parental fallacy," as we shall expand upon in the chapter of that name, is hard to avoid. The fantasy of parental influence on childhood follows us through life long after the parents themselves are faded into photographs, so that much of their power comes from the *idea* of their power. Why do we cling to the parental fallacy? How does it still parent us, comfort us? Are we afraid to admit the daimon into our own lives, afraid that it might have called us once, might still be calling, so we hide out in the kitchen? We retreat to parental explanations rather than face destiny's claims.

If Colette could postpone her destiny or acknowledge it by the intensity of her resistance, Golda Meir, who led Israel during the 1973 war, was launched straight forward by hers while in fourth grade in the Milwaukee public schools. She organized a protest group against the required purchase of schoolbooks, which were too expensive for the poorer children, who were thus denied equal opportunity to learn. This child of eleven (!) rented a hall to stage a meeting, raised funds, gathered her group of girls, prepped her little sister to declaim a socialist poem in Yiddish, and then herself addressed the assembly. Was she not already a Labor party prime minister?

Golda Meir's mother had pressed her to write out her speech first, "but it made more sense to me just to say what I wanted to say, 'speeches from my head.' "[12]

The future life does not have to arrive so overtly. Golda Meir, a woman of determination and leadership, came right out with it. Her daimon set the path and kept her to it. At about the same age, Eleanor Roosevelt, another woman of great determination and leadership, was entering the world of her future, not through action but by withdrawing into fantasy.

Eleanor Roosevelt declared herself an "unhappy child," whose early years were "gray days." What a quieting, polite term for what she endured. "I grew up with a fear of insanity."[13] She lost a mother who never liked her, a younger brother, and a playboy father, all before she was nine. "She is such a funny child, so old-fashioned, that we always call her 'Granny.' " From the time she was five, if not earlier, her natural reserve tightened; she became more sullen, stubborn, spiteful, sour, and unable (she could not read at seven, could not cook or sew, as was expected in her circles at that period). She lied; she stole; she threw antisocial tantrums in company. She was taught and subdued by a tutor, whom she "hated for years."[14]

All the while "I carried on a day-by-day story, which was the realest thing in my life."[15] In her story, Eleanor imagined that she was living with her father as the mistress of his large household and a companion in his travels. The story continued years after his death.

Today "the case of Eleanor R." would require therapy. Today, even if the family system were addressed, the child would almost certainly be treated by biopsychiatry's armamentarium of drugs, which would confirm with all the power of biology the child's feelings of being a "bad child." (Badness must be in my very cells, like an original sin or like a sickness. Else why would I be taking these pills to make me better, like the pills I take when I have fever and pains?)

Eleanor's elaborate daydreams would have no intrinsic value as exhibiting the imagination of her daimon, and her calling. Instead they would be reduced to escapes into unreality, verging on delusions. With drugs to reduce the strength and frequency of her images, psychiatric medicine could minister to a mind diseased, thereby proving by circular reasoning that what it had eliminated was indeed disease.

Another consultant, if called in on the case of Eleanor R., would suspect a connection between her early day-to-day fantasy and her later regular newspaper columns concerning social reality and called "My Day." This consultant would reduce her genius for democratic compassion, for human welfare, and her optimistic wide-angle vision to "compensation" for the isolated self-enclosed fantasies of her childhood's gray days.

Again a father. And again an opportunity to slip in a Freudian interpretation: Eleanor's Electra complex (love for the father and desire to replace the mother) caused both the gray depressions and the escapes from them in wishful omnipotence fantasies. Since the fantasies could have had other *content,* such as magical flights, secret pacts, romantic trysts, animal rescues, and royal weddings, the acorn theory proposes a very different understanding of young Eleanor Roosevelt's imaginings.

Their caring and managerial content was purposeful, preparation for the dutiful life she would later live. The fantasies were invented by her calling and were indeed more *realistic* in their orientation than her daily reality. Imagination acted as teacher, giving instruction for the large ministering tasks of caring for the welfare of a complex family, of a crippled husband, of the state of New York as the governor's wife, the United States as its first lady, and even of the United Nations. Her fantasies of attending to "Father" were a preliminary praxis into which she could put her call, her huge devotion to the welfare of others.

COMPENSATION THEORY

The theory of compensation—that Eleanor Roosevelt compensated her hopeless feelings with empowerment fantasies—pulls a lot of weight in psychobiography. Simply stated, the theory says the roots of later superiorities are buried in early inferiorities. Short, sickly, and sad children are driven by the principle of compensation to develop into towering leaders of activity and strength.

The biography of Generalissimo Francisco Franco, dictator of Spain from 1939 until 1973 (he died two years later), fits easily into the frame of compensation theory. As a boy he was "excruciatingly shy," of "fragile build" and "diminutive size." "At fifteen, tiny and baby-faced, he entered the Infantry Academy at Toledo, and one of the instructors . . . handed him a short-barreled musketoon instead of the heavy regulation rifle." Franco drew himself up and said: "Whatever the strongest man in my section can do, so can I."[16] This insult stayed with Franco, for he was a man to whom dignity was central. Besides the evident compensation for early frailty, he competed ("sibling rivalry") with his extraverted brothers, who were cheerful, successful, and talkative. So Franco overcame early inferiorities with victories, oppression, and a ruthless hand.

We can put on parade, one after another, eminent men of accomplishment and bravery who as children gave quite opposite indications. Erwin Johannes Eugen Rommel—the Desert Fox, a heroic soldier, decorated with the highest medals for bravery under fire in two world wars, a field marshal, campaign veteran, tactician, and inspirer of his men in campaigns in Belgium, France, Romania, Italy, and North Africa—as a little boy was known in his family as the "white bear" because he was so pale, dreamy, and slow of speech. Falling behind his classmates in primary school, he was considered lazy, inattentive, and careless.[17]

Robert Peary, who walked the Arctic wastes until he "discovered" the North Pole, was the only son of a widow. He stayed close to his mother, at home in the yard, "to evade boys who called him 'Skinny' and teased him about his fearfulness."

Vilhjalmur Stefansson, another heroic polar explorer, was called "Softy" by his classmates and spent hours alone, sailing a toy boat in a tub of water.

Mohandas K. Gandhi was a short, thin, ailing, ugly, and frightened child, afraid especially of snakes, ghosts, and the dark.[18]

The theory of compensation that these figures supposedly exemplify begins with Alfred Adler, the third, least-known, and shortest-lived member of the great therapeutic triumvirate of Freud, Jung, Adler. His studies of gifted personalities universalized the idea of compensation into a basic law of human nature. His evidence, gathered in art schools at the beginning of this century, claimed to show that 70 percent of art students had optical anomalies, and that there were degenerative traces in the ears of the great composers Mozart, Beethoven, and Bruckner.

According to the Adlerian theory, challenges of illness, birth defects, poverty, or other untoward circumstances in youth provide the stimulus for all higher achievements. Each person—in less spectacular fashion than the eminent and extraordinary—compensates for weaknesses with strengths, transforming inabilities into empowerment and control. The human mind is basically constituted to think in the constructs of strength/weakness, superior/inferior, striving to stay on top.[19]

The little anecdote of the Spanish dictator shows the more simple Adlerian notion of compensation. A more subtle and dangerous notion links it with the Freudian theory of sublimation. The Freudian theory holds that early weaknesses are transformed not simply into strengths, but into products of art and culture—at the bottom of which, nonetheless, are the dregs of early childhood wrongs that can be detected in the product as its true originating seed.

This pernicious mode of interpretation can be readily put to use: Jackson Pollock (1912–1956), who "invented" the drip calligraphy of abstract expressionist action painting. He painted on expansive white canvases, laying them on the floor and walking around and dripping colors from his brush as he moved, flinging interlacing arcs, wiggles, curves, and splotches, a vast tracery of rhythmic patterns. He is said to have said: "When I am painting, I am not aware of what I am doing."

But the wise psychologist, of course, can trace Pollock's traces on white canvas back to a signal inferiority in childhood. The youngest of five brothers on a Wyoming farm, little Jackson was referred to by his brothers "as 'baby' up into his teenage years, and he *hated* it."

> Like most farmhands, the Pollock boys shunned the outhouse whenever possible, preferring to make evanescent designs on the nearest patch of dry, dusty ground [and white winter snow]. Young Jackson often saw his brothers urinating . . . competing to see who could reach farthest. Too young to compete, he would retreat to the outhouse . . . even to urinate—a habit that persisted for the rest of his life, even after he was old enough to make the same long yellow arcs his brothers made.[20]

Although the painter does not know what he is doing, every smart analytical psychobiographer does know! The later arcs are sublimations of piss marks in the dust, piss marks that have remained in the shamed unconscious of the artist. The analytical psychobiographer denies what the artist himself says (and therefore perhaps knows—that is, that he does not, perhaps cannot, know the invisible source of his work). Also, the interpreter ignores the meaning of the very word he relies on for the interpretation: "unconscious." If you already know what the unconscious contains and what it is doing—sublimating phallic competition and sibling rivalry by action painting—then the source is not unconscious at all, and Pollock is implementing a program, proving a theory, of the psychobiographical interpretation.

A theory so degrading to inspiration deserves the derision I am giving it. Compensation theory kills the spirit, by robbing extraordinary persons and acts of their sui generis authenticity. Superiorities emerge from a lower source rather than expressing a more significant image. For, as almost every extraordinary life shows, there is a vision, an ideal that calls. To what precise actuality it calls usually stays vague if not altogether unknown.

If all superiorities are nothing more than overcompensated inferiorities, and all gifts but reformed wounds and weaknesses in nobler disguise, which can be unmasked by analytical acumen, then Franco is nothing but a short man, *really*, still caught in competing with his brothers, and Pollock, too, is but a "baby." They are nothing but the theory itself; and so too is everyone else, a "nothing but." There is no gift and there is no daimon who gives it. We are each alone on the planet, without an angel, subject to our hereditary flesh and all the oppressor's wrongs of family and circumstances, which only the willpower of a "strong ego" can overcome.

With compensation theory torched and discarded, let's go back and review from the perspective of the acorn theory the childhood characteristics of Gandhi, Stefansson, Peary, and Rommel, reading backward as we did with Manolete's early shyness. Gandhi was afraid of invisible presences and the dark because the daimon that held his destiny knew of the lathi charges and beatings, of the long imprisonments in dark cells, and knew that death would be his steady companion on the road. Assassination was written in Gandhi's script. Were Peary and Stefansson already rehearsing in their odd, childish ways the barren loneliness at the icy top of the world? And Rommel (who said to his son, "Even as an army captain I already knew how to command an army")[21]—perhaps that pale, slow, lazy, inattentive "white bear" of a boy was retreating in a kind of precognitive shell shock from the overwhelming artillery fire of El Alamein, the poundings and bombings he was to meet in two world wars, including the strafing that fractured his skull in Normandy and the suicidal poison the SS required him to take for his suspected part in the plot to kill Hitler.

Franco's pretentious posturing, too, can be reread less as an Adlerian compensation and more as a demonstration of the dignity of the daimon. "I am not a little baby-faced boy. I am El Caudillo of all Spain and must be accorded the respect of my calling." Whatever the calling—for not only caudillos demand respect (murderers do, too, as we learn in the chapter on the Bad Seed)—the daimon stands in dignity. Don't dis the daimon. A child defends its daimon's dignity. That's why even a frail child at a "tender" age refuses to submit to what it feels is unfair and untrue, and reacts so savagely to abusive misperceptions. The idea of childhood abuse needs to be expanded beyond the sexual kind—which is so vicious not principally because it is sexual, but because it abuses the dignity at the core of personality, that acorn of myth.

MOTIVATION THEORY

Although I condemned the compensation theory of calling, the theory of motivation finds support in our anecdotal evidence. Eminent people whose lives present the most striking examples of calling are characterized, according to the study of creativity by Harvard professor of psychiatry Albert Rothenberg, by one supreme factor. He rules out intelligence, temperament, personality type, introversion, inheritance, early environment, inspiration, obsession, mental disorder: All these may or may not be present, may contribute, may be strongly dominant, but only motivation is "absolutely, *across the board,* present in *all.*"[22]

Is not psychology's "motivation" the push in the acorn of the oak—or, better, the oakness of the acorn? Oaks bear acorns, but acorns are pregnant with oaks.

Motivation appears in odd ways, as indirectly as Eleanor Roosevelt's daydreams and as violently as in this story from the very early childhood—he was five—of Elias Canetti, a Bulgarian-born thinker and writer who was awarded a Nobel Prize for literature in 1981.

> My father read the . . . *Neue Freie Presse* every day; it was a grand moment when he slowly unfolded it. . . . I tried to find out what it was that fascinated him in the news-

paper, at first I thought it was the smell. . . . I would climb
up on the chair and greedily smell the newsprint. . . .
[Later he] explained that the important thing was the letters, many tiny letters, on which he knocked his fingers.
Soon I would learn them myself, he said, arousing within
me an unquenchable yearning for letters. . . .

[My cousin] was learning how to read and write. She
solemnly opened the notebook in front of me; it contained letters of the alphabet in blue ink, they fascinated
me more than anything I had ever laid eyes on. But when
I tried to touch them . . . She said I wasn't allowed to. . . .
all I could get from her with my tender pleading was that
I could point my fingers at letters without touching
them. . . .

Day after day, she let me beg for the notebooks; day
after day, she refused to give them to me. . . .

On the day that no one in the family ever forgot, I
stood at the gate as usual, waiting for her. "Let me see the
writing." . . . I tried to catch her, running after her all over
the place, I begged, I pleaded for the notebooks . . . by
which I meant both the notebooks and the writing, they
were one and the same for me. She lifted her arms with
the notebooks far over her head . . . up on the wall. I
couldn't get at them, I was too little. . . . All at once, I left
her there and walked the long way around the house to
the kitchen yard, to get the Armenian's ax and kill her
with it. . . .

I raised the ax high and . . . marched back over the
long path into the courtyard with a murderous chant on
my lips, repeating incessantly: *"Agora vo matar a Laurica!
Agora vo matar a Laurica!"*—"Now I'm going to kill Laurica! Now I'm going to kill Laurica!"[23]

Extraordinary people display calling most evidently. Perhaps that's why they fascinate. Perhaps, too, they are extraordinary because their calling comes through so clearly and
they are so loyal to it. They serve as exemplars of calling and
its strength, and also of keeping faith with its signals.

They seem to have no other choice. Canetti had to have letters and words; how else could he ever be a writer? Franco had to be as physically tough as any cadet in the school. Barbara McClintock and Yehudi Menuhin demanded real tools; they had to get their hands started. Extraordinary people bear the better witness because they show what ordinary mortals simply can't. We seem to have less motivation and more distraction. Yet our destiny is driven by the same universal engine. Extraordinary people are not a different category; the workings of this engine in them are simply more transparent.

Our interest therefore is less in these people and their "personalities" than it is in the extraordinary factor of fate itself—how it arrives and shows itself, what it demands, and its side effects. We look to these biographies for manifestations of destiny.

Clearly then, we are not engaged in a worship of the rich and famous or in a study of creativity and genius, of why Mozart and van Gogh were as they were. A genius belongs to everyone. No person is a genius or can be a genius, because the genius or daimon or angel is an invisible nonhuman escort, not the person with whom the genius lives.

A VISION OF CHILDREN

During early life person and daimon often are taken to be one and the same, the child absorbed by the genius, a confusion which is understandable since the child has so few other powers and the daimon comes with so much. Then the child is set apart as exceptional, special, a prodigy—or as a dysfunctional troublemaker, potentially a violent criminal, to be tested, diagnosed, and weeded out.

A connection between pathology and exceptionality also follows the Romantic tradition that likes to link genius with insanity, thereby giving license to all sorts of fooleries: The crazier you appeared, the more certain your genius. But our move is more responsible and even inspiring. It gives our ordinary lives and their strange deviant moments a sense of an innate image, which holds the pieces together in a pattern of meaning. Each anecdote from the early life of exceptional people is told here not to illustrate *their* childhoods only, but to shed light on yours and on those of the children we care for and worry about. Each vignette offers an intuition of calling within the blatant symptomatic peculiarities. Could we begin to look at children with this vision in mind? It would give pause to our diagnostic approach to the character and habits of children.

The War Against Children, as Peter and Ginger Breggin entitle their recent book, threatens American children with an epidemic of troubles caused by the methods that would cure them of their troubles.[24] The familiar evils of other ages reappear in the guises of helping programs, pharmaceutical prevention, and apartheid segregations. It's all back again— eugenics, white racism, sterilization, forced removal, banishment to beggary, punishment, and starvation. As in colonial days, drugs to ease the coolies' pain and increase their indifference will be provided by those who cause the pain.

Children have become the sacrificial victims of Saturn-Moloch, as in the ancient Mediterranean. They are also the scapegoats for scientistic fears of the anomalous, of the excessive, and of the paradigm-shifting movements of imagination that first appear as new—that is, in the young. What is already taking place in our "mental health facilities," where drugs are dispensed with less shame than condoms, would have benumbed during their childhoods probably every one of the extraordinary people told about in this book.

The vicious inadequacy of treatment is not intended by practitioners, who mean well. It results willy-nilly from the inadequacy, or viciousness, of theory. So long as the statistics of normalizing developmental psychology determine the standards against which the extraordinary complexities of a life are judged, deviations become deviants. Diagnosis coupled with statistics is the disease; yet diagnosis coupled with statistics is the very name—*Diagnostic and Statistical Manual* (or *DSM*)—of the universally accepted guide produced by the American Psychiatric Association and used by the profession, the health care providers, and the insurance payers.[25] Yet the whole of that thick, heavy, and lightweight book provides accounts of the various ways the daimons affect human fate and how sadly and strangely they often appear in our civilization.

This book prefers to connect pathology with exceptionality, exchanging the term "abnormal" for "extraordinary" and letting the extraordinary be the vision against which our ordinary lives are examined. Rather than case history, a psychologist would read human history; rather than biology, biography; rather than applying the epistemology of Western understanding to the alien, the tribal, and nontechnological cultures, we would let their anthropology (their stories of human nature) be applied to ours. I want to reverse our thinking in psychology as it is taught and practiced, ambitiously seeking to redeem this field from some of its sins.

EMINENT AND EXCEPTIONAL

The stories that punctuate this chapter and the entire book show the book's focus: mainly our early years. They show its method: mainly anecdotal. They show its passion: the extraordinary.

This passion needs some explaining. The extraordinary reveals the ordinary in an enlarged and intensified image. The study of the extraordinary for the sake of instruction has a long trail, from biographies of classical greats by Varro, Plutarch, and Suetonius, through later exemplars like the Church fathers[26] and Vasari's lives of Renaissance artists, and across the Atlantic to Emerson's *Representative Men*. This tradition is accompanied all along by the moral lessons to be drawn from the stories of biblical types such as Abraham, Ruth, Esther, and David, and from lives of the saints—all heightened examples of character.

All along, too, the theatrical tradition set forth extraordinary persons—from Oedipus, Antigone, Phaedra, Hamlet, Lear, and Faust to Willy Loman—as exemplars for reflection in our own lives.

Although this book wraps Nobel laureates and statesmen under the same cover with pop stars, murderers, and talk show hosts, this copresence and the equal time given all do not imply that celebrity equals creativity. Eminence exemplifies the extraordinary power of calling to a particular path. So this book simply makes use of the eminent for its own purpose: to make more evident by means of their fates what also calls in ours.

We use these figures as they are always used by a culture: to inspire ordinary lives by displaying their own potentialities. Extraordinary people excite; they guide; they warn; standing, as they do, in the corridors of imagination—statues of greatness, personifications of marvel and sorrow—they help us carry what comes to us as it came to them. They give our lives an imaginary dimension. That's what we look for when buying biographies and reading the secret intimacies of the famous, their luck, their errors, their gossip. Not to pull them down to our level, but to lift ours, making our world less impossible through familiarity with theirs. Without these exemplars of the daimon we have no other category of the extraordinary except diagnostic psychopathology.

These personifications of heightened imagination burn right into the soul and are its teachers. Not only the hero and hero-worship, but tragic figures too, beauties and comics and crones and handsome leading men. The stagy exaggeration of character traits displayed by extraordinary people belongs to the Romantic tradition. When the tradition of Romantic grandeur, with its cast of lunatics, lovers, and poets, is downsized by egalitarianism, deconstructed by academic cynicism, or labeled grandiosity by psychoanalytic diagnostics, then the vacancy in the culture is occupied by pop-star squatters, Trumped-up magnificoes, and Batman, civilization left with only tinsel celebrities to model its culture.

So this book wants to set psychology back two hundred years, to the time when Romantic enthusiasm was breaking up the Age of Reason. I want psychology to have its base in the imagination of people rather than in their statistics and their diagnostics. I want the poetic mind applied to case histories so that we read them for what they are: modern forms of fiction, and not scientific reports.

Case histories do demonstrate more what's wrong with psychology than with its cases. The clinical stories show how usual psychology—and we are each affected by its style of thought—draws its conclusions by working backward from the ordinary to the extraordinary, taking the "extra" right out of it.

Among the epigraphs at the opening of this book was one by Edgar Wind, perhaps the greatest scholar of the Renaissance imagination. It's worth repeating:

> A method that fits the small work but not the great has obviously started at the wrong end. . . . the commonplace may be understood as a reduction of the exceptional, but the exceptional cannot be understood by amplifying the commonplace. Both logically and causally the exceptional is crucial because it introduces . . . the more comprehensive category.[27]

If the exceptional is the more comprehensive category, then we may comprehend more, by studying an extraordinary person, about the deeps of human nature than by studying even the largest sample of accumulated cases. A single anecdote lights up the whole field of vision. Manolete in the kitchen cowering from the bulls in his destiny; Canetti taking to the ax for the sake of words. Then we may see disturbances in children less as developmental problems than as revelatory emblems.

Each biographical bit exemplifies in a nutshell this book's main thesis: We need a fresh way of looking at the importance of our lives. I am intending to assault the conventions of biographical perception, which insist that time and the past determine your day.

Ever since Herodotus and Thucydides invented history and the Bible told who begat whom, all Western things are chronicled by time. About time, the Hebrews and the Hellenes agree; time really counts. Progress depends on it, evolution requires it, measurements, without which we would have no physical sciences, are based on it. The very notions of "new" and "improved" that lure your consumer desire are inventions of time. The Western mind has trouble stopping its clock. It conceives its inmost life as a biological clock and its heart as a ticker. The electronic gadget on the wrist encloses in a concrete symbol the Western time-bound mind. The word "watch" is cognate with "awake" and "aware." We do believe that all things move through time, which carries on its river all the world, all the species, and each individual life. So when we look at anything, we see it in time. We even seem to see time itself.

To change how we see things takes falling in love. Then the same becomes altogether different. Like love, a shift of sight can be redemptive—not in the religious sense of saving the soul for heaven, but in a more pragmatic sense. As at a redemption center, you get something back for what you had misperceived as merely worthless. The noisome symptoms of every day can be revalued and their usefulness reclaimed.

Symptoms in our culture mean something "bad." The word itself merely means a combination (*sym*) of accidental happenings, neither good nor bad, that coalesces this with that into an image. As judgment of their value need not be moral, so their province need not be medical. As accidental happenings, symptoms do not belong first to disease but to destiny.

If symptoms—even if they show suffering—are not primarily regarded as something wrong or bad in a child, then we can release imagination from its focus on fixing a child's symptoms. We can end that perversion of the medical adage

"Like cures like": Doing something wrong to a child to get rid of the wrong that is the symptom. If the symptom is not "bad" we do not have to use bad methods to make it go away.

Sophisticated and superstitious therapists often wonder where a symptom goes when it goes away. Is it really gone? Will it come back in another form? And now that it's gone, what might it really have been trying to express? These wonderings show a sense that there is a "something else" in a symptom besides its asocial, dysfunctional, and handicapping badness.

These wonderings open the eye toward an invisible intention in a symptom, so that we can regard the symptom less anxiously, less (moralistically) as a wrong, and more simply as a phenomenon (which meant, originally, something that shows, shines, lights up, brightens, appears to be seen). A symptom wants to be looked at, not only looked into.

A restructuring of perception is what I am after in this book. I want us to see the child we were, the adult we are, and the children who require us in one way or another, in a light that shifts the valences from curse to blessing, or if not blessing at least symptom of calling.

BEAUTY

Of all psychology's sins, the most mortal is its neglect of beauty. There is, after all, something quite beautiful about a life. But you would not think so from reading psychology books. Again, psychology fails what it studies. Neither social psychology, experimental psychology, nor therapeutic psychology find a place for the aesthetic appreciation of a life story. Their tasks are investigation and explanation, and should an aesthetic phenomenon pop up in any of their material (and not only in the aesthetically dedicated, like Jackson Pollock, Colette, or Manolete) it will be accounted for by a psychology that is without aesthetic sensitivity to begin with.

Each twist of fate may have its interpretation, but it also has its beauty. Just look at the image: Menuhin stomping away from the metal-stringed toy; Softy Stefansson sailing his boats in a tub; jug-eared and bony Gandhiji with all his fears. Life as images does not ask for family dynamics or genetic dispositions. Even before there are life stories, lives display themselves as images. They ask first to be seen. Even if each image is indeed pregnant with meanings and subject to dissecting analysis, should we jump to the meanings without appreciating the image, we have lost a pleasure that cannot be recovered by the very best of interpretations. We have also taken the pleasure out of the life we are regarding; the display of its beauty has become irrelevant to its meaning.

By psychology's "mortal" sin, I mean the sin of deadening, the dead feeling that comes over us when we read professional psychology, hear its language, the voice with which it drones, the bulk of its textbooks, the serious pretensions and bearded proclamations of new "findings" that could hardly be more banal, its soothing anodynes for self-help, its decor, its fashion, its departmental meetings, and its tranquilizing consulting rooms, those stagnant waters where the soul goes to be restored, a last refuge of white-bread culture, stale, crustless, but ever spongy with rebounding hope.

Neglect of beauty neglects the Goddess, who then has to steal back into the departments as sexual harassment, into the laboratories as "research" experiments with sex and gender, and into the consulting rooms as seductive assignations. All the while psychology, without beauty, becomes victim of its own cognitive strictures, all passion spent in pushing for publication and position. Without beauty, there's little fun and less humor. Grand motivations are lost to psychological categories like grandiosity and inflation, while the adventure of ideas is cut to fit experimental designs. Whatever romance might still be left appears in the desire to help suffering people by entering a "training program" for therapists. But if helping is the calling, then better to apprentice with Mother

Teresa than to expect a psychology without soul, beauty, or pleasure to train you to help the suffering. Psychology has no self-help manual for its own affliction.

As evidence of this book's attempt to exit the mortuary is the absence from these pages of the contemporary language of psychology. Except where set apart in quotation marks to keep from contaminating a sentence with psychological morbidities, you will not find any of these infectious agents: performance, growth, creativity, thresholds, continuum, response levels, integration, identity, development, validation, boundaries, coping measures, operant conditioning, variance, subjectivity, adjustment, verifiable results, test results, emergence, hope. You will find few diagnostic labels and no acronyms. This is a psychology book without the word "problem." Little mention of "ego," of "consciousness," and none of "experience"! I have also tried to prevent the most pernicious term of all, "self," from creeping into my paragraphs. This word has a big mouth. It could have swallowed into its capacious limitlessness and without a trace all the more specific personifications such as "genius," "angel," "daimon," and "fate." And finally, I boast this triumph: a book with passionate psychological intent whose passion was not diverted into the indulgences of the gender war. As civilization subsides into its own waste deposits, it doesn't matter whether you are feminine or masculine or any composite of them. We all dissolve together. Far more urgent matters than gender call out to the passion of psychology.

So this book wants to join psychology with beauty. Though this redemptive move is a consummation devoutly to be wished, it becomes possible in general only when we make particular moves with our individual biographical images— taking our life as an image into a connection with beauty.

Looking for the acorn affects how we see each other and ourselves, letting us find some beauty in what we see and so love what we see. Thereby we may come to terms with the oddities of human character and the claims of its calling. To love this calling and to live with its demanding love on us, our very marriage to it till death, if that does, us part—that vision informs this book.

By looking at ourselves as examples of calling, at our destinies as manifestations of a daimon, and at our lives with the imaginative sensitivity we give fictions, we might put a stop to the worry, the fever, and the fret of searching out causes. Like dogs chasing our own tails, we are bedeviled by the "why" question, which conjures up its twin, the devilish "how"— how to change. The pursuit of happiness becomes the pursuit of answers to the wrong questions. We little realize to what feverish extent all psychologies promote anxiety—in parents, in children, in therapists, in researchers, and in the field itself as it extends its searchings into ever more "problem areas." Everything seems to call for studies, research, analyzing: aging, business management, sports, sleep, and the methods of the research itself. Restless inquiry is not the only kind of knowing, self-examination not the only kind of awareness. Appreciation of an image, your life story as studded with images since early childhood, and a deepening into them slows the restlessness of inquiry, laying to rest the fever and the fret of finding out. By its very definition, given by Thomas Aquinas in his *Summa theologica,* beauty arrests motion. Beauty is itself a cure for psychological malaise.

That longing in the human heart for beauty must be recognized by the field that claims the human heart to be its province. Psychology must find its way back to beauty, if only to keep itself alive. Amazingly, even studies of creative personalities in the arts seem to regard the desire for beauty—if they mention it at all—as only a variable factor. How can the modes of biographical writing that leave out the propelling force of beauty (doesn't the acorn want to be a beautiful oak?) ever meet the hunger of the readers who search biographies for clues to living. Only if the story itself transmits this sense of beauty can it satisfy the life it is written about.

Like cures like: A theory of life must have a base in beauty if it would explain the beauty that life seeks. The

Romantics grasped this essential truth. Their exaggerated overreach toward cloudy glories meant to bring into this world forms of the invisible they knew were necessary for imagining what a life is.

A last member of these Romantics, the Connecticut poet Wallace Stevens, makes clear these cloudy thoughts:

> . . . The clouds preceded us
>
> There was a muddy centre before we breathed.
> There was a myth before the myth began,
> Venerable and articulate and complete.[28]

The tale we take from Plato about the soul choosing its particular destiny and being guarded by a daimon ever since birth is such a myth—venerable, articulate, complete; and it is there before you began the other myth you call your biography.

———

To come down and look back: Let me put in a nutshell what we may so far cautiously attribute to the acorn theory. It claims that each life is formed by its unique image, an image that is the essence of that life and calls it to a destiny. As the force of fate, this image acts as a personal daimon, an accompanying guide who remembers your calling.

The daimon's "reminders" work in many ways. The daimon motivates. It protects. It invents and persists with stubborn fidelity. It resists compromising reasonableness and often forces deviance and oddity upon its keeper, especially when it is neglected or opposed. It offers comfort and can pull you into its shell, but cannot abide innocence. It can make the body ill. It is out of step with time, finding all sorts of faults, gaps, and knots in the flow of life—and it prefers them. It has affinities with myth, since it is itself a mythical being and thinks in mythical patterns.

The daimon has prescience—maybe not of particulars (that Rommel and Pollock would commit suicide, that

"Granny" Eleanor would be first lady, that Canetti would receive a Nobel Prize), because it cannot manipulate happenings to accord with the image and fulfill the calling. Its prescience is therefore not perfect, but limited to the significance of the life in which it has its embodiment. It is immortal, in that it doesn't go away and can't be killed off by merely mortal explanations.

It has much to do with feelings of uniqueness, of grandeur and with the restlessness of the heart, its impatience, its dissatisfaction, its yearning. It needs its share of beauty. It wants to be seen, witnessed, accorded recognition, particularly by the person who is its caretaker. It is slow to anchor and quick to fly. It can't shed its own supernal calling, sensing itself both in lonely exile and in cosmic harmony. Metaphoric images are its first unlearned language, which provides the poetic basis of mind, making possible communication between all people and all things by means of metaphors.

We will be elaborating the acorn theory and discovering other effects of the daimon in other chapters of this book.

— 🎵 —

CHAPTER 2

GROWING DOWN

The ladder whose ascent implies spiritual progress has a long pedigree. The Hebrews, Greeks, and Christians all gave special value to the heights, and our spiritually influenced compass of Western morality tends to put all better things up high and worse things down low. By the last century, growth became inexorably caught in this ascensionist fantasy. Darwin's thesis, *The Descent of Man,* became, in our minds, the ascent of man. Each immigrant moved upward in social class as buildings moved upward with their elevators to more expensive levels. Industrial refining of buried minerals—coal, iron, copper, oil—increased their economic value and the financial status of their owners simply by raising these basic stuffs from below to above. By now, the upward idea of growth has become a biographical cliché. To be an adult is to be a grown-up. Yet this is merely one way of speaking of maturity, and a heroic one at that. For even tomato plants and the tallest trees send down roots as they rise toward the light. Yet the metaphors for our lives see mainly the upward part of organic motion.

Hasn't something critical been omitted in the ascensionist model? Birthing. Normally we come into the world headfirst, like divers into the pool of humanity. Besides, the head has a soft spot through which the infant soul, according to the traditions of body symbolism, could still be influenced by its origins. The slow closing of the head's fontanel and fissures, its hardening into a tightly sealed skull, signified separation from an invisible beyond and final arrival here. Descent takes a while. We grow down, and we need a long life to get on our feet.

The enormous difficulty small children have growing down into the practical, their tight won't-let-go grip, their fear, their strain to adapt, and their puzzled wonder over the little things of the earth around them show us every day how hard it is to grow down. Japanese ideas of caring for infants call upon the mother or caregiver to be present all the time. The child is to be kept close, brought into the human community because it has come from so far away.

Symbol systems like that of the zodiacal cycle in both Western and Asian astrology start headfirst. The most refined, the most subtle, is the last sign, of the Fish (West) and the Pig (East). The symbolic body-locus of this last sign is the feet. It seems the feet are the last to arrive. And they are the first to go, if we follow, for instance, the slow dying of Socrates. The hemlock poison he was required to drink first numbed and chilled his lower limbs, as if he began to be drawn away from this world feet first. To plant a foot firmly on earth—that is the ultimate achievement, and a far later stage of growth than anything begun in your head. No wonder the faithful revere the Buddha's footprint in Sri Lanka. It shows he was truly in the world. He had really grown down.

In fact, the Buddha had begun the process of growing down early in his life, when he left his protected palace gardens to enter the street. There the sick, the dead, the poor, and the old drew his soul down into the question of how to live life in the world.

These familiar stories of Socrates and the Buddha, and the images of astrology, give another direction to growth and another value to "down." For, in its most common usage, "down" is nothing but a downer. The soul has to drag its feet with doubts and second-guessing, if not symptoms, when pressed to accommodate itself to the upward push of career. College kids with bright promise sometimes suddenly find their "personal computer" is down. They fall off the fast track. They want to "get down." Or drinks, drugs, and depression set in like Furies. Until the culture recognizes the legitimacy of growing down, each person in the culture struggles blindly to make sense of the darkenings and despairings that the soul requires to deepen into life.

Organic images of growth follow the favorite symbol for human life, the tree, but I am turning that tree upside down. My model of growth has its roots in heaven and imagines a gradual descent downward toward human affairs. This is the Tree of the Kabbalah in the Jewish and also Christian mystical tradition.

The Zohar, the main Kabbalist book, makes it clear that the descent is tough; the soul is reluctant to come down and get messed by the world.

At the time that the Holy One, be blessed, was about to create the world, he decided to fashion all the souls which would in due course be dealt out to the children of men, and each soul was formed into the exact outline of the body she was destined to tenant. . . . Go now, descend into this and this place, into this and this body.

Yet often enough the soul would reply: Lord of the world, I am content to remain in this realm, and have no wish to depart to some other, where I shall be in thralldom, and become stained.

Whereupon the Holy One, be blessed, would reply: Thy destiny is, and has been from the day of thy forming, to go into that world.

Then the soul, realizing it could not disobey, would unwillingly descend and come into this world.[1]

The Kabbalist tree, as first elaborated in thirteenth-century Spain, imagines the descending branches to be conditions of the soul's life, which becomes more and more manifest and visible as it descends. The lower it gets, the more difficulty we have grasping its meaning, according to Charles Ponce, a recent psychological interpreter of Kabbalah. As he says, the upper regions and symbols are not as occult as the worldly ones; "the legs remain a mystery."[2] It's easy to see the ethical implications of this upside-down image: A person's involvement with the world gives evidence of the descent of the spirit. Virtue would consist in downwardness such as humility, charity, teaching, and not being "stuck up."

The Tree of the Kabbalah repeats two of the most enduring creation myths of our civilization, the biblical and the Platonic. The Bible reports that God took six days to make the whole cosmos. The first day, as you will recall, God was busy with huge abstractions and higher constructions such as separating dark and light, getting his basic orientation. Only toward the end of the process, as it moved downward during days five and six, do we get to the multitudes of animals and to the human being. Creating progresses downward from the transcendent to the teeming here of immanence.

Plato's tale of descent is the Myth of Er which I shall condense from the last chapter of his *Republic:*

The souls are all hanging around in a mythical world, having arrived there from previous lives, and each has a lot to fulfill. This lot is also called a portion of fate (Moira) that is somehow representative of the character of that particular soul. For instance, the myth says the soul of Ajax, the intemperate and mighty warrior, chose the life of a lion, while Atalanta, the fleet young woman runner, chose the lot of an athlete, and another soul chose the lot of a skillful workman. Ulysses' soul, remembering its long life of trials and tribulations, "and tired of ambition, went about a long time seeking the life of a private man of no business, and with difficulty found it lying somewhere, neglected by the rest.

"When all the souls had chosen their lives according to their lots, they went before Lachesis [*lachos* = one's special lot or portion of fate]. And she sent with each, as the guardian of his life and the fulfiller of his choice, the genius [*daimon*] that had been chosen." Lachesis leads the soul to the second of the three personifications of destiny, Klotho (*klotho* = to twist by spinning). "Under her hand and her turning of the spindle, the destiny of the chosen lot is ratified." (Given its particular twist?) "Then the genius [*daimon*] again led the soul to the spinning of Atropos [*atropos* = not to be turned, inflexible] to make the web of its destiny irreversible.

"And then without a backward glance the soul passes beneath the throne of Necessity," sometimes translated as the "lap" of Necessity.[3]

Precisely what a "lot" (*kleros*) is imagined to look like does not come clear from the text. The word *kleros* combines three closely connected meanings: (a) piece of the earth, like our sandlot, car lot, empty lot, which expands to mean (b) that "space" which is your portion in the overall order of things, and (c) an inheritance, or what rightfully comes down to you as an heir.[4]

I understand these lots in the myth to be images. Since the lots are each particular and encompass a whole style of fate, the soul must be perceiving intuitively an image that embraces the whole of a life all at once. It must be choosing that image which attracts: "This is the one I want, and it is my rightful inheritance." My soul selects the image I live.

Plato's text calls this image a *paradeigma,* or "pattern," as translators usually say.[5] So the "lot" is the image that is your inheritance, your soul's portion in the world order, and your place on earth, all compacted into a pattern that has been selected by your soul before you ever got here—or, better said, that is always and continually being selected by your soul, because time does not enter the equations of myth. ("Myth," said Sallust, the Roman philosopher of paganism, "never happened but always is.") Since ancient psychology usually located the soul around or with the heart, your heart holds the image of your destiny and calls you to it.

Unpacking the image takes a lifetime. It may be perceived all at once, but understood only slowly. Thus the soul has an image of its fate, which time can show only as "future." Is "future" another name for fate, and are our concerns about "the future" more likely fantasies of fate?

Before the souls enter human life, however, they pass through the plain of Lethe (oblivion, forgetting) so that on arrival here all of the previous activities of choosing lots and the descent from the lap of Necessity is wiped out. It is in this condition of a tabula rasa, or empty tablet, that we are born. We have forgotten all of the story, though the inescapable and necessary pattern of my lot remains and my companion daimon remembers.

The greatest of all followers along the Platonic line, Plotinus sums up the myth in a few lines: "Being born, coming into this particular body, these particular parents, and in such a place, and what we call external circumstances . . . form a unity and are as it were spun together."[6] Each of our souls is guided by a daimon to that particular body and place, these parents and circumstances, by Necessity—and none of us has an inkling of this because it was eradicated on the plains of forgetting.

According to another Jewish legend, the evidence for this forgetting of the soul's prenatal election is pressed right into your upper lip.[7] That little crevice below your nose is where the angel pressed its forefinger to seal your lips. That little indentation is all that is left to remind you of your preexistent soul-life with the daimon, and so, as we conjure up an insight or a lost thought, our fingers go up to that significant dent.

Images such as these fill the mind with lovely speculations, and have for centuries. Why is She called Necessity and why does He pay so much attention to sea monsters and creeping things one whole day before getting to humankind? Are we best because last? Or are we least, like an afterthought?

These cosmological myths place us in the world and involve us with it. The cosmologies of today—big bangs and black holes, antimatter and curved, ever-expanding space going nowhere—leave us in dread and senseless incomprehensibility. Random events, nothing truly necessary. Science's cosmologies say nothing about the soul, and so they say nothing to the soul, about its reason for existence, how it comes to be and where it might be going, and what its tasks could be. The invisibilities that we feel enmeshing our lives with what is beyond our lives have been abstracted by the cosmologies of science into the literal invisibility of remote galaxies or waves. They can't be known or perceived, because they are measured by time, and our lives are mere nanoseconds in the vast panoply of science's myth. What's the purpose of anything?

These "invisibles" of the physical universe can't be known or perceived, only calculated, because they are light-years away and because by definition they are indeterminate. Here it is worthwhile noting that some ancient philosophy considered the indeterminate (*apeiron*) to be the basis of evil.[8] Explanation by the physical sciences of the ultimate origins of and reasons for our life may not be such a good way to go. Any cosmology that begins on the wrong foot will not only produce lame accounts; it will also lame our love of existence. The creation myth of random events in unimaginable space keeps the Western soul floating in a stratosphere where it cannot breathe. No wonder we look to other myths, like that of Plato's Er, the book of Genesis, and the Kabbalist Tree. Each of these gives a similar mythical account of how things are: They found us in myths, and the myths unfold downward into one's personal soul. No wonder, too, that Plato says this about his "fable": "It may preserve us, if we are persuaded by it."

STARDOM I: JUDY GARLAND

The descent into the world may be painful and costly. Costly, especially, to the family. The price of calling is often paid by the very circumstances in which the acorn has taken root— the body, the family, and the immediate participants in the life of the calling, such as husbands and wives, children and friends, collaborators and mentors. Often the demands of the calling ruthlessly wreak havoc on the decencies of a well-lived life.

Of course, not only the eminent are called. Who doesn't feel the pressure of taking on too much and going too far, whatever the profession? All of us worry that we could still have done more—another vegetable for Thanksgiving dinner or another half hour on piano practice or on the exercise machine. The addiction to perfection is another term for the call of the angel. The voice that cautions speaks only part of the daimon's message. Another part calls to the ideal. So the blame placed on modern stress, money needs, superego commandments, and dreadful deadlines tries to reduce the archetypal nature of the indefatigable inhuman angel and its relentless claims. Though everyone feels at times the press of calling, it is in the exaggerated life of celebrities where these demands are most apparent and best documented.

Riches and acclaim never compensate; stars always seem displaced persons, always needy, estranged, haunted by an unspoken tragedy that is blamed on parents or betrayals in love, on ailments or forced inhuman schedules. The blame belongs to the angel, to the difficulty of the inhuman attempting to come down into the human. Addictions that keep stars estranged and "out of it," suicide attempts, and early death may result from the incommensurability between calling and life. In a well-measured world of human convention, how can I live the ahuman demands of what I am called to do?

To show the difficulties of growing down, I want to contrast the stories of two of the most widely recognized exceptional talents in show business. We'll begin with Judy Garland, or Frances Gumm of Grand Rapids, Minnesota, who entered our world June 10, 1922, by means of a show business family that promoted her almost as soon as she could stand up. Garland's calling announced itself when she was two and a half. As Baby Gumm, she joined her two older sisters onstage. Then, solo, she sang "Jingle Bells" to an audience that roared approval, brought her back again and again, to which she responded by singing and ringing her bells louder and louder. Her father had to haul her offstage. Immediate rapport. Immediate fans.

Baby Gumm had already seen an act of the Blue Sisters, three girls between the ages of twelve and five; "When the youngest Blue Sister started to sing, alone, the Gumms could all see how this was really going to send Frances into a fit. And it did. She sat transfixed. When it was all over, she turned to Daddy and—I'll never forget it—said, 'Can I do that, Daddy?' " Garland's sister Virginia reports that "even in her two-year-old head, she already knew *exactly* what she wanted."

Garland believed her calling "was inherited. Nobody ever taught me what to do on stage. . . . I just did 'what came naturally.' " Remembering her initial "Jingle Bells" performance, she compared the rush onstage to "taking nineteen hundred wake-up pills." Garland of the Hollywood Bowl and Carnegie Hall was already there in two-year-old Baby Gumm.

Her own explanation of "inherited" means less literally genetic (as we shall come to see in chapter 6) than innate, given "naturally," like her daimon and its calling. A thousand manipulating fathers cannot yield one Mozart any more than can the pushiest mother in the world produce one Judy Garland. I would rather attribute the startling magnetism of Frances Gumm, age two and a half, in Grand Rapids, to the acorn of Judy Garland awakening onstage, an acorn that "chose" exactly those show business parents and sisters and circumstances for beginning its life on earth.

But that life took its toll on Frances Gumm. Growing down followed a suffering course, a course that also followed an orbit among the "stars." One after another, the big names of show business who sang, danced, and filmed with her, and who reviewed her, gave her immense tribute. The crowd at her two-and-a-half-hour one-woman show at Carnegie Hall in 1961 included Richard Burton, Leonard Bernstein, Carol Channing, Jason Robards, Julie Andrews, Spencer Tracy, Anthony Perkins, Mike Nichols, Merv Griffin, and the like. Her recordings could outsell Elvis Presley's, and an expensive double album stayed in the "Top Forty for an astonishing seventy-three weeks." Superlatives belonged to her. "The greatest artist who ever lived and probably ever will live"—Fred Astaire; "the most talented woman I ever knew"—Bing Crosby; "the finest all-round performer we ever had in America"— Gene Kelly. Elia Kazan describing greatness in performance lists Caruso and Callas, Raimu and Garbo, and "Judy Garland at the end of her life." "All my life," said Garland of herself, "I've done everything to excess."

But below her yawned the snake pit: ambulances to the hospital, stomach pumps, blackmail, throat slashed with broken glass, stage fright, shouting matches in public, pills by the handful, a bad drunk, promiscuous sex, sequestered salary, turned out in the street, bleak despair, and paralyzing terror. The descending part was aging, embodied, entangled, and dying.

During the social distress and democratic idealism of the thirties and forties—the Great Depression, the New Deal, the war effort—Judy Garland lived Hollywood. She did join in, but did she grow down? She contributed to the American war machine by maintaining America's most valued and tenacious antidepressant drug, without which it cannot fight a war, produce, or have a nice day: the myth of innocence, the psychology of denial. So she did not have to step out of character or desert her chosen lot while raising funds for war bonds by singing and by entertaining at army bases. Her image pinned to bunk beds and bulkheads and folded into the wallets of the dead as "the girl back home" still kept her up rather than growing down. Although her image projected the small town and high school of Frances Gumm, Judy Garland did not find a Yellow Brick Road into the world. The days were spent cutting records, making movies such as *Meet Me in St. Louis,* negotiating, and falling apart.

The making of two particular films gave her opportunity for, and show her difficulty with, growing down: *The Clock* (1945) and *Judgment at Nuremberg* (1961). Her role in *The Clock* was that of an ordinary working girl meeting and marrying a soldier. In *Nuremberg* she had a small, poignant role as a tragic and frowsy hausfrau who had befriended a Jew. These two films afforded Garland with a way down from magical child and star-struck success, from Dorothy and Little Nelly Kelly. But these opportunities were few and she resisted them when they came. Her acorn belonged "over the rainbow." Even in her final stage appearances, when she was bloated or frail, incoherent or terrified, it was that particular song from *The Wizard of Oz* that entranced the audience, keeping her, and them, ascending.

The critic Clifton Fadiman was able to see into the essential image, the innate "excess," in Garland's heart, the ageless, genderless, bodiless, deathless genius itself:

Why did we call her back again and again and again, not as if she had been giving a good performance, but as if she had been offering salvation.

As we listened to her voice . . . as we watched her, in her tattered tramp costume . . . we forgot—and this is the acid test—who she was, and indeed who we were ourselves. As with all true clowns (for Judy Garland is as fine a clown as she is a singer) she seemed to be neither male nor female, young nor old, pretty nor plain. She has no "glamour," only magic. She expressed a few simple, common feelings so purely that they floated about in the dark theatre, bodiless, as if detached from any specific personality.[9]

The usual way of coming to terms with the tragic messes of Garland's life is to accuse "Hollywood" and its pressures of agents, studios, and pseudo-realities. Only this can explain how a star so gifted, who "had it all," could "sink so low."

I would rather see each of these sinkings as attempts at descent, at misbegotten ways of growing down. It is as if the world that she never reached kept pulling her into it by means of its usual instruments: sex and money, dealers and lovers, brokers and contracts, marriages and failures. Down, down even to testifying in a murder trial and her final scene of death on a toilet during the night of June 21–22, the apogee of the solar year, its brightest moment and shortest night.

Where most of the population never "make it" in the Garland sense and dream lifelong of becoming stars, or just of touching one once, the reverse in Garland's case is striking. She wanted to enter the regular world, to live with a man in a stable marriage, to have children (she had three, but in her forties said, wistfully, "I suppose it's too late for me to have another child"), to have friends and not only fans. What kept her going was none of these normalcies, but the ruthlessness of her calling, which opposed them.

The standard modern dilemma of home versus work, family versus career takes on in Garland's case the archetypal dimension of a cross, preventing her calling from growing down into life. The vertical dimension stretched between hellish suffering and heavenly miracles, unable to settle into the flat and level of the daily world. Her star was never quite born. Hollywood magnified the calling, demanding that her life comply wholly with her otherworld's acorn, for which Hollywood acts as collective agent. It expected her life to take care of itself. But Frances Gumm did not know how to keep house, be married, raise children, cook a meal, or make anything with her hands. She could not even find the right clothes to put on.

James Mason, who was her leading man in *A Star Is Born,* said at her funeral: "She who gave so much and richly . . . needed to be repaid, she needed devotion and love beyond the resources of any of us." An inhuman demand: the need of the inhuman for a human world.

Garland gave this account of the dilemma her acorn posed: "Maybe it's because I made a certain sound, a musical sound, a sound that seems to belong to the world. But it also belongs to me because it comes from within me."

We are back to a general principle: The heart's image requires efforts of *attachment* to every sort of anchoring circumstance, whether these anchors be the loyalty of friends, the stability of contracts, the reliability of health, the schedules of the clock, the facts of geography. Because "the sound seems to belong to the world" and comes through as an invisible gift, there can never be enough world in which to sink its roots. Why do stars "sink so low"—becoming commercial face-lifted drunks, sex freaks, religious paranoids? Are these not desperate attempts to touch the common ground? Every symptom is a compromise, as Freud saw. Symptoms attempt the right aim but accomplish it in the wrong way. The heights seek the depths; one way or another they want to come down, even if by suicide, by ruinous contracts and bankruptcy, by entangling emotional messes. No soft landings. "The middle road was never for her," said Garland's daughter Liza Minnelli at the funeral.[10]

LONELINESS AND EXILE

The "Judy Garland story" tells of solitude in the midst of world acclaim. How do we account for the loneliness that accompanies every life? Loneliness is not specific to stars in huge Hollywood houses, or reserved for aged seniors in nursing homes. Loneliness belongs to childhood, too. That loneliness in a child's heart may be aggravated by fears of the dark, punishing parents, or rejecting comrades. Its source, however, seems to be the solitary uniqueness of each daimon, an archetypal loneliness inexpressible in a child's vocabulary and formulated hardly better in ours.

Moments of dejection drop us into a pool of loneliness. Waves of intense loneliness occur as aftershocks of childbirth, of divorce, of the death of a long-lived partner. The soul pulls back, mourns alone. Twinges of loneliness accompany even a marvelous birthday celebration and a victorious accomplishment. Are these mere hangovers—compensatory falls after unusual heights? Nothing seems to hold against the drop. All the networking that has interlaced our extension outward and downward into the world—family, friends, neighbors, lovers, little routines, and the results of years of work—seem to count for nothing. We feel ourselves curiously depersonalized, very far away. Exiled. No connection anywhere. The spirit of loneliness has taken over.

To guard against these moments we have philosophies that explain them and pharmaceuticals that deny them. The philosophies say the uprooted and hurried condition of modern city life and impersonal work have created a social condition of anomie. We are isolated because of the industrial economic system. We have become mere numbers. We live consumerism rather than community. Loneliness is symptomatic of victimization. We are victims of a wrong way of life. We should not be lonely. Change the system—live in a cooperative or a commune; work in a team. Or build relationships: "Connect, only connect." Socialize, join recovery groups, get involved. Pick up the phone. Or ask your doctor for a prescription for Prozac.

Deeper than social philosophy and social remedy is the account of moral theology. It recognizes in loneliness the sin of the Fall. We are cut off from Eden and from God owing to the Original Sin of humankind. When we feel alone and lost in the valley, we are stray sheep that have wandered from the path of redemption, out of grace and out of faith and therefore out of hope. We can no longer hear the call of the shepherd or obey the bark of his persistently nipping dog hounding our conscience with guilt. We are alone purposely, in order to hear the still small voice whose whispering is drowned out by the madding crowd. Even worse: Loneliness is evidence of damnation for our personal sins committed in the corruptible body of flesh. Of course Judy Garland was homeless, needy, broke, and lonely. These are the wages of sin.

Moral theology from the East considers the suffering of isolation to be the task imposed on this life by past karmic actions in another incarnation or as a preparation for the next. Moral theologies whether Eastern or Western subtly transform the sense of loneliness into the sin of loneliness, exacerbating its unhappiness. Grin and bear it. Or repent.

Existentialism, another way of accounting for loneliness, accepts the suffering of isolation as basic to its theory of human existence. Heidegger or Camus, for instance, places the human being into the situation of "throwness." We are merely thrown into being here (*Dasein*). The German word for "thrown" (*Wurf*) combines senses of the throw of the dice, a projection, and a litter of pups or piglets cast by a bitch or a sow. Life is your project; there is nothing to tell you what it's all about, which of course leaves you feeling existential anxiety and dread. It's all up to you, each individual alone, since there is no cosmic guarantee that anything makes sense. There is neither God nor Godot to wait for. You make a life out of the deepest feelings of meaninglessness. The heroic ability to turn loneliness into individual strength is the way that Judy Garland failed to find. She was too dependent, too weak, too fearful to combine "solitary" and "solidary," a motto proposed by Camus in one of the tales collected in his aptly titled work *The Exile and the Kingdom*. Garland's desperation demonstrates the truth of existential nihilism. Such would be the existentialist reading.

These ways of thinking about loneliness—social, therapeutic, moral, existential—make two assumptions that I cannot accept. First, each says that loneliness equates with literal aloneness and consequently is remediable by some sort of human action, such as repenting for sins, therapeutic relating, building the project of your life with your own heroic hands. Second, each assumes that loneliness is fundamentally unpleasant.

But if there is an archetypal sense of loneliness accompanying us from the beginning, then to be alive is also to feel lonely. Loneliness comes and goes apart from the measures we take. It does not depend on being literally alone, for pangs of loneliness can strike in the midst of friends, in bed with a lover, at the microphone before a cheering crowd. When feelings of loneliness are seen as archetypal, they become necessary; they are no longer harbingers of sin, of dread, or of wrong. We can accept the strange autonomy of the feeling and free loneliness from identification with literal isolation. Nor is loneliness mainly unpleasant once it receives its archetypal background.

When we look—or, rather, *feel*—closely into the sense of loneliness we find it is composed of several elements: nostalgia, sadness, silence, and a yearning imagination for "something else" not here, not now. For these elements and images to show, we first have to focus on them rather than on remedies for being left literally alone. Desperation grows worse when we seek ways out of despair.

These conditions of nostalgia, sadness, silence, and a yearning imagination are the stuff of Judy Garland's songs, her voice and phrasing, her body language, her face and eyes. No wonder her performances reached the common heart as no others did. Nostalgia, sadness, silence, and imaginative yearning are also the inmost stuff of religious and romantic poetry in many languages and many cultures. They remind the acorn of its origins. Like E.T. in the Spielberg film, the acorn seems nostalgic, sad, silent, and filled with yearning for an image of "home." Loneliness presents the emotions of exile; the soul has not been able to fully grow down, and is wanting to return. To where? We do not know, for that place the myths and cosmologies say is gone from memory. But the imaginative yearning and the sadness attest to an exile from what the soul cannot express except as loneliness. All it can recall is a nostalgia of feeling and an imagination of yearning. And a condition of want beyond personal needs.

Therefore, when we look again at Judy Garland, we can begin to understand why even when she was hardly able to find the words or hit the notes. The crowd called for those lyrics, "Somewhere, over the rainbow," and for the song's last yearning question, "Why can't I?" We can begin to understand as well how Garland was able to keep her fans and professional admirers, despite the shaming collapses and infuriating, erratic petulance of drunken, drugged, messed-up Frances Gumm. She made each of her listeners aware of what they, too, most intimately were longing for: the awakened image in the heart of the exiled and its yearning for what was not in this world.

We can also read again the last phases of her life as conditions appropriate to exile, like that of a wanderer on the road, a vagrant or a pilgrim, a member of the Diaspora, a Sufi poet-beggar, or a wine-drunk Zen monk. The daimon's home is not on the earth; it lives in an altered state; the body's frailty is a basic precondition of the soul's life on earth; and don't we each leave the world with debts unpaid? Drop the sociology and the psychoanalysis and Garland stands among the few who could never fully grow down because it was her acorn not only to sing and dance in the theatrical spotlight, to be the magical child and enact the otherworld's presence as the white-faced clown, but also to be the representative of exile and its longing.

STARDOM II: JOSEPHINE BAKER

Another equally miraculous woman, whose movement down the Kabbalistic Tree took a different course, was born in St. Louis Social Evil Hospital in 1906, also in June. From this degraded entry into the world she first had to rise to the stars before she could begin her remarkable downward course. As Frances Gumm bore the genius of "Judy Garland," Freda J. McDonald (or Tumpy, as she was called as a child) bore "Josephine Baker."

This, too, was a woman of fascination and extravagance. Josephine Baker burst into the world at the Theater of the Champs-Elysées (Elysian Fields of heavenly paradise) in Paris in October 1925, nude but for a few feathers. The motions of her frenzied dancing body "gave all of Paris a hard-on." She was then nineteen.

By thirteen she had already been married. That first husband, a steelworker, was earning, but Josephine "spent every penny he brought home on dresses." As the success following the Paris opening brought in money, her "dresses" expanded: Now she had dogs she traveled with, a monkey on her shoulder, an ostrich cart. She loved cars, although she could not drive. Among those she owned was a rare and expensive Bugatti. In January 1928 she and her manager left Paris for Vienna taking along, besides hangers-on, lovers, and relatives, "a secretary, a chauffeur, a maid, a typewriter, two dogs, 196 pairs of shoes, assorted dresses and furs, 64 kilos of face powder, and 30,000 publicity shots for the fans."

The body into which her soul descended was one thing, its early circumstances quite different. Scarce food, bedbugs; sleeping on the floor with the dog, hired out, as a child, to work where she and a dog shared the same food and fleas. The woman she worked for beat her, and kept her naked because clothes cost too much. Still a child, she was pawned off to another house to work, and sleep with, a white-haired old man. That she'd gotten this far was already an accomplishment. Records of the health department in St. Louis show that three out of five children died before the age of three.

She was dancing even then, in a basement where she set up a little stage and box benches. She slapped the other kids around so they would sit still and pay attention while she performed. She spent every minute she could watching performances at the local clubs and halls, and hung around the show people when they came through.

Once she carried a snake into a funeral where the coffin lay open. The snake got loose and panicked the mourners; the coffin tipped over, the corpse rolled, and the snake was bashed to death by the angry people. Tumpy—or was it already Josephine, protector of animals?—screamed, "You've killed my friend!" It's not so unusual for children to feel an animal's soul. Yet we also should recall that the snake is perhaps the most ancient and universal carrier of the genius spirit, the figure of a protective guardian, the "genius" itself. Had she already made friends with her acorn?

Finally, one more extravagant tale of Josephine:

> In Stockholm, she played before the king. "But if you asked me how he looked, I couldn't tell you. When I dance, I dance, I don't look at anyone, not even a king." . . .
>
> Crown Prince Gustav-Adolf, then a young man of twenty-eight, was also present. . . . the crown prince invited Josephine to the palace, and led her through a secret door into a room with a four-poster bed covered in precious furs. She lay down, naked, and the prince summoned a servant who came in with a silver tray heaped with jewels, and one by one, the prince covered Josephine's body with diamonds, emeralds, rubies. . . . this story is by now part of the country's folklore.

Josephine Baker's star life shows many similarities to that of Judy Garland: the huge public acclaim and the public eclipse; the mesmerizing performances; the need to "be in love"; the struggle with men as lovers, partners, and exploiters (one young man shot himself right in front of her and died at her feet); money running through her fingers; the show-business whirl and its glamorizing effect on personal habits and health;

the ascent from nowhere; the complete lack of a normal education; obsessions with physical inferiorities (Garland worried over her weight and build, Baker over her hair); and sex.

Sexual relations were essential to Josephine Baker's performances: She did it in the wings; standing up before going on; with every dance partner, gay or not; with big shots who paid; with the famous; with everyone she wanted, wherever she wanted, whenever she wanted. Once she lay on the floor of her stateroom to entice an indifferent codancer: "Look at my body, all the world is in love with that body, why are you so arrogant?"

The writer Georges Simenon, creator of the detective Maigret, and one of Baker's innumerable lovers as she was one of his *mille et trois,* described the secret of this body: its particular *croupe.* "In French, *croupe* means a horse's hindquarters, a rump, hips. Josephine's *croupe,* Simenon tells his readers, is the sexiest in the world. . . . Why? 'By God, it's obvious, that *croupe* has a sense of humor.' "

Garland's biographers indicate some of the same compulsive eroticism. The main similarity lies in both women's ability to fascinate, to represent a transcendent aspect of the human soul that calls to each soul in the audience. It is as if they can show off the daimon, let it be seen and heard. Garland's daimon was "Over the Rainbow," Baker's "La Danse de sauvage."

The parallels part. Josephine Baker grows down. This movement must not be explained away by her down-and-dirty act, her down-and-out childhood, the downfall of her career, or by the easy racist explanation that, since she was black, down was her way. She was not put down, nor did she fall down; Josephine Baker grew down.

She moved step by step into the political and social world. First, it was the war that began in 1939; she was then thirty-two. She wanted to do all she could for her adopted country, France. This meant risking her life for the French underground by smuggling information, hidden in musical scores, across the borders of France and Spain into Portugal. Being black, she was banned from the theater and was in danger of deportation, even execution. In Morocco, where she was kept royally by relatives of the ruling family, she worked at saving Jews from roundups; for a while she wore a yellow Star of David on her coat, a far cry from pink plumes. During the cold winter after the liberation of Paris she scavenged hundreds of pounds of meat, bags of vegetables, and coal to help the poor. She was awarded the Légion d'Honneur and the Croix de Guerre for her contributions and was congratulated by de Gaulle.

The next step down was her return to America, where she began to align herself with her St. Louis circumstances. She was an early participant in the civil rights movement; she insisted blacks be hired as stagehands; she joined the 1963 March on Washington; she visited black inmates in a New Jersey prison. For her efforts on behalf of integration she was praised by Martin Luther King, Jr., and Ralph Bunche. She also visited Castro's Cuba; the FBI's file on her ran to a thousand pages.

Baker's last step down was supporting eleven adopted children from many nations and of many colors, fighting to keep them together and to see they were fed, housed, and schooled. She toured and performed, appealing for funds to hold on to the country estate that was their home and into which she had sunk her last money. Saved once by Grace Kelly and another time by Brigitte Bardot, finally she was foreclosed and physically thrown out in the rain. Broke, homeless, aging, she gave her last show to wild acclaim, in Paris a few days before she died, April 12, 1975, at the Salpêtrière hospital. Her death there recapitulated her birth at the St. Louis Social Evil Hospital, for the Salpêtrière had been built for outcast women, prostitutes, syphilitics, indigents, criminals.

Rise and fall. It is one of the archetypal patterns of life, and one of its most ancient, cosmic lessons. But *how* one falls, the style of coming down, remains the interesting part. Judy Garland's was a heroic and sad decline into collapse. Her efforts aimed at the comeback; she tried again and again to connect with the upper world of stardom, a struggle that ironically led to that dismal death in a London flat. The thirty-minute ovation Josephine Baker received in Paris that final week was both for the daimon in her body ("the people did not want to leave the theater") and for her long and slow history of growing down into this world of "social evils": fascism, racism, abandonment of children, injustice.[11]

The Platonic myth of growing down with which we began this chapter says the soul descends in four modes—via the body, the parents, place, and circumstances. These four ways can be instructions for completing the image you brought with you on arrival. First, your body: Growing down means going with the sag of gravity that accompanies aging. (Baker told people she was sixty-four while she was still in her mid-fifties; she wore old clothes and gave up covering her baldness.) Second, admitting yourself to be one among your people and a member of the family tree, including its twisted and rotten branches. Third, living in a place that suits your soul and that ties you down with duties and customs. Last, giving back what circumstances gave you by means of gestures that declare your full attachment to this world.

— 🦗 —

CHAPTER 3

THE PARENTAL
FALLACY

If any fantasy holds our contemporary civilization in an unyielding grip, it is that we are our parents' children and that
the primary instrument of our fate is the behavior of your
mother and father. As their chromosomes are ours, so are
their mess-ups and attitudes. Their joint unconscious psyche—the rages they suppress, the longings they cannot fulfill,
the images they dream at night—basically form our souls, and
we can never, ever work through and be free of this determinism. The individual's soul continues to be imagined as a
biological offspring of the family tree. We grow psychologically out of their minds as our flesh grows biologically out of
their bodies.

If sharp definitions of parenting and parents have begun to
melt owing to the infiltrations of law, demographics, and bio-
chemistry, the idea of parenting and parents is more hardened
than ever in the minds of moral reformers and psychothera-
pists. The shibboleth "family values," expressed by catch-

phrases like "bad mothering" and "absent fathering," trickles down into "family systems therapy," which has become the single most important set of ideas determining the theory of societal dysfunction and the practice of mental health.

Yet all along a little elf whispers another tale: "You are different; you're not like anyone in the family; you don't really belong." There is an unbeliever in the heart. It calls the family a fantasy, a fallacy.

Even the biological model has puzzling gaps. Contraception is easier to account for and practice than conception itself. What goes on in that massive, virginly intact, single, round ovum that allows only this particular minuscule sperm among millions to enter? Or is the question more correctly addressed to the sperm? Is one of you more wily, more pushy, and more sympathetically congenial? Or is it just the randomness of "luck"—and what is luck, really? We know about DNA and the results of joinings, but we are left with the mystery that Darwin spent a life with, the mystery of selection.

The acorn theory suggests a primitive solution. It says: Your daimon selected both the egg and the sperm, as it selected their carriers, called "parents." Their union results from your necessity—and not the other way around. Does this not help to understand the impossible unions, those antipathies and misalliances, the quick conceptions and sudden desertions occurring between the parents of so many of us, and especially in the biographies of the eminent? The couple came together, not for their personal unity, but to beget the unique person, endowed with a specific acorn, who turns out to be you.

Take for instance the tale of Thomas Wolfe, that gigantic, verbose, romantic Smoky Mountain novelist, born October 3, 1900. The parents of Wolfe, says his biographer Andrew Turnbull, were joined in "an epic misalliance. Two people more temperamentally unsuited could scarcely be imagined."[1] The father was "lavish, sensual, expansive"; the mother, "flinty, parsimonious, repressed."

How did they ever get together? Some sixteen years before Thomas Wolfe's arrival on earth, his mother, Julia Westall, age twenty-four, country schoolteacher, came into the shop of once-divorced, once-widowed W. O. Wolfe, a marble cutter who made tombstones. She came a-calling to sell books (her moonlighting way of picking up the extra penny).

Having glanced at the book she was selling, he put his name down for it. Then he asked if she ever read novels.

"Oh, I read most everything," she answered. "Not the Bible as much as I should though."

W.O. said he owned some fine love stories, and that afternoon . . . he sent her Augusta Jane Evans' *St. Elmo.* A few days later when Julia was starting out to sell another book . . . W.O. pressed her to stay for lunch, after which he took her into the parlor and showed her his stereopticon slides of the Civil War. . . . he took her hand, said he had been watching her for quite a while as she passed his shop, and proposed.

Julia . . . protested that they barely knew each other. W.O. was so adamant, however, that she finally said she would open the book she was selling at random and abide by the middle paragraph of the right-hand page. "Just a bit of foolishness on my part," she remembered long afterwards, and hit on a description of a wedding with the words "till death do us part." "Oh, that's it!" cried W.O. "That's the very thing! We're going to let it stand!" The wedding took place in January, a scant three months after his headlong proposal.

Many explanations for this sudden misalliance: opposites attract; youth and age; simple utility (she needed an economic foothold; he needed a housekeeper); sado-masochistic compulsion; reenactment of parental dramas; societal pressures on the single . . . Are you convinced?

Why not at least entertain that they met "through the book"? She approached him proposing a book; he countered, sending her a book; it was decided by opening a book, and they brought forth, as fruit of their bookish union, Thomas Wolfe, writer of books. When he was two, it was a parental "parlor trick to have [him] 'read aloud' for guests." Julia believed she had invisibly brought about his literary ability, for during her pregnancy, she had "spent the afternoons reading in bed."

As for Wolfe's six living brothers and sisters, they had other acorns, which chose those parents for other proclivities. Again, it is mainly in the exceptional that the acorn shows itself most clearly.

So Thomas Wolfe was called to that household in Asheville, North Carolina, and his parents were called to each other to make that household so that he could do what had to be done. How else could he have done what he did had he not "known" his parents before they knew him? An angel's finger opened the page conceiving them to be his parents before they conceived him, their child.

MOTHERS

Julia Wolfe believed in her determining influence on her son Tom. And I wouldn't ever contest the impression of a mother's character, whatever it be, makes upon her natural-born child. She is so indubitably there that it needs no argument, no affirmative evidence. So a whole step in this discussion can be bypassed. As the mathematician G. H. Hardy said, "A serious man ought not to waste time stating a majority opinion." Let us then put Mother behind us, as she is always behind us anyway, a great silent idol center stage, against which the biographies in this book take place.

As for the power in this idol and our idolatrous worship of it, let me repeat an oft-told tale:

Identical twin men, now age thirty, were separated at birth and raised in different countries by their respective adoptive parents. Both kept their lives neat—neat to the point of pathology. Their clothes were preened, appointments met precisely on time, hands scrubbed regularly to a raw red color. When the first was asked why he felt the need to be so clean, his answer was plain.

"My mother. When I was growing up she always kept the house perfectly ordered. She insisted on every little thing returned to its proper place, the clocks—we had dozens of clocks—each set to the same noonday chime. She insisted on this, you see. I learned from her. What else could I do?"

The man's identical twin, just as much a perfectionist with soap and water, explained his own behavior this way: "The reason is quite simple, I'm reacting to my mother, who was an absolute slob."[2]

How shall we arrange the three components of this tale—the facts of perfectionism, the theory of reactive causality, and the myth of Mother? Proponents of innate geneticism might claim that this tale is superb anecdotal evidence for the dominating role of heredity. Advocates of the importance of early environment might still claim that, indeed, the two men reacted to their mothers, but in two different ways—one in accord, the other in opposition—and that their mothers indeed were the crucial influence in forming their obsessiveness.

For me, this tale illustrates myth substituting for theory and accounting for facts. For let's not overlook that what the identical twins have in common besides their perfectionism is their identical theory of that perfectionism: their mutual assertion that "Mother" is behind it all. The myth of Mother in our culture carries the higher dignity and force of theory, and we are a nation of Mother-lovers in the support we give her by adhering to the theory.

If we can so readily accept the Mother-myth, then why not another myth, a different myth, the Platonic one this book proposes? It cannot be the resistance to myth that makes us balk at the acorn theory, since we so gullibly swallow the

myth of Mother. The reason we resist the myth of the daimon, I believe, is that it comes clean. It is not disguised as
empirical fact. It states itself openly as a myth. Furthermore,
it challenges us to recognize our individuality as a birthright
without the fallback pillow of Mother as comforting ground
and archetypal support.

As nuclear one-on-one motherhood wanes, the myth
hangs in there, clutching at the archetypal breast. We still believe in Mom even as we watch everything change: day-care
centers, spread-out families, daddies doing diapers, homeless
kids caring for younger siblings, teenage mothers of two or
three kids, forty-five-year-old mothers of their first. It's all
changing: demographics, economics, legal definitions of par-
enthood, conceptions, adoptions, drugs, diagnoses, guidance
books.

Nonetheless, the myth of the mother as the dominant in
everyone's life remains constant. For behind each birth-giver
and care-provider sits the universal Great Mother, upholding
the universe of that belief system I am calling the parental fallacy, which keeps us bonded to her. She appears shaped by the
style of your personal mother, and she is as bad as she is good.
Smothering, nourishing, punishing, devouring, ever-giving,
obsessive, hysterical, morose, loyal, easygoing—whatever her
character, she too has a daimon, but her fate is not yours.

Yet biography loves mothers. It loves to tell of marvelous
or malevolent mothers as the agents of destiny behind men
and women of eminence. Cole Porter, carrying his mother's
name Kate Cole Porter, also carried "her own life-long
dream—to become a professional musician."[3] She saw to it
that the little boy of eight performed and at ten traveled thirty
miles by train for his music lessons. Frank Lloyd Wright's
mother knew exactly that her son was to be an architect and,
say the biographers, influenced him in that direction by hanging pictures of buildings in her baby's room. It was to cheer his
depressed mother that James Barrie began the ad hoc storytelling that led to his writing inventions like Peter Pan.

Pablo Casals, one of eleven children in a poor family in a Catalan village, was taken by his mother to Barcelona some forty miles away to go on with his music; "and until Pablo was twenty-two the home was fragmented, burdened, impoverished by the weight of the mother's consuming drive to see the talent of her son actualized and recognized."[4]

One day the mother of Edward Teller, the physicist hawk of nuclear arms, was walking in a Budapest park, heavy with her unborn child. Her companion asked why her pace had slowed and why she was studying the landscape. Teller's mother replied, "I have a feeling this time it will be a son, and I'm sure he will be famous, so I'm looking for the best site to build his monument."[5] Our usual psychology says Teller was pushed to fame by his mother. But why not imagine that Ilona Teller intuitively picked up on the daimon inhabiting her womb?

Krishnamurti, the philosopher-teacher, lost his mother when he was still a boy, but he "frequently saw her after she died, I remember once following my mother's form as it went upstairs. . . . I saw the vague form of her dress and part of her face. This happened almost always when I went out of the house."[6]

Krishnamurti's sighting of his mother's form demonstrates clearly the blending of the memorial mother, her actual being, and the spirit of the mother, her daimon, which often merges with or participates with the daimon of the child, even as it grows into majority and eminence. It is the rare mother who can see the seed, encourage its emergence, and yet not mess with its individual direction.

Van Cliburn, the master pianist, was taught music by his mother. She makes clear the distinction between mentoring the spirit and mothering the child:

> With the realization of Van's unusual gifts, our relationship while at work became that of teacher and pupil rather than mother and child. . . .

From the outset I cautioned young Van against "show-ing off"... reminding him that his ability was a divine gift for which he should be deeply grateful, without tak-ing undue credit for himself.

Cliburn confirms this: "From age three, she gave me a piano lesson every day of my life. Every single day. We'd sit down to the piano and she'd say, 'Now just forget I'm your mother. I'm your piano teacher, and we must be very serious.' "

The greatness of the mother's power is indisputable, espe-cially when it can recognize and defend—and, as in cases like Cliburn's, serve to instruct—her child's daimon.

The daimon, however, predates the mother, maybe even predetermines the mother—or at least so says the acorn the-ory. For little Van was already a musician by the age of two; he had picked up by ear, simply by listening to lessons going on in another room, a "complex little number" that required "crossing left hand over the right" with "tricky rests and syn-copations."[7] And so the acorn theory says also that his dai-mon chose just the right mother, one who knew what to do with a wunderkind. Would young Cliburn from Kilgore, Texas, have gone to Moscow, knocking the judges dead and winning the International Tchaikovsky Piano Competition, had he been born, say, to your mother or raised in your house?

But is eminence caused by the mother? Do mothers cre-ate their children as they carry them, bringing their spirits to birth as they bring their bodies to term? If we do not differ-entiate her daimon from her child's, then mother must also be declared a monster maker, whose daimon or demon lives out its life in her physical child. Hitler, Mao, Nasser of Egypt were deeply attached to their mothers. Kwame Nkrumah of Ghana was lifted out of village life and given a Western edu-cation because of the persuasion of his mother. Whether a charismatic leader is actually seen into and helped by a mother, or whether a leader needs to believe in the mother myth, which he honors by tribute to a personal mother, cannot be ascertained. But somehow the mother myth likes big dictators.

Woodrow Wilson, Harry Truman, Dwight D. Eisenhower, Lyndon Johnson, Richard M. Nixon—they too were favored by or favored their mothers. Remember Nixon, confused and broken, leaving the White House in disgrace, paying maudlin tribute to his mother in that last speech.

My mother, once meeting Sara Delano Roosevelt, Franklin D.'s mother, was asked how many children she had. My mother answered, "Four," to which the senior Mrs. Roosevelt replied, "I had only one, but he did very well." And Sara Delano Roosevelt saw to it that he did, perhaps noticing his genius very early, following it or pushing it every difficult step of the way as long as she lived.

What about those mothers who had no understanding of their children's calling and misperceived their natures? And what about the eminent people who fought with Mother, hating her mind, her habits, and her values? Differences of this sort seem to make no dent in the parental fallacy. The myth still holds whether Mother gave positive unconditional support or lived her life in selfish narcissistic indifference. Biographies twist contrary facts toward the same end, which shows that biographers, including ourselves in our own accounts of why we are as we are, remain as enthralled by the parental fallacy as were those twins who stated that Mother was the reason for their raw red hands.

George Lukács, a Hungarian Marxist writer and influential critic, was at odds with his mother from the start. In the last year of his life (1971), he "still remembered her . . . unkindly." All along he had refused to extend her even "formal courtesy." Lukács wrote: "At home; absolute alienation. Above all mother; almost no communication." Because she was conventional, shallow, and mainly interested in social life, Lukács's biography connects his Marxist sympathy for the oppressed and his antibourgeois rebelliousness with this antagonism to his mother. The acorn theory, of course, regards his mother as necessary for his genius: He needed an enemy within the walls who represented the values his daimon innately abhorred. "Very early I was ruled by feelings of strong opposition."[8]

This kind of radical opposition to the conventional mother appears in the biographies of the composer Igor Stravinsky, for instance, and the photographer Diane Arbus.

Stravinsky's mother chided her son for not "recognizing his betters, like Scriabin," and she did not hear *Le Sacre du Printemps,* one of the pathbreaking works of the century, until its twenty-fifth anniversary performance, a year before she died. Even then she told friends she did not expect to like it, that he did not write "her kind of music."[9]

Gertrude, the mother of Diane Arbus, was concerned about her children; "like any good mother, she wanted them only to do the 'right thing,' 'the correct thing,' and to have all the advantages."[10] Arbus was an original outsider, a portrayer of freaks, who eventually killed herself; Stravinsky lived a long, extraordinarily productive life, composing not "[his mother's] kind of music."

Stravinsky and Arbus strayed far from their mothers' narrow path. But we may not claim it was that path which forced them so far out. We may not assume that a conventional mother produces a freaky child, any more than that a freaky child produces a conventional mother—or that a wild and woolly mother produces a normal child. As researchers report, all sorts of mothers have all sorts of offspring. The two generations cannot be tied together by a neat knot.

Mothers and children may worship at very different altars and serve very different gods, even if they are placed all day long in the same family. No matter how close physically, they may have immensely different fates. Roy Cohn, one of those sleazy, clever power pushers who slide to the forefront throughout history, received protective, conventional parenting. "My parents were forever trying to provide me with a 'normal' childhood."[11] Summer camp; Park Avenue apartment; the Horace Mann school; Columbia Law. An only child, Cohn lived, traveled, and kept company with his mother, Muddy, until she died when he was forty. Throughout, she looked out for him; a careful, watchful, accommodating mother who called her son "the child." The "normal" child she sought became a notoriously shady mess.

Hannah Arendt's mother, too, was caring and watchful, keeping a diary of observations of and reflections upon Hannah's behavior from birth well into the teen years. She restrained Hannah from sitting up too soon and from freely moving her legs, swaddling her, as was the custom, in a *Wickelteppich,* or wrapping rug. She fostered her daughter's education in every respect. Two closely attentive mothers attempting to give their children the best; yet Cohn turned out ruthless, vain, and amoral, while Arendt became one of the leading moral philosophers of this age, friend of Karl Jaspers, lover of Martin Heidegger; she remained a "sunshine child" with a "genius for friendship" and a principled commitment to "neighborly love," an idea that lies at the heart of her enduring thought.[12]

Then there is the neglectful mother. "My mother used to put a pillow on the floor and give me one toy and just leave me there," said Barbara McClintock. Later, her overburdened mother sent her daughter out of state to live with relatives.[13] Edna St. Vincent Millay's mother, a nurse, yanked her daughter out of eighth grade after a dispute with the principal. Edna had been doing excellently in school and enjoyed her friends, but now she was left alone at home all day and often at night while her mother worked.[14] Tina Turner said: "I had no love from my mother or my father from the beginning. . . . *Alienation, rejection*—I didn't know those words. I just knew I couldn't communicate with my mother. . . . And that was the beginning for me. I didn't have anybody, no foundation in life, so I had . . . to discover my mission in life."[15]

Though neglected by their mothers, these children were not left alone by their daimons, which proved to be their foundations. For it was solitude that McClintock and Millay needed for their callings, and neglect that Turner required to discover hers. These acorns evidently picked mothers of the neglecting kind to provide the right environment for these young girls.

Whether their subject receives support from the mother (Casals, Wright, Roosevelt) or has differences with the mother (Lukács, Arbus, Stravinsky), or is neglected by the mother (McClintock, Millay, Turner), biographers tend to enlarge Mother with mythical greatness, confusing the power of her archetypal image with the force of the individual acorn.

DECONSTRUCTING THE PARENTS

The parental fallacy depends largely on this fantasy of one-way vertical causality, from larger to smaller, from older to younger, from experienced to inexperienced. Yet, just as actual motherhood is waning in the face of social changes that alter its conventions, so the theory of Mother's importance is being undermined by evidence against vertical causality within families.

Another twice-told tale. This one reports the behavior of a family of rhesus monkeys on an unpopulated Japanese island, where researchers left fresh sweet potatoes on the beach.

> Imo spat out the sand clinging to her sweet potato, put it into the sea, and rubbed it vigorously with her free hand. She ate the cleaned potato, enjoying its salty taste. Nearby, Nimby watched—and thrust her potato into the sea. She

didn't get all the sand off, but it still tasted better than ever before. The two young playmates' example taught others; soon their age-mates, both male and female, had caught on to the potato-washing routine. Imo's mother also learned, and soon was teaching potato washing to Imo's younger siblings. Imo's father, though he enjoyed a reputation for toughness and leadership, was too stubborn to try the new trick.[16]

The researcher David Rowe wants us to see that innovation and the transmission of ideas take place in various ways: horizontally within the family (sibling to sibling); vertically, but reciprocally, child to mother and mother to child; outside the family, as young monkeys learn from one another. Some—the old males—seem not to learn at all, or at least not about washing potatoes.

But one crucial question is not asked: How did Imo get the idea? How come she washed that first potato? What prompted that bit of behavior? Her daimon, of course— which inspired the whole event to begin with, and also the oft-told report. Imo's genius continues to teach you and me by means of this story. Yes, animals, too, have angels. As far back as we can imagine cultural history, it was widely believed that animals were the first teachers. Our earliest language, our dances, our rituals, our knowledge of what to eat and what not to eat, passed into our behavior through theirs.

Suspicion of vertical causality, particularly suspicion of the mother as primary factor in determining fate, comes from another direction as well. Diane Eyer calls mother-infant bonding (which gives her book its title) "a scientific fiction" (her subtitle).

Bonding is, in fact, as much an extension of ideology as it is a scientific discovery. More specifically, it is part of an ideology in which mothers are seen as the prime architects of their children's lives and are blamed for whatever

problems befall them, not only in childhood but throughout their adult lives.

Later in her book, Eyer says: "I would like to urge the impossible—that we discard the word [bonding] entirely . . .
[which] would force us to notice that children are not merely
putty in our hands. They are born with vastly different personalities and capabilities." Eyer's "scientific fiction" is my
"parental fallacy"; her perception of children's "vastly different personalities" is my vision of uniquely distinct acorns. Far
more than parents shape our lives:

> Children are profoundly affected by an array of people
> who interact with them, by the foods they eat, by the
> music they hear, by the television they watch, by the
> hope they see in the adult world. . . . People can connect
> with each other intellectually, emotionally, through daily
> caretaking, through games, through music and art,
> through formal learning and from long distances. There
> are many, many dimensions to the nurturance of our
> children.[17]

Eyer's net of nurturance could be cast wider, to include
the spiritual and religious phenomena arising autonomously
in children and reported in detail by Robert Coles. Also to be
included are the machineries and interiors that children live
within, the streets and their sounds, the explanations and values taught them, and the invisibles displayed by nature. All
this not only provides children with stimulation and input.
All this also expresses the meaning of the world, to which
each of them must respond. That some respond in unexpected ways, or refuse to respond at all, cannot logically be attributed to insecurities and disturbances in their tie with
parents. For any one of us, child or adult, the question eclips-
ing all others is: How does what comes with you to the world
find a place in the world? How does my meaning fit with the

meanings to which I am asked to conform? What helps growing down?

The parental fallacy does not help anyone grow down. It pulls us away from the acorn and back to Mom and Dad, who may already be dead and gone though we remain stuck with their effects. I am then a mere effect myself, a result of their causes. For all our heroic individualism America still clings to a mother-based developmental psychology that states we are fundamentally results of parenting and, as such, fundamentally victims of what happened in the past and left indelible stains. Psychologically, as a nation, we seem ever to be trying to put the past behind us, trying to recover from past abuses. Perhaps recovery begins only when we have put the mother myth behind us. For we are less the victims of parenting than of the ideology of parenting; less the victims of Mother's fateful power than of the theory that gives her that fateful power.

John Bowlby's immensely influential *Child Care and the Growth of Love* states that theory. An archetypal voice of the Great Mother sounds through it, with dire warnings of evil and death if the theory be unheeded, the mother's power dishonored.

> The evidence is now such that it leaves no room for doubt regarding the general proposition—that the prolonged deprivation of a young child of maternal care may have grave and far-reaching effects on his [sic] character and so on the whole of his future life. It is a proposition exactly similar in form to those regarding the evil after-effects of German measles before birth or deprivation of vitamin D in infancy.[18]

It is not your mother who holds dominion over your adult life, but the ideology that proclaims that each of us has been determined in the first hours after birth, or during birth itself, the ideology that proclaims a series of tiny causes and accumulating effects lead to how you are today and how you will affect your own children. You are the direct cause of damage to their lives, damage resulting not merely in their frustration and failure, but in crimes and madness. This ideology traps women in the parental fallacy and children in mother-blame. Eyer's caustic criticism deconstructs this ideology. But her deconstruction is not destructive. Like mine, it aims to dissolve the fallacy that has made bonding a bondage. "The fallacy," says David Rowe,

> is in believing that what forms human nature is a fourteen-year period of rearing, rather than a heavier weight of cultural history and ultimately human evolutionary roots. In broader terms, cultural traditions can be passed in many ways other than exposure to idealized nuclear families. The adolescents who signed up enthusiastically for Nazi youth groups before World War II did not have souls bent and torn by poor rearing in early childhood; indeed, their families were stolidly middle-class and emotionally supportive. If a nation's youth can be changed by a few years of great cultural change, why emphasize childhood?[19]

The elevation of the parents, of the mother in particular, to the neglect of all other realities—societal, environmental, economic—shows that adulation of an archetype can obliterate common sense. Eyer notes that worldwide authorities on mothering (Bowlby and T. Berry Brazelton) attribute the hollow-eyed lassitude and sadness of young children in Cambodia and in post–World War II Europe to the loss of their mothers and to other disturbances in the mother-child relationships, taking no note of the overwhelming horrors in the world encompassing these mothers and children. Had these children been "well-bonded," with "good-enough mothers," secure in their "attachments," the devastation, genocide, and despair would have been incidental to their deplorable condition! Again the archetypal myth of the completely surrounding mother, insulating from all influences, prevails over the actual world of collective pain. The mother myth encloses as well the minds of the scientific observers. Mother-based theories comfort and suffocate, both.

A very different sort of observer, Mary Watkins, points out that the major psychological theorists—D. W. Winnicott, Melanie Klein, René Spitz, John Bowlby, Anna Freud—who lay such stress upon the mother-child relation as *the* determinant of life ever after worked out their ideas while bombs were falling and buildings burning in England, or just before and just after World War II. It is not unusual to retreat to the mother when in danger, but must psychoanalytic "science," too, hide behind her skirts?

Eyer's remark that children are "profoundly affected . . . by the hope they see in the adult world" may be the key to the dismay and disorder of children. What hope do they see in the adult world? Pinning hope on a child and its future is easier than finding a larger hope for the adult world itself. Archaic peoples and tribal communities offered their children constancy, an unlimited time span of continuities. Cyclical changes and nomadic migrations did not shake the foundations. Myths made life livable, and hope was not even a category of archaic existence. Hope enters history, and our psychology, as trust in continuity fades.

Our main myth is apocalyptic, as the Revelation of St. John, the last book of our Bible, says, and our children today live among and act out images of catastrophe.[20] Of course suicide among children shows a startling rise. How troubling it must be for a child to tie its star to a collapsing structure of depletion, extinction, and loss that cannot be repaired by bonding people together in satisfying human relationships. It's all beyond people, says this myth. The only hope, according to the authorized version of the catastrophe, is in a divine redemption and a second chance. In face of that cosmic science fiction of Armageddon, psychology's scientific fiction narrows the cause of devastated children to dysfunctional parenting, while a world with all the parents in it edges toward the cliff.

ABSENT THE FATHER

"Dad! Are you home? Is anybody here?" No. Dad is out to lunch. And he should be—as I shall claim. His job is elsewhere—as I shall explain—because his fundamental value to the family is maintaining the connection to elsewhere.

When we watch Dad on TV sitcoms and the accompanying ads, he's a rather foolish man. He's not quite with it; a piece of him is astray. Commentators on contemporary fatherhood complain that he is being deliberately made to look foolish and antiquated, because this weakened image helps take down the stuffed-shirt power of the patriarchy, makes more equal the relations between the genders, and blurs the hierarchical differences between fathers and children. Therefore wives are shown to be more practical and connected, children to be more with it and savvy. Even if he's a good guy, Dad is a little dumb.

I want to suggest that something more is going on than shifting social conventions and softening of the patriarchal father. The comedy played out on TV has a subtle subplot with appropriate foundations. Maybe Dad's true task is *not* knowing about coffee, bleach, and mouthwash or how to resolve pubescent dating dilemmas, and maybe his dumbness shows that this is truly not his world. His world is not shown in these sets, for it's offstage, elsewhere and invisible. He must keep one foot in another space, one ear cocked for other messages. He must not lose his calling or forget obligations to the heart's desire and the image that he embodies.

Of course, this is not an obligation only of men; but it is men who are defined as "absent." So our psychological task is to explore this absence beyond the usual charges of desertion, workaholic addiction, negligent unrelatedness, lack of child-support payments, double-standardism, and patriarchal pomp which are rightly laid at the feet of many fathers.

Fathers have been far away for centuries: on military campaigns; as sailors on distant seas for years at a time; as cattle drivers, travelers, trappers, prospectors, messengers, prisoners, jobbers, peddlers, slavers, pirates, missionaries, migrant workers. The work week was once seventy-two hours. The construct "fatherhood" shows widely different faces in different countries, classes, occupations, and historical times.[21] Only today is absence so shaming, and declared a criminal, even criminal-producing, behavior. As a social evil, the absent father is one of the bogeys of the remedial age, this historical period of therapy, recovery, and social programs that try to fix what we do not understand.

The conventional father-image, of a man at his job, coming home at dusk to his family, earning, sharing, and caring, with quality time for his kids, is another fantasy of the parental fallacy. This image is way off its statistical base. As of 1993 only a very few families in the United States fit the pattern of a working husband-father earning for a family consisting of a stay-at-home wife-mother and their own two children. Everyone else is doing something different. The statistical pull in a father is thus preponderantly *not* to fulfill this image, just as for a woman it is *not* to fulfill the image of a stay-at-home, wife-mother. If "family values" mean parents' togetherness with their natural children in their own house, these values have little to do with how the American people actually live.

Rather than blaming fathers for their absenteeism and the concomitant unfairness of loading extra burdens onto mothers, mentors, the schools, the police, and taxpayers, we need to ask where Dad might be when he's "not at home." When he is absent, to what else might he be present? What calls him away? Rilke has an answer:

> Sometimes a man stands up during supper
> and walks outdoors, and keeps on walking,
> because of a church that stands somewhere in the East.

And his children say blessings on him as if he were dead.

And another man, who remains inside his own house,
dies there, inside the dishes and in the glasses,
so that his children have to go far out into the world
toward that same church, which he forgot.[22]

Rilke accounts for the father's absence. What about the quality of his presence—that anger, that hatred? Why is Father such an abusive, brutal family destroyer? What is this rage?

Is it really his wife he hates, his children he wants to beat, because no one does what he says and they cost so much? Or might there be another factor, less personal and more demonic, that has him and doesn't let up?

I have come to be convinced that the parental fallacy itself has harnessed Father's spirit to a false image, and his daimon turns demonic in kicking against the traces. He is trapped in a construct called American fatherhood, a moral commandment to be the kind of good guy who likes Disneyland, and kids' food, gadgets, opinions, and wisecracks.

This bland model betrays his necessary angel, that image of whatever else he carries in his heart, glimpsed from childhood into the present day and which this book would confirm for him. The man who has lost his angel becomes demonic; and the absence, the anger, and the paralysis on the couch are all symptoms of the soul in search of a lost call to something other and beyond. Father's oscillations between rage and apathy, like his children's allergies and behavior disorders and his wife's depressions and bitter resentments, form part of a pattern they all share—not the "family system," but the system of rip-off economics that promotes their communal senselessness by substituting "more" for "beyond."

And so his absences—physical, mental, spiritual—call him away from the cage of American delusions that crush the angel's wings. Without inspiration, what's left is bare, aimless ferocity. Without desire for an ideal, what's left is lustful fantasy and the seduction of free-floating images that find no anchor in actual projects. Present in body and absent in spirit, he lies back on the couch, shamed by his own daimon for the potentials in his soul that will not be subdued. He feels himself inwardly subversive, imagining in his passivity extremes of aggression and desire that must be suppressed. Solution: more work, more money, more drink, more weight, more things, more infotainment, and an almost fanatic dedication of his mature male life to the kids so that they can grow up straight and straight up the consumer ladder in the pursuit of their happiness.

A "happy" child was never and nowhere the aim of parenting. An industrious, useful child; a malleable child; a healthy child; an obedient, mannerly child; a stay-out-of-trouble child; a God-fearing child; an entertaining child—all these varieties, yes. But the parental fallacy has trapped the parents also in providing happiness, along with shoes, schoolbooks, and van-packed vacations. Can the unhappy produce happiness? Since happiness at its ancient source means *eudaimonia,* or a well-pleased daimon, only a daimon who is receiving its due can transmit a happy benefit to a child's soul. Yes, I am saying that "care of soul," as Thomas Moore has written, may thereby help the child's soul prosper.

Should the onus of soul-making in the parent shift to making the soul of the child, then the parent is dodging the lifelong task set by the acorn. Then the child replaces the acorn. You feel your child is special, and you care for it as your calling, seeking to realize the acorn in your child. So your daimon complains because it is avoided, and your child complains because it has become an effigy of the parents' own calling. Your mother, as I said, may be a demon, but she is not your daimon; so your child, too, is not your daimon.

I have learned, through years of work with patients and in men's retreats, and from listening to what cautions me, that when a child substitutes for your daimon you will resent that child, even grow to hate it, despite goodwill and high ethics. The novelist and brilliant social critic Michael Ventura writes that Americans hate their children.[23] His observation seems preposterous. What culture in history ever spoke more as a child, felt more as a child, thought more as a child, or was more reluctant to put all childish things away? And what culture today campaigns more to save the children globally, provides more emergency help for preemies and for surgical transplants in infants whatever the cost, and engages in more frontline defense of the fetus? Yet all this is a cover under which hides an appalling neglect.

Just look at the evidence. Of the 57 million children (under fifteen years of age) living in the United States, more than 14 million are living below the official poverty level. The United States ranks below Iran and Romania in the percentage of low-birth-weight babies. One of every six children is a stepchild, and half a million make their "homes" in residential treatment centers and group and foster homes. More children and adolescents in the United States die from suicide than from cancer, AIDS, birth defects, influenza, heart disease, and pneumonia *combined.* Each day, at least 1 million "latchkey children" go home to where there is a gun.[24]

Besides these children who find their way into sociological statistics, there are those from all economic classes in treatment for attention deficit disorders, hyperactivity, obesity, defiance, bulimia, depression, pregnancy, addiction . . .

Gross economic injustice, political passivity, and the delusions of circuses (without bread) are responsible for the plight of children. But also I accuse the parental fallacy of sponsoring this negligence. Parents' deficient attention to the individual call they brought with them into the world and the hyperactivity of their distraction from this call betrays their reason for being alive. When your child becomes the reason for your life, you have abandoned the invisible reason *you* are here. And the reason you are here as an adult, as a citizen, as a parent? To make a world receptive to the daimon. To set the civilization straight so that a child can grow down into it and its daimon can have a life. This is the parenting task. To carry out this task for the daimon of your child you must bear witness first to your own.

Any father who has abandoned the small voice of his unique genius, turning it over to the small child he has fathered, cannot bear reminders of what he has neglected. He cannot tolerate the idealism that arises so naturally and spontaneously in the child, the romantic enthusiasms, the sense of fairness, the clear-eyed beauty, the attachment to little things, and the interest in big questions. All this becomes unbearable to a man who has forgotten his daimon.

Instead of learning from the child, who is living evidence of the invisibles in everyone's life, the father capitulates to the child, disturbing its growing down into civilization by setting it up in a toy world. Result: a child-dominated fatherless culture with dysfunctional children with pistol-packing power. Like the vampires that so fascinate them, children in our culture, sentimentalized for their innocence and neglected on account of the bother they cause, drain away the blood of adult life.

ANCESTORS

The belief that parents shape my world from the beginning strikes me as a variety of "misplaced concreteness." I take the term from the English philosopher Alfred North Whitehead. Misplaced concreteness does not keep "abstract" and "concrete" distinct enough. Cosmic mythical parents and personal mothers and fathers get mixed up. Then the formative powers and mysteries assigned to abstractions such as heaven and earth, Sky God and Earth Goddess (or vice versa, in Egyptian myth) become concrete mothers and fathers, while mothers and fathers are divinized, causing effects of cosmic proportion.

The displaced powers of the mythical couple who sustain the world, like Zeus and Hera, become the "family romance," as Freud called the fallacy. Involvements with parents make us or break us. Moreover, you believe you belong only to this personal story and your parents' personal influence on it, rather than to the invisible myths parents have displaced. Being shaped so fatally by the parental world means having lost the larger world-parents, and also the world at large as parent. For the world too shapes us, nurtures us, teaches us.

If today our civilization is turning toward the environment to stave off ecological disaster, the first step of this rapprochement with nature is to cross the threshold of the parental house into the home of the world. We are parented by everything around us—if "parenting" means watching, instructing, encouraging, and admonishing. Do you really believe that humans invented the wheel out of their big brains alone, or fire, or baskets, or tools? Stones rolled downhill; bolts of fire shot from the sky and out of the earth; birds wove and probed and pounded, as did apes and elephants. The sciences that master nature were taught by nature how it could be mastered.

The more we cling to the overriding importance of parents and the more cosmological power we accord them, the less we notice the fathering and mothering afforded by the world every day in what it sends our way. As J. J. Gibson's psychological school at Cornell University maintained, the world affords nesting and sheltering, nourishing and quenching, adventuring and playing. The world is made less of nouns than of verbs. It doesn't consist merely in objects and things; it is filled with useful, playful, and intriguing opportunities. The oriole doesn't see a branch, but an occasion for perching; the cat doesn't see a thing we call an empty box, it sees safe hiding for peering. The bear doesn't smell honeycomb, but the opportunity for delicious feeding. The world is buzzing and blooming with information, which is always available and never absent.

Children, especially, recognize this nurturance and instruction offered by nature. According to the observations of the brilliant pioneer of ecology Edith Cobb, the imagination of children depends wholly on this contact with the environment.[25] Imagination does not grow all by itself in the household, or even out of imaginative tales told by parents. Children are "by nature" at home in the world; the world invites them to grow down and take part. And this is not merely a statement prompted by Jean-Jacques Rousseau, Friedrich Froebel (the originator of the kindergarten), and Alice Miller—for I am not saying children are naturally good or whole, only that their imaginations and minds feed on a nature that is also their parent. Therefore, if our children today are disordered, it isn't so much parenting they need as, perhaps, less parentalism, which keeps them from trust and pleasure in the actual, physical world.

The more I believe my nature comes from my parents, the less open I am to the ruling influences around me. The less the surrounding world is felt to be intimately important to my story. Yet even biographies begin by locating the subject in a place; the self starts off amid the smells of a geography. The moment the angel enters a life it enters an environment. We are ecological from day one.

So the coming ecological disaster we worry about has already occurred, and goes on occurring. It takes place in the accounts of ourselves that separate us from the world by attaching us to parentalism, the belief that what's out there is less of a factor than my close family in the formation of who I am. The parental fallacy is deadly to individual self-awareness, and it is killing the world.

Until this psychological fallacy is set straight, no compassionate campaigns of multiculturalism and environmentalism, no field trips, Peace Corps, bird-watching, or whale songs can fundamentally reattach me to the world. First I must make that psychological reconstruction, that leap of faith out of the house of the parents and into the home of the world.

Psychotherapy compounds this fault. Its theory of developmental damage owing to the family actually turns the patient away from everything else that might give comfort and instruction. To what does the soul turn that has no therapists to visit? It takes its trouble to the trees, to the riverbank, to an animal companion, on an aimless walk through the city streets, a long watch of the night sky. Just stare out the window or boil water for a cup of tea. We breathe, expand, and let go, and something comes in from elsewhere. The daimon in the heart seems quietly pleased, preferring melancholy to desperation. It's in touch.

The "facilitating environment" so necessary to the fantasy of adequate parenting, according to D. W. Winnicott (the gentle, down-home clinical philosopher of sensible therapy), is the *actual* environment, were it not so neglected and therefore feared. By leaving the actual world out of its main theoretical constructs, psychological theory imagines that world out there as objective, cold, indifferent, even hostile (therapy as protective refuge, consulting room as sanctuary). Thus the world receives the projection of the bad mother, the killing mother, which its theory has invented. We're back to a world of nature as conceived by Descartes four centuries ago, a bare *res extensa,* an extended field of matter void of soul, inhospitable, mechanical, even demonic.

Of course there are demons out there to be propitiated. Disasters lurk, but these powers behind the door and in the bush are also ancestors, not merely germs, spiders, and quicksand. As we have misplaced the cosmological parents, so we have lost the ancestors too. The parents have swallowed them up.

Our biographies and case histories begin with the facts of our parents and the place of our birth. They sometimes go back through the parents to the bloodline of four grandparents, in the best cases even to the eight great-grandparents. Most stop their genealogy at Mom and Pop, some even at Mom alone—since Pop is always absent.

Thus the idea of ancestors filters through actual parents. Besides their divinization as the movers and shakers of your heaven and earth, parents have also usurped the protective duties and the demands for attention traditionally accorded to the invisible ancestors. "Ancestry" in our culture implies chromosomal connection; ancestors are those humans from whom I have inherited my body tissues. Biogenetics replaces the spirit world.

In other societies an ancestor could be a tree, a bear, a salmon, a member of the dead, a spirit in a dream, a special spooky place. These may be addressed as "Ancestor" and an altar home built for them, away from the home you inhabit. Ancestors are not bound to human bodies and certainly not confined to physical antecedents whose descent into your sphere allowed only via your natural family. Only if a member of the natural family (itself not always determinable), say a grandparent or an uncle or an aunt, is worthy enough, powerful enough, knowledgeable enough, may he or she become an ancestor in the sense of a guardian spirit. To be an ancestor you do not need to be dead, but you do need to know the dead—that is, the invisible world and how and where it touches the living.

As spirits, ancestors are concerned with other spirits, the community as a whole, the things they live with, the locations in their environments, and the particular image in the heart that keeps your person hale and sees you through. When you boil over rashly or grow lax and impotent or become quarrelsome and petty, specific ancestors may be called on to ward off bad influences and set things right. None of these dysfunctional states is attributed to your parents. Whatever is wrong with you comes from elsewhere: spells; taboo breaking; rituals unperformed; bad airs, waters, places; a distant enemy; an angry divinity; a neglected duty or forgotten offense. But never, never could the state of your soul be attributed to what your mother or father did to you some thirty years ago! They simply were the necessary occasion for your appearance in the community, their having performed the necessary rites that allowed your soul to enter the world.

Without a sense of ancestors, what can we propitiate as having a direct and controlling influence over our lives, but our parents? We take literally the commandment to "Honor thy father and thy mother," which shows decency and kindness. But let's not forget that the Fifth Commandment, along with the ones preceding it, aims to eliminate all traces of pagan polytheism, to which ancestor worship is essential. The text makes it clear that these "parents" are not just human Mom and Dad. They have huge powers and are to be honored as guarantors of fate, "that thy days may be prolonged, and that it may go well with thee, upon the land which the Lord thy God hath given thee" (Deut. 5:16). Like ancestor spirits, they are protective guardians of a long life, bearers of good fortune, and nature spirits inhabiting the land itself. By command, henceforth and forever more, the parental fallacy is established. The primordial spirit world has been reduced to the all-too-human concrete statues of personal figures.

This reduction by official religion of that splendid archaic menagerie of ancestors has taken centuries. We call it civilization. Gaia and Ouranos, Geb and Nut, Bor and Bestla shrunk to this small measure of Mom and Pop, not in heaven at all, just one easy flight up above our daily commerce. Our horizons have been cut down to their scale, and their scale magnified by what they replace. And our rituals wither to once-a-year Hallmark days in honor of them, care for their health and welfare, and phone calls, even if we continue to attribute immense determining power to their magical influence over our intimate lives.

"Honor thy father and thy mother," yes, indeed; but do not confuse them with creator-destroyer gods, or with ancestors. It is laborious to "work through" the "parent-problem" because it is not a mere logical error or misplaced concreteness, or a difficult step in a therapeutic process toward individual self-determination. Working through the parental fallacy is more like a religious conversion—out of our secularism, out of our personalism, out of our monotheism, developmentalism, and belief in causality. It requires a step backward into the old connection with invisibilities and a trusting step out and over the threshold into the rich profusion of influences afforded by the world. "Religion," Whitehead also said, "is world loyalty."[26] This could imply disloyalty to a belief long held dear by society as a whole, by therapy in general and by you in particular: the belief in the power of parents.

— ❧ —

CHAPTER 4

BACK TO THE
INVISIBLES

Since the acorn can't even be seen under a microscope, we postulate its invisible reality. To learn more about it we need first to study the nature of invisibility. Invisibility perplexes American common sense and American psychology, which hold as a major governing principle that whatever exists, exists in some quantity and therefore can be measured. If an image in the heart that calls you to your fate exists, and may be strong and long-lasting, has it measurable dimensions? A passion to cage the invisible by visible methods continues to motivate the science of psychology, even though that science has given up the century-long search for the soul in various body parts and systems. When the searchers failed to find the soul in the places where they were looking, scientistic psychology gave up also on the idea of soul.

There are other approaches to the soul, other accounts of fate-determining invisibilities. Swedes tell a folktale of the forests. The lumberjacks of northern pine, fir, and spruce used to work pretty much alone, felling trees, lopping branches. They drank, too, in the short days of white cold. Coffee. *Snaps* . . . Sometimes Huldra would appear. She was an exquisitely formed creature, delicate, enchanting, and irresistible. Sometimes, a woodcutter would stop his work, even drop his ax to follow her beckoning farther into the woods. As he approached, she turned her back—and vanished. Once Huldra turned her smiling face away, there was nothing. She had no back, or her back was invisible. And he, drawn too deeply into the forest, unable to find familiar markings or get back to a clearing, lost his bearings and froze.

MYTHICAL THINKING

I am opening this chapter with a mythical tale of the siren— the wood nymph, the tree-soul—and of the simple human at his chores who at her disappearance loses direction and motion and dies. The interpretation of the tale in terms of male and female roles, of archetypal anima, of losing the soul to fantasy projections, of the enchanted forest as mother domain, of archaic vegetative spirits taking revenge on man the destructive ax-murderer—these do not take the tale back far enough, back to the absent back of Huldra.

Behind each and every interpretation of the tale is the tale. The tale provides the invisible backdrop against which all analyses parade their brilliance. Myth lies behind every account we give of it, and it gives no account of itself. Myths fall back on invisibility. They show an enchanting face, but their backing disappears under scrutiny. Nothing's there. We are lost in the woods.

We can all tell tales of how myths came into being: out of dreams; out of primitive "man's" attempt to explain the cosmos and its natural phenomena; as ways of establishing tribal law by reference to fearful powers; from shamanistic visions and revelations; or just in portentous elaborations of simple stories told by old women, after beer in the firelight, to pass the time or lull the young to sleep. . . . Whatever the account of the origin of myth, what's behind myths remains inscrutable.

Great philosophical questions turn on the relations of visible and invisible. Our religious beliefs separate heaven and earth, this life and the afterlife, and our philosophical thinking cuts apart mind and matter, all of which forces a chasm between the visible and the invisible. How to bridge the chasm? What means are there for transporting the unseen into the seen? Or the seen into the unseen?

There are three traditional bridges: mathematics, music, and myths. Mysticism might be considered a fourth. However, mysticism unites visible and invisible; all things are transparent and proclaim their invisible ground. So for the mystic there is no chasm and no problem. Engineering a rational connection between the realms may only push them further apart. That is why mystics recommend contemplating a dilemma rather than trying to fix it.

The equations of math, the notations on a musical score, and the personifications of myth cross the limbo land between two worlds. They offer a seductive front that seems to present the unknown other side, a seduction that leads to the delusional conviction that math, music, and myths *are* the other side. We tend to believe that the real truth of the invisible world is mathematical and might be put into a single unified field equation, and/or that it is a musical harmony of the spheres, and/or that it consists in mythical beings and powers, with names and shapes, who pull the strings that determine the visible. The three modes transpose the mystery of the invisible into visible procedures we can work with: higher math, musical notations, and mythical images. So enchanted are we by the mystery transposed into these systems that we mistake the systems for the mystery; rather, they are indications pointing toward it. We forget the old lesson, and mistake the finger that points at the moon for the moon itself.

We believe Huldra's invisible back must be as beautiful as her front. What is the relation between what we see and what we don't? Is her back displayed in her front, and does the smile of beauty therefore lure because it is the best possible representation of the invisible?

Beauty could be a bridge, but we can't be so sure. Huldra's back may be a horror; after all, the woodsman dies lost and frozen. So, though beauty has been defined by Neoplatonists[1] as invisible presence in visible form and the divine enhancement of earthly things, it offers no structure and no permanence. Tracking its definitions through history will not lead us where we are now heading. Besides, beauty has been reduced to the other three bridges: mathematical proportion, harmony of parts, and the radiance of the goddess Aphrodite. Curious how the search for Huldra's back leads so deep into the mythical forest. And we can't get out by searching for familiar facts. The invisible shows no facts.

The stories that myths tell cannot be documented in histories; the gods and goddesses, and the heroes and their enemies, are told about in stories inscribed in clay and carved in statues, but have they ever been physically seen? The fabulous places of myth are not in this world—all invented, just fables. The long-lasting and ever-renewing vitality of myths has nothing factual behind it. Nothing but invisibles lies behind all myths' strength. "Myth is a mixture of truth and poetic fancy. This fading into uncertainty belongs to the very nature of myth," says the Plato scholar Paul Friedländer.[2] Perhaps Huldra, fading into the forest, is myth personified, the basic truth of myth captured in a single poetic image.

Usual life, too, is backed by invisibles, those abstractions of high-energy physics that compose all the visible, palpable, and durable stuff we bump into; the invisibles of theology we kneel to; the invisible ideals that take us to war and death; the invisible diagnostic concepts that explain our marriages, our motives, and our madnesses. And what about time; has anyone seen it recently? All these invisibles, which we take so for granted, seem much harder and firmer than the flimsy fantasies of myth.

We live among a throng of invisibles that order us about: Family Values, Self-Development, Human Relationships, Personal Happiness, and then another, more fierce set of mythical figures called Control, Success, Cost-Effectiveness, and (the biggest and most pervasively invisible) the Economy. Were we in old Florence or ancient Rome or Athens, our invisible dominants would have statues and altars, or at least painted images, as did the Florentine, Roman, Athenian invisibles called Fortune, Hope, Friendship, Grace, Modesty, Persuasion, Fame, Ugliness, Forgetfulness. . . . But our task here is not to restore all the invisibles but to discriminate among them by attending to the one that once was called your daimon or genius, sometimes your soul or your fate, and now your acorn.

Perhaps these other sorts of daily invisibles that we accept without thinking receive their hardness from our attachment to them. If we cling like barnacles to our favorite set of invisibles, then they must serve as rocks and feel as solid. Philosopher Henri Bergson explained why we prefer particles to myths: "The human intellect feels at home among inanimate objects, more especially among solids, where our action finds its fulcrum and our industry its tools; . . . our concepts have been formed on the model of solids, . . . our logic is preeminently, a logic of solids."[3] Bergson concludes, therefore, that intellect is unsuited for actual living and for the account of life. All the while, this same inadequate intellect fights furiously against other sorts of accounts, such as myth, which it condemns with solid arguments, buttressed with facts, supported by evidence, and structured by logic.

William Wordsworth saw through the logic of solids, perceiving the invisible within them:

> To every natural form, rock, fruit, or flower,
> Even the loose stones that cover the highway,
> I gave a moral life: I saw them feel
> Or linked them to some feeling: the great mass

Lay bedded in some quickening soul, and all
That I beheld respired with inward meaning.[4]

"Authentic tidings of invisible things!" adds William James in his essay entitled "On a Certain Blindness in Human Beings," where he quotes Wordsworth among passages from Ralph Waldo Emerson, W. H. Hudson, Josiah Royce, Robert Louis Stevenson, Leo Tolstoy, and Walt Whitman as witnesses to the presence of the invisible.[5]

James ironically praises and blames this "certain blindness." On the one hand, he condemns our usual perception, which cannot see the invisible inwardness of rock, fruit, and flower. On the other hand, precisely this blinding of the usual intellectual mind and the blunting of its sharp edge permits us to say, with Wordsworth, "I saw them feel."

The Wordsworth passage is a statement of mythical *thinking* and not merely a feeling. "I saw them feel" shows a softer sensibility in intellect itself that can receive and understand the authentic tidings of invisible things. Just this sensibility in intellect, which I am also calling mythic sensibility, allows you to notice the quickening soul in which our lives are bedded. For Wordsworth and for mythic sensibility in general, the acorn is not embedded in me, like a pacemaker in my heart, but rather I am embedded in a mythical reality of which the acorn is but my particular and very small portion. What the Romantics called the "quickening soul" is today named psychic reality. It is all over the place, although we insist it is invisible.

INTUITION

The traditional mode of perceiving the invisible and therefore of perceiving the acorn is intuition. Intuition also includes what I have called mythic sensibility, for when a myth strikes us, it seems true and gives sudden insight.

In psychology intuition means "direct and unmediated knowledge," "immediate or innate apprehension of a complex group of data."[6] Intuition is both thoughtless and also not a feeling state; it is a clear, quick, and full apprehension, "the significant feature being the immediacy of the process."[7] Intuitions "occur to a person without any known process of cogitation or reflective thinking."[8]

Our perceptions of people are mostly intuitive. We take them in as a whole—accent, clothes, build, expression, complexion, voice, stance, gestures, the regional, social, and class cues—all delivers itself at once, as a full gestalt, to intuition. The old diagnosticians of internal medicine used intuition; so do photographers and astrologers and personnel managers and baseball scouts and deans of admission, and probably also CIA analysts, retrieving the field information and seeing in a mass of tedious data an invisible significance. Intuition perceives the image, the *paradeigma,* a whole gestalt.

Intuitions occur; we do not make them. They come to us as a sudden idea, a definite judgment, a grasped meaning. They come with an event as if brought by it or inherent in it. You say something, and I "get it," just like that. You show me a short, complicated poem, and "I see." We go to the blockbuster retrospective at the art museum, and without reading the blurb sheet or plugging in the audio lecture, I suddenly find myself gasping "Aha" in front of a painting on the wall. I've been struck.

Your sentence that I intuitively grasp, the complex poem, and the picture on the museum wall are each expressive forms and quite visible. The rapid understanding that seizes me, bringing me to what psychology calls the "aha *Erlebnis,*" that gasping response of sudden insight, pulls or pushes my breath out of me by the force in the picture. Mythical thinking attributes this forcefulness, which produces my insight, to a power in the thing. The power in the thing establishes the reality, even the physicality, of the invisible.

Another important characteristic of intuition is the way it works. It does not expand slowly as a gradual suffusion of mood; nor does it advance by thought, step by step; nor does it come to its insight by a careful examination of sensate details that compose the whole object before me. As I said, intuition is clear, quick, and full. Like a revelation it comes all at once, and fast. It is quite independent of time—just as myths are timeless, and fall apart when we ask of them temporal questions such as "When did this occur?" "What is the origin?" "Did the myth develop?" "Are there no new myths?" "Don't they result from historical events?" And so on. The historian bound by the data of time never can quite get into mythical sensibility.

Because intuitions are clear, quick, and full, and therefore so convincing, they can be wholly wrong, missing the mark just as quickly and completely as they can get it right. Jung, who placed intuition (with thinking, feeling, and sensation) among the four functions of consciousness, made a major point of intuition's need for its brother and sister functions.[9] Alone, it can pick the wrong horse as surely as the right one, or go off with paranoid certitude, oblivious of logic, feeling, and fact. But Jung's ironic realism regarding intuition was not shared by the idealist strain of intuitionist philosophers. Baruch Spinoza, Friedrich Schelling, Benedetto Croce, Henri Bergson, Edmund Husserl, and Alfred North Whitehead ennoble it one way or another as an axiomatic and quasi-divine gift that is, as well, a philosophical method of knowing truth.

Intuition is also called upon for explaining creativity and genius, the inexplicable accounted for by a process that is itself inexplicable. But the idolization of intuition neglects especially its darkest shadow, the intuitive opportunism of the sociopath, and the clear, quick, and full seizures of the psychopathic criminal whose unmediated and self-evident propositions produce wholly arbitrary and casual deeds of violence, without logic, feeling, or appreciation of the real facts.

Intuition may propose a way, but does not assure right action or even accurate perception. This we know from any of our immediate, self-evident moves such as falling in love with the wrong person, making false accusations and issuing rash dismissals, and arriving at those sure self-diagnoses of medical conditions that prove wholly hypochondriacal. Though certain, intuition may not be accurate. Our mythic sensibility may pick up the authentic tidings of inward things, but authenticity can be assured only by checking the facts, looking back at tradition, thinking carefully, and valuing by feeling. For centuries the Roman Catholic church has used these methods for testing intuitive claims of sanctity and examining miracles.

This excursus on intuition was necessary for three reasons. First, we needed an acceptable term for the kind of perception that sees mythically ("I saw them feel"), that sees through the visible, and that claims insight into the invisible. We needed to make psychologically plausible the idea of mythical sensibility, equivalent to that of math and music, so that reliance on myth in this book may carry conviction. To grasp or be grasped by myth you need intuition. The relevance of a myth to life strikes like a revelation or a self-evident proposition, which cannot be demonstrated by logic or induced from factual evidence. The best evidence is anecdote, the telling example that lights up an obscure idea in a clear intuitive flash.

The second reason for this excursus was to show a common function at work in the three bridges, math, music, and myth, and also in the realm of aesthetics or beauty. It is intuition that gives them each their instantaneity and sureness. Kant's theory of aesthetics relies on intuition, as does Mozart's description of composition. Authorities who have examined poetic inspiration and mathematical invention show the immediate certitude of intuition in the examples they present—e.g., the mathematician Henri Poincaré's oft-cited statement that "Most striking at first is this appearance of sudden illumination."[10]

The third reason takes us again to biographies and to a terrible tension between intuition and tuition in many exemplars of the acorn. Emerson wrote: "We denote this primary wisdom as Intuition whilst all later teachings are tuitions."[11] Emerson opposes the two, seeing *intuition* as *not*-tuition. Insight and learning, the heart's imagination and classroom study, do not have to be opposed. Nevertheless, Emerson correctly intuited that strong division in many of the eminent who chose intuition over tuition. They quit school; they hated it; they wouldn't or couldn't learn; they were thrown out; their teachers walked out on them: intuition at war with tuition.

SCHOOLDAYS AND NIGHTMARES

Cradles of Eminence, a delightful (and well-documented) report on the childhoods of four hundred famous modern persons, states that three fifths of the subjects "had serious school problems": "Rejection of the classroom is an international phenomenon and has little to do with whether the schools are public or private, secular or clerical, or with the philosophy of teaching employed in the various schools."[12] Nor does the school difficulty of these eminent persons have anything to do with their families' attitudes, economic circumstances, or educational level. Hating school, failing school, expulsion from school afflicts all sorts, for better or for worse.

Thomas Mann, who was awarded Nobel recognition largely for a novel he wrote in his early twenties, described school as "stagnating and unsatisfactory"; the great Indian scholar and poet Rabindranath Tagore (who, like Mann, came from an educated and well-to-do background) quit school at thirteen because he suffered so much there. "I was fortunate enough to extricate myself before insensibility set in." "Of his schooldays Gandhi said that they were the most miserable years of his life . . . that he had no aptitude for lessons and rarely appreciated his teachers . . . and might have done better if he had never been to school." The Norwegian novelist Sigrid Undset declared: "I hated school so intensely. I avoided the discipline by an elaborate technique of being absent-minded during classes." The Nobel Prize–winning physicist Richard Feynman called his early school "an intellectual desert." The actor and director Kenneth Branagh so feared school when he was about eleven that he tried throwing himself downstairs to break a leg rather than go. Later he withdrew into his room and read and read. The German filmmaker Rainer Werner Fassbinder simply "could not remain in the company of normal children" and eventually was put in a Rudolf Steiner school. Jackson Pollock, "who flouted . . . school requirements as blithely as he ignored its dress code" was expelled from Los Angeles High School. John Lennon was expelled from kindergarten.

The saddest story I have found of the miseries of the schoolchild comes from the English poet Robert Browning. He was sent off to a boarding school at the age of eight or nine. It so depressed him that "he chose a leaden cistern in the school for his 'place of burial.' It had on it a raised image of a face. He imagined this face as his epitaph, passing his hands over it again and again and chanting, 'In memory of unhappy Browning.'" As for the lessons, Browning said "they taught him nothing there."

The imaginative existentialist writer Paul Bowles "did not get along with his new teacher, Miss Crane. He resented her authoritative style and . . . he adamantly refused to take part in class singing and as a method of revenge devised a system to do what to him were meaningless assignments without really doing them: he simply wrote everything perfectly, but backwards."

For Bowles, the activity most detested was singing, for others it will be Latin or algebra or sports or English composition. The acorn draws the line, and no one can force it to cross into the territory of its incompetence. It is as if the oak cannot bend or pretend to be a lovely poplar. As the acorn brings gifts, it sets limits, and only if the school allows intuition into the tuitional methods of the teacher can a bridge be thrown across, allowing the gift to emerge from the limits.

School failures are common; is this because the child fails school or because school fails the child? Either way, the gap widens between the innate intuitive ability of the child and the formalized tuition of school. As the writer William Saroyan put it: "I resented school, but I never resented learning." All the while he had trouble in school he was reading on his own "nearly every book in the Fresno, California, public library."

The composer Edvard Grieg said: "School developed in me nothing but what was evil and left the good untouched." Thomas Edison said, "I was always at the foot of the class." Stephen Crane, Eugene O'Neill, William Faulkner, and F. Scott Fitzgerald all failed courses in college. For Ellen Glasgow, author of *On Barren Ground* and a Pulitzer Prize–winning writer, school was "intolerable." Willa Cather, Pearl Buck, Isadora Duncan, and Susan B. Anthony also disliked school. Paul Cézanne was rejected by the École des Beaux-Arts in Paris. Marcel Proust's teacher considered his compositions disorganized, and Emile Zola got a zero in literature, also failing in German language and in rhetoric. Albert Einstein wrote of his middle school (which he attended from age nine and a half): "I preferred to endure all sorts of punishments rather than to learn gabble by rote." Earlier, at primary school, he was not especially noticeable and was called Biedermeier, meaning a little dull, a little simple, a little "unclever." His sister wrote that "he wasn't even good at arithmetic in the sense of being quick and accurate, though he was reliable and persevering." Some of these characteristics were due to his slowness of speech.

General George S. Patton was dyslexic and was kept back; Winston Churchill, at Harrow, "refused to study mathematics, Greek, or Latin and was placed in the lowest form—in what today would be termed the remedial reading class, where slow boys were taught English. His English, however, was not poor; his knowledge of Shakespeare was unusual and self-motivated."

The gap between what is seen by the school and what is felt by the child can work in two ways. Mostly, the child following his or her invisible track is perceived as "out of it," unteachable, obstinately difficult, even stupid. But pressure can build the other way as well. Diane Arbus, the quirky and extraordinary photographer, said: "The teachers always used to think I was smart and it would torment me because I knew that I was really terribly dumb." Whether the child is perceived as "dumb," like Einstein, or "smart," like Arbus, the gap in perception between child and school remains unbridged. When perception of the invisible in the child does occur, as in the cases of Truman Capote, Elia Kazan, and James Baldwin (chapter 5), it feels like an unforgettable miracle.

Examinations especially can be a trial. The master bacteriologist Paul Ehrlich had to be excused from school compositions because of his "complete ineptness." Giacomo Puccini consistently failed exams. Gertrude Stein would not take her final in a class at Harvard. Anton Chekhov refused to study classics, and failed his school exam twice. These failures at school gave him nightmares. "All his life he was to be haunted by dreams of teachers trying to 'catch him out.' " Pablo Picasso, "who could never remember the sequence of the alphabet," left school at ten "because he stubbornly refused to do anything but paint"; even his private tutor gave up on him because Pablo could not learn arithmetic.[13]

Often it was not in school, but outside of it—in extracurricular activities or during time spent altogether away from school—that calling appeared. It is as if the image in the heart in so many cases is hampered by the program of tuition and its timebound regularity. Henri Matisse began to paint during a convalescence. H. G. Wells was slated for the retail trade; he broke his leg when he was eight, began to read, and was "saved" from commerce for literature. Chief Justice of the Supreme Court and candidate for the presidency Charles Evans Hughes wandered the streets of New York City for six months while waiting to be accepted into college. William Randolph Hearst and the artist John La Farge added to their learning by "wasting time" in Manhattan streets. At fifteen, Marie Curie had a whole year in the country free from school.[14] Who can prescribe where the acorn learns best or where the soul puts you to the test?

Exams are a ritual moment, anything can happen. They mark transitions from one state of being to another, the way a wedding does, or like giving birth for the first time. Examination panics, together with the strange ceremonies of food and fetishes the night before "the final," further show the ritual background of the test. An exam tests more than your endurance, ability, and knowledge; it tests your calling. Does your daimon want the path you have chosen? Is your soul really in it? If doing well on the test may be a confirmation, a failed exam may be how the daimon lets us know we've been headed wrong.

Omar Bradley, a five-star general who held in mind vast campaigns involving millions of men and tons of supplies, was near the bottom on his test scores—in group twenty-seven of twenty-eight—when he entered West Point. Through plodding and grinding he worked his way up to graduate forty-fourth in a class of 168 (in the same class, Dwight D. Eisenhower was sixty-first and James Van Fleet ninety-second). Tuition helped Bradley's intuition. Intuition also helped him get into West Point when he had to sit through four days of four-hour exams each day.

> I had a terrible time with algebra. At the end of two hours I had solved no more than 20 percent of the necessary 67 percent of the problems required to pass. . . . That was it, complete failure. There was no way I could finish or pass. Utterly discouraged . . . I gathered up my papers and walked up to the officer in charge. . . . I saw he was deeply engrossed in a book. Not wishing to disturb him, I returned to my desk thinking I might as well give it one more try. Then, almost magically, the theorems started to come to me.[15]

Bradley made it. He "hung on through the rest of the exams" and was accepted by West Point.

Sometimes the acorn, like a good angel, "magically" enters the exam room at a fateful moment. (Compare Barbara McClintock's exam, recounted in chapter 8.) Reading life backward we might say that Bradley *had* to pass that exam: His military ability was essential to victory over Germany in 1943–1945, and later to serving as Army Chief of Staff.

Rush Limbaugh failed Speech 101. When he retook the course, he held his fellow students at Southeast Missouri State spellbound; his professor, however, gave him a D, despite his inventive talent, his confidence, and "his instinct for instant analysis." The professor said: "I felt a smugness, that he was not ready to listen to a teacher."[16] Limbaugh's grasp of the audience was intuitive; for him tuition only interfered.

The conflicts between school and student show up sharply in the area that belongs most closely to the acorn's image, as in the case of Limbaugh. Bernard Baruch, advisor to presidents in the fields of banking, finance, and international economics, did well enough at Harvard, though he finished in the bottom half of his class in political economy and number crunching (math).[17]

Finally, Woody Allen: "I paid attention to everything but the teachers."

> He demonstrated his abhorrence of school in some predictable ways. When he first attended P.S. 99 he was placed in an accelerated class because of his high IQ, but since the strictures of the classroom did not allow him to express himself in his own way and to use his imagination in his lessons, he instead expressed himself by becoming a troublemaker. . . . He played hooky. . . . He failed to do his homework. He was sometimes disruptive in class and rude to the teacher, who in turn lowered his grades for his behavior.[18]

The angel who reads a life as a total image hears these complaints and troubles and says: "Of course school was a horror, Woody. You were already making films and writing jokes about these situations, so why have to go through them so concretely?" Billy Graham "could see no point to going to school at all. Literature . . . gave him a lot of trouble."[19] He was "the last of everybody to get" Milton's *Allegro*. Of course! The world's most renowned evangelist doesn't need to get Milton and all that literature because he has already received the True Word. Paul Bowles had lots of imagining to do and so little time left for such extras as schoolwork. As for Rush Limbaugh, he already had a national listening audience by the throat, so of course he couldn't take instruction from a Southwest Missouri State teacher of speech. Browning, writing his epitaph in school, was already reading his life backward. And why wouldn't Branagh prefer a dramatic fall downstairs (such as you see on stage and in the movies) to school? Wasn't he already a remarkable actor of heroic parts? As for Churchill, of course he had language problems. How could a person who was awarded a Nobel Prize in literature and whose eloquence in 1940 and 1941 saved Western civilization for a while take on this huge daimon? It was far too much for a small-sized schoolboy. Invisible fates may show as visible failures.

Maybe we should read the data of learning disorders and the cases of school problems differently. Instead of "failed at school," see "saved from school"—not that this is my personal recommendation. I ask only that the sadnesses of children in school be imagined not merely as examples of failure but as exemplars of the acorn. The daimon's intuition often cannot submit to the normalcy of schooling and becomes even more demonic. When we read life backward, when we look at the gestures of the acorn from the taller perspective of the full tree, we can gauge tuition against the importance of intuition.

But what parent and what counselor can perch so high and see so well? And what child—even a gifted "genius"—can stick stubbornly enough to its intuitions, unless driven there by complete misunderstanding or by incapacitating symptoms like dyslexia, attention deficit disorder, allergies, asthma, or hyperactivity, any of which can keep a child from school. From school, yes, but not from learning; from tuition, but not from intuition, not from that certain blindness which allows seeing of other sorts. Not every child will see, not every child will profit from missing school, but for us who watch over them and supposedly guide them, this door to the invisible factors at work in their disorders must be kept open, just in case it is an angel knocking and not merely a malady.

Remember Jung's remark: "The Gods have become diseases." To see the angel in the malady requires an eye for the invisible, a certain blinding of one eye and an opening of the other to elsewhere. *It is impossible to see the angel unless you first have a notion of it;* otherwise the child is simply stupid, willful, or pathological. Even in the sciences, you only begin to see the phenomenon in the sky or under the microscope if someone first describes what you are looking for; we need instruction in the art of seeing. Then the invisible becomes suddenly visible, right in your squinting eye.

There is in each of us a longing to see beyond what our usual sight tells us. A revelation of the invisible in an intelligible form leads us to the astrologer. How can the invisible and unbelievable planetary transits parading through their zodiacal houses make my day? Please, explain my dream; alter my state. We would see a sign. Weekend workshops invite us to open the doors of perception and invite the invisibles in. A long and serious tradition, however, warns against throwing the doors wide open, especially in a culture that cannot tell Waco from wacko.

BRIDGING REALMS

The main teaching in cultures where spirits visit frequently and the world itself is a bridge—such as those of Haiti, West Africa, Melanesia, and the circumpolar peoples we group together as Eskimos—focuses upon knowing the distinct nature and name of the different visitors, their rank, their powers, their spheres of action. These cultures have gatekeepers and bouncers, who know ways of holding off what doesn't belong at this place in this moment. We had them too, once. Platonic philosophers (Iamblichus, Proclus, Porphyry) listed all sorts of angels and archons and daimones.[20] The world was quite permeable, inhabited by both physical and imaginal bodies. The psychologist of religion David Miller[21] reviews these "ghosts" or *Geists* (spirits) in our tradition to show their importance. But that permeability existed long ago in another kingdom of consciousness. Since then, the retraction of our interest from what rational consciousness calls magical, mystical, and mythical merges all the imaginal bodies indiscriminately into the monstrous. Result: The invisible becomes "alien." The alienation of the invisible makes it more eerie and distant, and more represented by werewolves, time warps, and abductions in the Stephen King–dom of our culture. Our modern passages are so narrow and with such low ceilings, the invisibles must twist themselves into freakish shapes in order to come through.

Maybe what comes from elsewhere will make me do crazy things; maybe that invisible world is demonic and should be excluded. What I can't see, I can't know; what I don't know, I fear; what I fear, I hate; what I hate, I want destroyed. So the rationalized mind prefers the chasm to the bridge; it likes the cut that separates the realms. From inside its concrete debunker, all invisibles appear the same—and bad.

According to the teaching of St. Paul, discrimination of the spirits is a sign of true spiritual consciousness. You have to be able to tell one invisible from another. One method the church used for refining this discernment was its proliferation of official angels and saints. The variety of figures showed many qualities, a host of different natures and areas of operation. (The more recent rationalized church has been downsizing the invisible realm, submitting its imagination to historical criteria. Every invisible saint had to have a visible forebear with a historical pedigree. So we lost St. Christopher and others who were "sheer myths.")

There are yet further questions regarding the relations between visible and invisible. Why make a bridge, anyway? Plotinus said: "It's for them to come to me, not for me to go to them." Maybe they don't want to come visiting. Or, maybe they are already here, like the angels in Wim Wenders's films? We cannot know, since our theories of perception do not permit their appearance. They may not be invisible at all, but only seem so because declared so by our doctrinal blinding. Is it their nature or our vision that defines them as invisible?

In the kingdom (or is it a mall?) of the West, consciousness has lifted the transcendent ever higher and farther away from actual life. The bridgeable chasm has become a cosmic void. The gods have withdrawn, said the poets Hölderlin and Rilke; it takes a leap of faith, said Søren Kierkegaard. Not even that will do, for God is dead, said Nietzsche. Any bridge must be of superhuman proportions. Well, *that* kind of bridge our culture has ready to hand; the greatest bridge, some say, ever constructed between visible and invisible: the figure of Jesus Christ.

Once invisibility has been removed from backing all the things we live among, so that all our accumulated "goods" have become mere "stuff," deaf and dumb and dead consumables, Christ becomes the only image left in the Kingdom for bringing back to our culture the fundamental invisibility upon which cultures have always rested. Fundamentalism attempts, literally and dogmatically, to recover the invisible foundations of culture. Its strength lies in what it seeks; its menace in how it proceeds.

Christ as bridge (and isn't the pope, vicar of Christ, still called the pontiff from *pons,* bridge), because the Incarnation means the presence of the invisible in the common matter of walking-around human life. A god-man: visible and invisible become one. Centuries of huge and vicious debates have attempted to split the unity by coming down on one side or the other: Jesus is really a divinely inspired but visible man; Christ is really the invisible God borrowing human shape.

Some glue, some independent link was required to hold these two theological incommensurables together, a third term that was different from the other two and that could join mortal and immortal. This third person, Christian theology named the Holy Ghost. But this figure, too, belongs among the invisibles, which still tilts the balance away from the world. So the debate goes on, as it should, because the relation between these two terms gives rise to metaphysical speculation and religious practices that keep the problematic idea of the invisible from slipping away. Besides, the debate gives rise to this chapter's focus upon the often strained relation during school years between the invisible acorn and the life of the person with whom it lives.

The theological debates can teach us a major psychological lesson. What we learn is less about belief in the union of the two incommensurables or about explanations of their mysterious connection, than about what happens *when they part*.

Psychopathology prompts sharper psychological insight than do spiritual ideals and formulae. A negative approach sheds the harshest light. The most pathologized moment in the entire incarnational story is the cry on the cross, which tells of the agony when one is encompassed only by the visible world. Enemies surrounded Jesus all through his thirty-three years, and though he was opposed and pursued, he was never so besieged as at that moment. The world of humans, of nature, and of things had become savage and hostile.

Hitherto, the world had been permeated with invisibilities, a condition that Christianity called paganism. When the invisible forsakes the actual world—as it deserts Job, leaving him plagued with every sort of physical disaster—then the visible world no longer sustains life, because life is no longer invisibly backed. Then the world tears you apart. Isn't that the simple lesson taught by the withering and collapse of tribal cultures once they are robbed of their spirits in exchange for goods?

The copresence of visible and invisible sustains life. We come to recognize the overriding importance of the invisible only when it deserts, when it turns its back and disappears like Huldra in the forest, like YHWH at Golgotha.

The great task of a life-sustaining culture, then, is to keep the invisibles attached, the gods smiling and pleased: to invite them to remain by propitiations and rituals; by singing and dancing, smudging and chanting; by anniversaries and re-membrances; by great doctrines such as the Incarnation and by little intuitive gestures—such as touching wood or by fin-gering beads, a rabbit's foot, a shark's tooth; or by putting a mezuzah on the doorpost, dice on the dashboard; or by qui-etly laying a flower on a polished stone.

All this has nothing to do with belief, and so it also has nothing to do with superstition. It's merely a matter of not forgetting that the invisibles can go away, leaving you with nothing but human relationships to cover your back. As the old Greeks said of their gods: They ask for little, just that they not be forgotten. Myths keep their daimonic realm invisibly present. So do folktales, like that of the woodsman who dropped his ax and its cutting edge, going deeper and deeper to keep close to that smiling.

— 🜲 —

CHAPTER 5

"ESSE IS *PERCIPI"*:
TO BE IS
TO BE PERCEIVED

Manolete was called to bullfighting, but this calling needed to be seen so that it could grow down into life. The perception was provided by a mentor, José Flores Camará, who "saw beyond," and who became Manolete's guide and manager, staying with him to the end.

> The decisive thing in Manolete's career took place. José Flores Camará happened to see him perform. . . . When he saw Manolete in the ring, he somehow saw beyond what the boy was to what he could someday become.
>
> He saw instantly that the boy was doing the wrong kind of passes for his build and personality. He saw that it was ignorance of terrains that was causing the boy to be tossed all the time.
>
> But he also saw that Manolete had tremendous courage. He saw that he killed better than anyone he had ever seen, killed in the old-fashioned dangerous, stylish,

straight-over-the-right-horn, up-to-the-hilt school of killing that had all but disappeared from the arenas.

Camará signed up Manolete, and as his manager he began to remake him. He took him out on the ranches with the calves and started him learning about bullfighting from scratch.[1]

Franklin Roosevelt also had this kind of vision, at least in regard to Lyndon Johnson:

In attempting to explain to me the basis for the President's rapport with the young congressman—a rapport almost unique in Roosevelt's life—one of Roosevelt's advisers, James H. Rowe, told me, "You have to understand that these were two great political geniuses. They could talk on the same level. Roosevelt had very few people he could talk to who could understand all the implications of what he was saying. But Lyndon, at the age of twenty-eight, could understand it all." Roosevelt, speaking of Johnson, once said to Harold Ickes, "You know, Harold, that's the kind of uninhibited young pro I might have been as a young man—if I hadn't gone to Harvard." Roosevelt also made a prediction. He said, "Harold, in the next couple of generations the balance of power in this country is going to shift to the South and the West. And that kid Lyndon Johnson could well be the first Southern President."[2]

George Washington also selected a young man, Alexander Hamilton, to be his aide-de-camp. This happened in 1777, during a dark winter of the Revolution, and when Hamilton was twenty-two years old. Their relation has caused, still causes, endless biographical and psychoanalytical speculation. What matters to us here is Washington's genial eye, which could see, and feel, for the young, cocky, but frail, artillery officer. Within a few months, Hamilton became, according to Washington's own words, "the principal and most confidential aide of the Commander in Chief."[3]

Battlefield appointments call for sharp eyes. Subalterns fall, the second in command is shot through the head—and instantly the one in charge must move someone up to fill the slot. On what basis does he make the decision? No personality inventory, no IQ test, no interview going into case history and childhood—instead, a rapid assessment of character, sometimes under fire; a perception of potential. Does crisis offer insight into the acorn?

How does a baseball scout perceive the uniqueness in a nineteen-year-old rookie infielder in the bush leagues, not only size him up in terms of skills, but also see a nature that will fit him into a team, maybe please the crowds, and be worth a large investment of money and time? What is this gift of perception?

I am going to put in here three of my own favorite tales of perceptive genius which today would likely be attributed to favoritism on the part of a professor or homosexual attraction between two men, or given some other explanation that reduces the gift of perception to petty self-interest. How little charity is left in our current accounts of what happens between two people, especially when one is younger, the other older, one with influence, one without. Having perhaps lost the power of perception we can only perceive power as the selective affinity between two persons. But to the tales:

At Harvard in the 1890's Professor William James had in his classes a rather wonky, stubby talkative Jewish girl from California. She was late for classes, didn't seem to understand what was going on, misspelled, knew no Latin—that sort of typical mess, the girl who couldn't get it together, a "typical neurotic" as we might say today. But William James let her turn in a blank exam paper, and gave her a high mark for the course, helped her through to medical studies at Johns Hopkins. He saw something unique in this pupil. She was Gertrude Stein, who found herself as the Gertrude Stein we know only ten years later far from Harvard, in Paris.

In a Southern small town a man named Phil Stone, who had some literary education at Yale, took under his wing as coach and mentor, a short, wiry, heavily drinking, highly pretentious lad of the town. This young fellow wrote poems, pretended to be British, carried a walking stick and wore special clothes—all in smalltown Mississippi during the First World War. Phil Stone listened to the boy, whom Jungian psychology might call today a "typical puer" and perceived his uniqueness. The man went on to become the William Faulkner who was awarded the Nobel Prize for literature in 1949.

And then this third tale of the perception that "saw beyond what the boy was to what he could someday become":

In the year 1831 one of those marvelous old-fashioned scientific expeditions was to set forth; a schoolmaster named John Henslow suggested that one of his former pupils be appointed naturalist. The lad was then 22; he had been rather dull at school, hopeless in maths, although a keen collector of beetles from the countryside; he was hardly different from the others of his type and class: hunting and shooting, popular member of the Glutton Club, aimed for the clergy. He had a "typical family complex" as we might say today, soft in the mother and dominated by a 300-pound father. But Henslow saw something and persuaded the parties involved, including the pupil named Charles Darwin, that he make this journey.[4]

For Charles Darwin it was his schoolmaster's eye that made the pivotal difference, as it was also for Elia Kazan and Truman Capote. The parents of these boys hardly knew what to do with them. Again, the acorn requires a mentor.

Kazan writes:

When I was twelve and we'd moved to New Rochelle, I had a stroke of luck—the accident of my eighth-grade teacher. Her name was Miss Anna B. Shank, and as much as anyone, she influenced the course of my life. She was in her late forties, which I considered very old indeed, and she took to me. . . . A deep-dyed romantic, she was the one who told me that I had beautiful brown eyes. Twenty-five years later, having seen my name in a newspaper, she wrote me a letter. "When you were only twelve," she wrote, "you stood near my desk one morning and the light from the window fell across your head and features and illuminated the expression on your face. The thought came to me of the great possibilities there were in your development and . . ."

Miss Shank set out zealously to turn me away from the eldest-son tradition of our people and the expectations of my father, to steer me off a commercial course that would feature bookkeeping and accounting toward an education in what they now call the humanities.[5]

Truman Capote's mother did not find her little boy an easy charge. She said he lied; he parroted her second husband's Cuban accent; he was effeminate, with "sissyish traits," and his voice never deepened, remaining as high as it had been when he was in fourth grade. As late as fourteen he was still throwing temper tantrums, "lying on the floor and kicking his legs in the air when he did not get his way." He walked in his sleep, boycotted gym, and combed his hair "all the time" while sitting in biology class. He flunked algebra, French, and Spanish. While only five or six he had a pencil and paper and scribbled notes to himself and carried a tiny dictionary with him wherever he went. He also accompanied a teacher to the movies and masturbated him in the dark. Mother sent him off to military school in Ossining (Sing Sing!) New York.

Enter Catherine Wood, English teacher,

who not only shared his faith in himself, but believed that it was her duty, her mission and sacred obligation, to help bring his talents to blossom.

He came to her attention as aggressively as he could manage. She was taking her students on a tour of the school library and had just picked out a book by Sigrid Undset to give to one of the girls. "Suddenly," she said, "this little fellow, who was not in my group, turned around from where he was sitting and interrupted me. 'Must be wonderful to read her in the original,' he said. 'Oh, I wouldn't think of anything else!' I replied, although of course I didn't know a word of Norwegian. From that time on I saw Truman, and when he came into my class the next year, in the eleventh grade, I saw him all the time."

A tall, gray-haired spinster . . . Miss Wood invited him often to dinner, read his stories, catered to him in class, and encouraged her colleagues to do the same. . . . "His mother couldn't understand this boy who liked such different things," she said. "I remember sitting in my little dining room and saying to her that it was hard for me to tell his own mother this, but that in years to come the other, regular boys, who do the usual things in the usual way, would still be doing those things while Truman would be famous."[6]

The eye may also belong to a member of the family—for instance, a sister. Golda Meir, a founding figure in the history of Israel and its prime minister during the 1973 war, had a sister, Sheyna, nine years older. Golda finished elementary school at fourteen, as class valedictorian. "Obviously I would go on to high school and then, perhaps, even become a teacher, which is what I most wanted to be." Her mother had other ideas. She wanted a "*dervaksene shein meydl* (a fine, upstanding girl), I could work in a shop . . . and start thinking about getting married, which, she reminded me, was forbidden to women teachers by state [Wisconsin] law."

In secret letters to her sister, who was dirt poor and tubercular and had moved out some years before after battling their mother, Golda Meir confessed her miserable dilemma. Sheyna wrote back: "No, you shouldn't stop school. . . . you have good chances to become something . . . should get ready and come to us . . . and we will do all we can for you. . . . come to us immediately."[7]

Golda Meir stole away from home at sixteen because Sheyna offered a home to what she perceived in her sister. Equally important in the Golda Meir story is the mother's intransigence, the parental fantasy of what the daughter should become. This helped unleash Golda's native daimon and its stubborn rebellious idealism, helping her on the road to what she essentially was.

The composer Alban Berg poured out his teenage heart to Hermann Watznauer, a member of the Berg family circle who became the boy's "friend, mentor and catalyst." When the relationship began, Watznauer was twenty-four, only ten years older than Berg, and he sympathetically accompanied the boy's confessions of soul and gushings from the heart in letters sometimes running on for thirty pages.[8] The mentor sees something essential. The poet Vladimir Mayakovsky's tutor, barely ten years older than his charge, said: "He liked working with adults and was annoyed if treated like a child. I observed that trait of his as soon as I met him."[9]

As a teenager, Arthur Rimbaud ("a boy who lived most of his life in the imagination . . . when he walked sedately from school to home he walked not the familiar streets but the deck of a ship, the cobbles of Rome, the pavements of the Acropolis") found his soul mate in his teacher Izambard, age twenty-one, to whom Rimbaud at last could "speak of poets and poetry." "This child," said Izambard, "treated from the first as a young comrade, little by little became a dear friend."

As Darwin's schoolmaster saw him, as Miss Wood saw Capote, so Izambard saw Rimbaud. Bainville, however, the most celebrated living poet of the day, to whom Rimbaud wrote an effusive appeal for approval, saying "We are in the month of love; I am nearly seventeen. . . . I've got something in me, I don't know what, that wants to soar," saw nothing.[10] Bainville filed away the poems and the letter. Matter closed. No catalyst, no mentor, no eye.

In these various *perceptual relationships* age and gender seem not to matter. In 1777 Washington was forty-five, Hamilton twenty; whereas Izambard and Rimbaud were scarcely six years apart. Today, to say age and gender seem irrelevant goes counter to the culture. A suspicion of homoerotic attraction between the elder Washington and the brilliant, slim Hamilton gives away a secret—not the secret of a supposed clandestine affair, but the secret of the source of the perceptive eye. It is the eye of the heart. Something moves in the heart, opening it to perceiving the image in the heart of the other. Roosevelt had "affection" for Lyndon Johnson. "The light from the window fell across your head," wrote Miss Shank. She saw. "Manolete was doing the wrong kind of passes for his build and personality." Camará saw. "That kid Lyndon Johnson could well be the first Southern President." Roosevelt saw.

In a "dreadful ancient . . . school house: dark dreary and scary at times," among a class of fifty children, mostly boys and mostly black, Orilla Miller—"a young white schoolteacher, a beautiful woman . . . whom I loved . . . absolutely, with a child's love," saw James Baldwin, ten years old. "They discovered a common interest in Dickens; both were reading him and anxious to exchange views. The young woman from the Midwest was amazed at the brilliance of the boy from the slums." They entered a friendship that allowed his daimon to come forth.

Baldwin also saw Miller. Years and years later, after he had become an important and famous writer, they connected again. He wrote her and "asked his old friend for a photograph": "I've held your face in my mind for many years."[11] Forty years after their first meetings in the Harlem schoolhouse and through the fiction of Dickens, Orilla Miller and James Baldwin went together to the movies to see (again) *A Tale of Two Cities.*

We can no longer quite believe in these relations of the heart's affections. We have learned to see with the eye of the genitals. We can't imagine attractions that are based in imagination. For our culture today, desires must really be unconsciously sexual, liaisons must really be copulations; open confessions, really seductive manipulations. But what drew these pairs together was a common vision; they fell in love with a fantasy. For Baldwin and Miller, Dickens. For Capote and Wood, Sigrid Undset in Norwegian! Roosevelt and Johnson's was a correspondence of geniuses: as Rowe said, "they could talk on the same level." Age, history, fact play no significant roles. Theirs was a conversation between two Presidents. Heart to heart. Acorn to acorn.

When John Keats writes, "I know nothing but the holiness of the Heart's affections and the Truth of the Imagination,"[12] he opens our own eye to see the workings of creative perception in human affairs. His phrase provides the transhuman ground for the art of mentoring. Mentoring begins when your imagination can fall in love with the fantasy of another. An erotic component is necessary, as it has been essential to education since Socrates, as it still is, though today either eliminated by computer learning or seen only with the genital eye as abuse, seduction, harassment, or impersonal hormonal need. The genital eye does not reveal what the acorn seeks.

Study, for instance, ads for partners in the personals columns. Once we pass through the sociological descriptions of body build, skin color, and sexual habits, of profession, age, and marital status, the Truth of the Imagination begins to emerge. Long walks, cooking, humor, movies, dancing, cuddling, and conversation: The ad states musical preferences, vacation dreams, tastes, and especially longings. We are asking for someone to accompany the acorn, not only for a companion in bed. A personal reveals "the holiness of the Heart's affections." The personal ad is a Romantic's dream. "A deep-eyed romantic, she was the one who told me that I had beautiful brown eyes," wrote Elia Kazan of Miss Shank, who saw "the great possibilities."

Seeing is believing—believing *in* what you see—and this instantly confers belief to whoever, whatever receives your sight. The gift of sight surpasses the gifts of insight. For such sight blesses; it does transformative work.

Therapy promotes the great delusion of insight. It preaches and practices the blindness of Oedipus. He asked questions about who he *really* was, as if you could find the true acorn of your being by self-questioning reflection.[13] This therapeutic fallacy builds upon another: that the acorn is out of sight, hidden, squirreled away in childhood, repressed, forgotten, and therefore can be redeemed only by active introspection in the mirror of the mind. Mirrors, however, tell only a half-truth. The face in the looking glass is only half the size of your actual face, merely half of what you in fact present and others see.[14]

The therapeutic search for true being might do better to follow carefully this chapter's maxim, stated in the passive voice, "to be perceived." You are a displayed phenomenon. "To be" is first of all to be visible. Passively allowing yourself to be seen opens the possibility of blessing. So we seek lovers and mentors and friends that we may be seen, and blessed.

Miss Shank saw Kazan in the light that "illuminated the expression on [his] face." Camará saw how Manolete moved, how he killed, how his motions were out of tune with the terrain. Watznauer walked with Berg, listened and looked. At the front the commander picking his replacements observes in broad daylight; the inner man stands in the outer display. How they come on, how they behave, how they are. And what is the first question we ask about the inward state of being of any person we meet? "How are you?" You are *how* you are, just as you are, in the saddle-back of the present moment, on parade. Your being, maybe all Being, is precisely "how" it appears to be, the how of just-so *Sein,* declaring who and what and where each event is. How it is says what it is. This is how it is; its gestures, style, colorings, motions, speech, expression—in short, the actual complications of the image—tell exactly how it is.

For all this insistence on the phenomenal I do not mean that there are no reserves, no shadows; I do not mean that an event is but a persona, the front it puts up, mere showcasing. Reserves and shadows are not invisible. They show in reticence, in circumlocutions and euphemisms, in shaded, averted eyes, in slips, in hesitancies of gestures, second thoughts, avoidances. There is nothing plain about a face, or simple about a surface. The supposedly concealed is also on view and subject to keen sight, making up part of what any event affords to a good looker. The image that a mentor spots in a pupil or apprentice is neither all front nor what's hidden behind, neither a false self nor a true one; there is no real you other than the reality of you in your image. The mentor perceives the folds of a complexity, those convex-concave, topsy-turvy curves of implication that are the truth of all imagination, allowing us to define an image as the *complete how of a presentation.* Here I am, right before your eyes. Do you read me?

So let's think again about the acorn as a concealed invisible potential. Instead, let's consider it to be thoroughly visible in the how of action—not *that* he fights bulls, but *how* he fights bulls is Manolete; not *that* Gertrude Stein writes, but *how* she writes is the uniqueness of her realized image. This invisibility of the acorn occurs in the how of a visible performance—in its traces, if you will. The invisible is thoroughly visible all through the oak and is not elsewhere or prior to the oak but acts like an implicate order folded all through the visible, like the butter in a French croissant or the fragrant air in risen bread: invisible, not literally as such, but the invisible visible.

Sometimes this invisible visible is referred to as the spirit of a place, the quality of a thing, the soul of a person, the mood of a scene, the style of an art. We like to take hold of it by accounting for it as context, as formal structure, or as an unclosed gestalt that draws us into it. Neither our concepts nor the eye that looks by means of them has been trained enough in imagination, in the perceptive art of reading images. We are not able to see how any one is when we try to see by means of types, categories, classes, diagnostics. Types of any sort obscure uniqueness.

The eye of the heart sees "eaches" and is affected by eachness, to borrow a term from William James. The heart's affections pick out particulars. We are moved by this one image: in a roomful of schoolchildren, only little Truman with his high voice. We fall for *this* one, not anyone.

But to see a particular person in terms of Irish or German, Jewish or Catholic, black or white, Alcoholic or Suicidal, Victim or Borderline, sees class concepts, not people. We are then talking sociology more than soul. We need an incredible number of words to read expressions. "Most people cannot 'say' what the person before them is like, but being unable to 'say' does not imply that one is unable to see," writes the philosopher José Ortega y Gasset.[15] So many words are available once we close the psychology book and open a novel, a travel diary, even a cookbook. Or a movie, in which we can watch adjectives and adverbs alive and well composed into images moving across the screen. "O for a Life of Sensations rather than of Thoughts," wrote Keats.[16] To see the acorn requires an eye for the image, an eye for the show, and the language to say what we see.

Failures in our loves, friendships, and families often come down to failures of imaginative perception. When we are not looking with the eye of the heart, love is indeed blind, for then we are failing to see the other person as bearer of an acorn of imaginative truth. A feeling may be there, but not the sight; and, as the vision clouds, so do sympathy and interest. We feel only annoyed, and we resort to diagnostic and typological concepts. But your husband is not "mother-bound"; he whines and expects and is often paralyzed. Your wife is not "animus-ridden"; she is peremptory, argues logically, and can't let go. *How* they are is who they are, and not *what* they are said to be by types and classes.

Some therapies try to correct imaginative myopia by promoting "empathy" and "syntonic countertransference identification." They also encourage psychodrama and role-playing in order to enable people to see through typical conceptions and into the heart of the other. Put yourself in your husband's place, your wife's, your child's. Imagine how they feel, how would it be to be them? Imagine! Maybe you can discover a kernel of truth in their behaviors if you look again by means of imagining.

Imaginative perception takes patience. As the alchemists said of their laborious frustrating experiments, "In your patience is your soul." How else meet the other's incomprehensible behavior, that oddness, that slowness? Dr. Edward Teller didn't speak until he was past three and was thought to be retarded. "One day Edward did talk, and it was in sentences, not words, as if he had been saving the effort until he had something to say." Dr. Benjamin Spock "spoke very little until he was over three, and when he did say anything he spoke with maddening slowness." Martin Buber, too, began to talk only at three. One of James Thurber's teachers "told his mother that he might be deaf." Woodrow Wilson, perhaps America's most bookish President, "had not learned his letters until he was nine years old and could not read until he was twelve." Former biographers blamed Wilson's relations with his mother and his father for this delay. Up-to-date biography prefers a psychiatric diagnosis, declaring "that Woodrow Wilson had *developmental* dyslexia," suggesting the blame be placed in his brain.[17]

Dyslexia, chronic lateness, distractability, hyperactivity make up "attention deficit disorder"—and what patience it demands. Yet how else contain and tease out what this "deficit" also shows? Children so categorized, and adults too, are often those with above-average intelligence, given to day-dreams, and with such widely open sensitive souls that their "ego" behavior is noncompliant and disorganized. Ritalin, Prozac, Xanax—of course, they work. But because they work against the deficit does not confirm the cause of it or disclose its meaning. Crutches work, but they can't account for your broken leg. Why is this disorder so prevalent today? What does the soul *not* want to attend to, and what might the daimon be doing when it is *not* reading, *not* speaking, and *not* fulfilling performance expectations? To discover this takes patience, and that imaginative perception that Henry James described as "a prolonged hovering over the case exposed."

—

"To be is to be perceived," said the Irish philosopher George Berkeley (1685–1753). We exist and give existence by virtue of perception. Berkeley meant that God's omniscient perception maintains all things. For a moralist—and Berkeley was a bishop—this could mean you're never out of the sight of God, so you'd better be good! For a metaphysician, "*Esse* is *percipi*" could mean that if God dozes off, blinks for even an instant, or is distracted by problems in another Brunian cosmos elsewhere, our world's being collapses into nothing.

An eristic rabbi might ask the bishop: Does God perceive himself? If he doesn't, then how can he be said to exist? And if he does, by what means? If he perceives himself in the mirror of nature, then either nature is a simulacrum of God and might be indistinguishable from God (as Spinoza proposed), or nature is percipient and endowed with a divine consciousness of its own, since it can make God exist. If the Almighty perceives himself by means of humans, then we have secular humanism: the existence of God is a result of human perception; God's existence depends on humans; we make him up. The rabbi might, no doubt, go on to suggest that maybe God's kind of existence does not require perception, but this limits his presence by leaving him out of the perceptual realm, separated, transcendent, neither omniscient nor omnipotent. And if God's existence does not require perception, then either your proposition, Bishop, is false, or God does not exist.

Berkeley, being Irish, educated at Trinity College Dublin, and having spent some good time in the American South, could give fine ripostes to these puzzles as well as spin out puzzles yet more complex. But there is one possibility he may have missed, since he hadn't read much Keats (unless in acorn?), and that is the psychological and ecological virtue of his wonderfully laconic and deservedly famous phrase. Perception bestows blessing—as the stories sketched in this chapter attempt to demonstrate. Perception brings into being and maintains the being of whatever is perceived; and when perception sees in "the holiness of the Heart's affections," again as these stories say, things are revealed that prove the Truth of the Imagination.

— 🪶 —

CHAPTER 6

NEITHER NATURE
NOR NURTURE —
SOMETHING ELSE

It's time to look at what hard-hat psychology says about falling in love, since that is when fate seems most clearly to be calling and an individual destiny decided. First we will need to examine how psychology conceives individuality as such. How can we claim that every single one of us is indeed a "single one"? Are we not deeply uniform, owing to genetic heredity and early environment? Studies of twins focus on this issue of individuality and on the variances in the biographies of even genetically identical twins sharing the same household. Besides nature and nurture, there seems to be something else. So we go first to research and then come to romance.

Scientific psychology carves the kingdom of causes into only two parts, nature and nurture. By definition, it eliminates the possibility of something else. Since the behavioral sciences, including molecular biology and pharmacological psychiatry, put all the reasons for our characters in these categories, and since we are imagining a third force in our lives, this third can only appear concealed within the other two. So we have not only to look at what behavioral sciences say, but also to look into how they say it. We have to proceed as if we were detectives searching for clues indicating the missing invisible person in statements by those who themselves do not believe anything is missing at all.

We do need to recognize at the outset that division into two alternatives is a comfortable habit of the Western mind. At its simplest level it's in the Bible: Us or Them. Abel and Cain, Jacob and Esau—good guy and bad—personify the division. Adversarial thinking did not begin with TV's shouting arguments, nor did our two-party political system arrive out of thin air. The twosome, with all its coupling and duplicity and pairing and opposing, feeds the "passion of the Western mind," to quote the title of Richard Tarnas's history of Western thinking.

Aristotelian logic cannot think in threes. From Aristotle's law of contradiction, also called the law of the excluded middle, to the binary logic—0 or 1—in our computer programs, our mind sets up its systems in pros and cons, in either-or's. Descartes did concede a tiny space for a third, right in the middle of the brain. He placed the soul in the pineal gland, attesting to its minuscule value vis à vis the two giant contenders in his system, the thinking mind inside and the extended space outside.

So this chapter will have to struggle with long-established and comforting habits of thinking in opposites that say: If behavior is not fully the result of genetic inheritance, then what's left over can be accounted for only by environmental influences, and vice versa. The introduction of "something else" violates our mode of thought and the convenience of its habitual operations. A "something else" disturbs minds that mistake comfortable thinking with clarity of thought.

After all, we can still be quite clear that from the evidence of our feelings, and from fateful idiosyncratic events, something else intervenes in human life that cannot be held within the confines of nature or nurture. The remarkable singularity of individuals, the differences among the billions of persons, even between newborn babies, siblings, identical twins, as well as those raised in the same circumstances and subject to the same influences—these facts ask for answers to the question of uniqueness.

TWINS

Let's turn first to heredity. The first great wave of genetic research, from Gregor Mendel (1822–1884) to James Watson and Francis Crick, has left its indelible traces and has receded. Most of us are convinced that we are made as much by our inherited structures of genes coded into chromosomes as we are created by God (theology), by economics (Marx), by past lives (Hinduism, Buddhism), by history (Hegel), by society (Durkheim and others). The undisputed evidence is in: The DNA corkscrew carries the code that plays a major part in the governance of our lives, physically, psychologically, and also spiritually.

Now the second wave of research has arrived. It is more differentiated in its methods and sophisticated in its questions. Research now asks more about differences, even among those who are genetically closely linked. How come twins have different characters, different fates?

Studies of difference find their best research material in identical (monozygotic) twins. These are a pair of people who have developed from the one and same fertilized ovum, rather than from two separate ova. Twins developed from separate ova are called fraternal (a patriarchal designation suggesting that there are only brothers in the brood). Monozygotic twins have identical DNA stuff; genetically they are the same. The same genetic information is coded in them both, equally; except for monozygotic twins, each person is genetically different from every other person.

We might, therefore, draw the obvious conclusion that identical twins must be exactly alike. But they aren't. They are only 90 percent concordant in ten physical characteristics such as hair color and hairline patterns, blood type, eye color, position of teeth, fingerprint ridge counts.[1] But the concordance begins to diminish as more psychic factors enter. Even height and weight and complexion do not show as high a concordance, whereas facial expression and susceptibility to diseases like diabetes, ulcers, breast cancer, and hypertension slide yet further away from concordance. Individuality comes more to the fore.

Why, then, aren't "identical twins" actually identical? What makes for even physical differences between these twins? "A simple answer is environment."[2] "We use' the term environment to refer to any nonhereditary influence." If it's not nature, it must be nurture. We'll take up the idea of environment shortly—but first, more on heredity.

When we arrive at cognitive abilities, such as reasoning, verbal fluency, and memory, differences become even more marked.[3] For ordinary sisters and brothers—not twins of either kind—"correlations are very low for all personality traits."[4] Seems people are individuals despite having the same parents and similar upbringing. Even Alzheimer's disease—a disease of the brain and not a personality disorder—shows 90 percent *difference* among siblings!

During the last fifty years an enormous amount of money and thought has gone into schizophrenia research, even though differential diagnosis of the schizophrenias (there are varieties) remains still a bit soft. Nonetheless, the main result of identical-twin studies regarding schizophrenia can be expressed by this clear sentence: "More than half of the genetically identical pairs of twins are discordant for schizophrenia."[5] If one twin succumbs, it is more likely that the other *will not* than that he or she will. Something else intervenes, differentiating the twins.

This something else is not, as we might jump to conclude, surely upbringing. When a pair of siblings is adopted and brought up in the same family and one of them is diagnosed schizophrenic, the other is not at any greater risk. "Shared family environment is not important. . . . This finding implies," say Judy Dunn and Robert Plomin, both highly competent researchers in the field of twin studies, "that the major reason why one person is diagnosed as schizophrenic and another is not must be the impact of environmental influences that are *not shared by family members*" (italics mine).[6] Since the factor influencing diagnosed schizophrenia is neither inherited genes nor shared family milieu, there is something else, something "not shared," something individual and unique to the particular person.

Three further findings in particular intrigue me. They bear upon our acorn theory of individuality. I invite you to give some imaginative thought to them. The findings concern creativity, traditionalism, and the fact that the genetic factor appears to get stronger during the middle years of childhood.

"One dimension of the cognitive realm [e.g., memory, verbal fluency, reasoning] that appears to show little genetic influence is creativity."[7] We will not bog down trying to define this vague and idolized term, nor will we inquire into the methods for measuring "creativity." We do know, however, from the accumulation of data and the anecdotes of life stories, that eminent persons usually stand out from their families, their peers, their home towns, their own children. The eminent are usually "different," unlike their closest kin (nature) and their milieu (nurture). That is, neither genes nor environment can be surely shown to determine eminence. The striking individuality of the eminent, who we suppose represent or partake in "creativity" (however it be defined), is not attributed either to nature or to nurture. Something else? An independent factor?

To avoid parsing out the "something else," and declaring for an independent factor, behavioral explanations blend nature and nurture. They propose a mysterious weaving of black and white threads whose result is so subtly entwined that we are confronted with a gray screen of uncertainty as to whether creativity is preponderantly genetic or environmental. In place of the eternal enigma of human creativity, this "gray" explanation offers less risk of shaking the two-party system with the introduction of a truly different component: the "calling" proposed by the acorn theory. It also offers less satisfaction to the imaginative mind.

If creativity shows little genetic influence, "traditionalism," surprisingly, seems rather strongly inherited. The research uses the term "traditionalism" for "the tendency to follow rules and authority and to endorse high moral standards and strict discipline."[8]

The data are apolitical as science must pretend to be, and so genetic "traditionalism" is not directly associated with actual political (Republican) or religious (fundamentalist, Orthodox) positions. Yet the description of traditionalism does suggest some genetic wiring at the core of conservative, even reactionary, party and church affiliations. Jerome Kagan's judicious studies of innate character[9] might speak of temperamental bias; astrology might imagine Saturn as an influence on the chromosomes; feminism might despairingly realize how immovable patriarchal attitudes are; Marxists might understand why it is so hard to awaken the peasants and proletariat to revolution; and the Church might take comfort: there will always be a genetic pool ready to flow uphill toward the Vatican.

Some forty years ago the anthropologist Paul Radin gave an explanation for the rise of monotheism. He said it was not a natural stage in the development of religions; rather, monotheistic thinking belonged to a priestly caste and cast of mind. Monotheism, he said, originates in a particular "temperament." He intuitively foresaw the determining role of the traditionalist attitude in character before genetics came up with the data about traditionalism.[10]

It becomes easier to see why it is so difficult to bring about change. Perhaps traditionalism is the conservative streak in human nature that appears as fundamentalism and single-mindedness in any culture, personified by the archetypal figure of the Old King. I find it a relief to know that holding the line with "high moral standards and strict discipline" is not necessarily the policy of the angel or the voice of a calling, but belongs to your frame like your skull and bones.

Assuming, then, that traditionalism has a strong genetic component, does this help to understand why the genius calls away from the traditional life? For many centuries, from the *Problemata* of Aristotle on melancholic frenzy (or *furor*, the exceptional mental state of "creative" people) through Cesare Lombroso in the nineteenth century, calling is compared with, even identified with, the untraditional and abnormal.[11] People like to imagine that novelty and originality are nontraditional, as if inspiration must by definition oppose order, discipline, rules, and authority—that is, "traditionalism." At least we may hazard the conclusion that there can be strong conflict between conservative genetic attitudes and something else that calls against and away.

A third intriguing finding says that the influence of heredity on intelligence (IQ measurements) increases *after* infancy, up to the middle years of childhood.[12] In fact, "the evidence seems to say that the heritability of IQ rises as one ages, all the way from early childhood to late adulthood."[13]

I would have thought that the genetic factor would be strongest and most determining of one's abilities, such as intelligence, at first entry into the world, before a person is bombarded by impacts from the outer world and able to select among them. I would have believed the early months and years to be when the genetic factors play the largest role. Yet findings in regard to the IQ of children show that as a child gets older—from age three to six or seven—heritability increases. It then begins to subside again, after about age seven. Furthermore, "IQ scores increase substantially during childhood, even though IQ is strongly correlated with heritability."[14] (We shall discuss the IQ issue in a moment.)

Why is the heredity factor less compelling at age two or three than at seven or eight? Is the individuality of intelligence more pronounced at birth, gradually to wane in middle childhood? The finding could suggest that an infant is less under the influence of both nature and nurture than an older child is and more indebted—at least in regard to native intelligence—to his or her own original gift. This reading of the data would support the Platonic myth that a person is born with an innate paradigm that is not identical with genetic endowment and that gradually gives way in middle childhood as genetic factors kick in. Moreover, "in late adulthood," when calling, character, and fate have become more inescapable, then, too, one's intelligence, and all that it serves, belongs more to the code of the soul than to that of the genes.

"Heritability appears to decline in early adolescence" also.[15] This is as we might expect. Many biographies bear witness to the sudden surprise of calling during the teen years. In other words, calling seems closest during the years three through eight and then again during adolescence—that is, if we imagine calling to be more evident when genetic influences recede. Some of the life stories in these chapters do show the daimon appearing in the early years, and in adolescence.

Speculations such as these are the frothy part of empirical and statistical studies. They make reading the literature fun. Taken straight, statistical studies stone the mind. So I present the findings not as they are presented to me, as evidence to harden the concrete. I offer them to spark speculation. Such speculation becomes even more important as the sciences of both molecular biology and statistics sophisticate and as the samples broaden. The imagination must expand to keep up with the data. Eleven thousand identical twin pairs are born in the United States each year. It becomes ever clearer that genetic influences are intensely complex and varied, even if we wish to plot them mechanistically or trap them under a bell curve.

With this we have landed in the IQ briar patch. "Although the issue of genetic influence on IQ scores has traditionally been one of the most controversial areas in the behavioral sciences, a recent survey of over a thousand scientists and educators indicates that most now believe *individual* differences in IQ scores are at least partially inherited."[16]

Do notice the word I emphasized: *individual*. Differences— not of gender, not of color, not of race, not of class, not of any group, but between individuals.

So I want to fault the comparison of IQ scores of so-called blacks and whites in at least four ways:

1. Who, genetically, is black and who white in our 350-year-old miscegenated culture, to say nothing of genetic mixing long before the Americas were invaded by Europeans and their imported Africans?
2. What are we actually "scoring" in IQ tests that is called "IQ"?
3. What is the psychological meaning of "test" in various social communities, and the relation between an IQ test as a ritual and other "test" rituals?
4. Besides these questions, which can be found in the endless arguments about IQ and its scores and tests, there is one that derives particularly from this book. If there is an acorn or daimon, and if this factor often resists compliance with socialization, as the stories of the eminent often show, could such resistance frustrate IQ test achievement? Would it not, perhaps, single out especially the IQ tests for its refusals, since high IQ scores are generally the right passport into a more acceptable part of the bell curve?[17]

INDIVIDUALITY

The individual identity of each human person is not only an article of religious faith or an axiom of the Western mind. Human individuality is also a statistical quasi-certainty.

Each of us has the capacity to generate 10^{3000} eggs or sperm with unique sets of genes. If we consider 10^{3000} possible eggs being generated by an individual woman and the same number of sperm being generated by an individual man, the likelihood of anyone else with your set of genes in the past or in the future becomes infinitesimal.[18]

Moreover, genetic research itself warns that the genes cannot be grasped by simplistic explanations. The timing of their interventions occurs in spurts and lags, their interrelation with environmental circumstances is infinitely involved. So research since the 1980s has focused more and more on separate lives, behavioral differences, nonshared orientations, or what you and I would call individuality.

To account for the genetic aspect of individuality, three theories have been growing in importance. These explanatory ideas, too, point toward "something else."

The first is called emergenesis. It is based in part on the startling data of genetic traits that do not run in families, yet appear in the tastes, styles, and idiosyncratic habits of identical twins reared apart.[19] Here are some examples of this amazing concordance in separately raised twins:

A pair of male MZAs [monozygotic adults], at their first adult reunion, discovered that they both used Vademecum toothpaste, Canoe shaving lotion, Vitalis hair tonic, and Lucky Strike cigarettes. After that meeting, they exchanged birthday presents that crossed in the mail and proved to be identical choices, made independently in separate cities.

There were two gunsmith hobbyists among the group of twins; two women who habitually wore seven rings; . . . two who obsessively counted things; two who had been married five times; two captains of volunteer fire departments; two fashion designers; two who left little love notes around the house for their wives . . . in each case, an MZA pair. . . .

The dizygotic separated in infancy and reared apart (DZA) twins whom we have studied, in contrast, seldom produced similar "coincidences."[20]

Emergenesis accounts for these convergent phenomena by saying that the similarities must be (a) genetic in origin (because they appear in identical twins) and (b) the result of a configuration of genes emergent uniquely in this or that particular pair. If these habits and tastes appeared in any single person, we would have no evidence of genetic influence. But since these habits and tastes appear in identical twins reared apart, the concordance can be due only to inheritance.

Emergenesis says that the genetic material results in a unique configuration inherited from the gene stuff of both parental lines. "You might receive the 10 and king of spades from Dad, and the jack, queen, and ace of spades from Mom, cards that had never counted for much in either family tree but whose combination in you might produce . . . a new Olympic record."[21] It is not just a pile of genetic stuff that makes for uniqueness, but the way your hand of cards fills out and forms a particular, and successful, configuration.

Our term for "configuration" was "pattern" or "image," the particular *paradeigma* that is your lot according to Plato's myth. Emergenesis accounts genetically and, I suppose, randomly for the paradigm that is yours. For who knows what makes you draw a winning hand? Or rather, the Fates know: Your configuration is the lot your soul chose before you ever took a breath.

The second theoretical idea goes by the name of "epistasis." It refers to the inhibitory effect of genes acting on one another in a staggering variety of combinations.

Behavioral differences among individuals involve many genes, perhaps hundreds. Each of these genes can make its own small independent contribution to the variability among individuals. . . . Epistasis . . . is like genetic luck. Luck of the draw at conception can result in certain unique combinations of genes that have extraordinary effects not seen in parents or siblings.[22]

An unpredictable "luck of the draw" plays its part in who we are. In Plato this random cause was named Ananke; the formidable goddess of necessity, she defied reason and, in Plato's myth, governed the lots our souls selected. And it was called Tyche and Moira, who are personifications of fate. From Roman times into the Renaissance this principle was called Fortuna—and it does seem odd to come, finally, to these archetypal figures to account for an individual's specific character and destiny. As if we knew it all the time, except that now we have a new name for it: chaos theory, the third idea now prominent in studies of heredity.

"In non-linear systems [and surely a life is a nonlinear system] tiny, seemingly trivial differences in input can lead to huge differences in output. . . . Chaotic systems are not predictable [and surely unpredictability, too, is a characteristic of life] but they are stable in their irregular patterns."[23] Chaos theory gives great importance to "sensitive dependence on initial conditions."

Have we not come home to the influence of the angel or genius, and the seemingly trivial, yet highly significant ways it works, like tiny Yehudi Menuhin's temper tantrum over the toy violin, like Ella Fitzgerald's sudden shift to singing on amateur night? I draw your attention further to the introductory phrase, "in non-linear systems." We cannot think of our biographies only as time-bound, as a progression along a line from birth to death. This is only one dimension, the temporal one, a linear one.

The soul moves in circles, said Plotinus. Hence our lives are not moving straight ahead; instead, hovering, wavering, returning, renewing, repeating. The genes work in lags and spurts. The sense of being "in the zone," in touch, opened out, blasted, seeing and knowing, comes and goes utterly unpredictably, yet with stable patterns.

I am different from everyone else and the same as everyone else; I am different from myself ten years ago and the same as myself ten years ago; my life is a stable chaos, chaotic and repetitive both, and I can never predict what tiny, trivial bit of input will result in a huge and significant output. I must always remain acutely sensitive to initial conditions, such as what or who came into the world with me and enters the world with me each day. On that I remain dependent.

LOVE

We seem not as unique in our loving as we might like to believe. People seem to have similar styles of loving. Adult identical twins show this similarity most clearly, for they tend to conceive of love in the same way.

By "styles of loving" I am referring to the models used in "love research." The broad concept "love" is sorted into a variety of baskets, such as responsible altruistic caretaking (agape), practical partnership (pragma), erotic intimacy (eros), and so on. Identical twins converge in these categories. Yet the reason for the similarity is not genetic.

> The findings from this first behavior genetic analysis of adult love styles are remarkable for two reasons. First, we know of no personality domain [stress tolerance, aggression, control, etc.] in which genetic factors play such a small role. . . . Second, we are aware of no attitude [religious beliefs, race biases, etc.] in which genetic factors play such a small role.[24]

Now here is a happy curiosity. These twins are in accord in all love styles *except for one:* mania, the obsessive, tormented feeling usually characteristic of romantic love. So we have to inquire into why the exception of manic romantic love. In this specific regard there seems to be an independence of the heart. Manic love is something else!

Since the explanation for the similarity of styles is not genetic, the research model allows only one alternative: environment. Look-alike twins who love alike have picked up identical love maps.

"Love maps" are one of the ways psychology tries to account for the mysteries of being seized by love. You grow up in a parental environment where certain features bring pleasure, meet needs, enhance vitality. These characteristics form a schema that you fall for when a person crosses your path who seems to have the attributes of the love map. "As you grow up, this unconscious map takes shape and a composite proto-image of the ideal sweetheart gradually emerges. . . . So, long before your true love walks past you in a classroom, at a shopping mall, or in the office, you have already constructed some basic elements of your ideal sweetheart."[25]

The love map consists of layers. Cross-cultural research claims that there is a collective level for love maps in general, such as a good complexion. In women, bodies that are plump and wide-hipped are universally attractive; in men, worldly goods, such as cars or camels. Then there are layers reflecting traditions, fashions, and local community norms. The theory of love maps suggests that environmental conditioning determines the object of your desire.

Other psychologists call this object choice a projection. According to Jungian psychology, the projection springs from an archetypal source as part of each soul's intimate essence. For Jungians, the love map has highly individualized features, because it is a complex image in the heart that brings about the "fall" and the feeling that this is a call of fate. The more obsessive and compelling the image, the more madly in love you become, which intensifies the conviction that indeed fate is calling. Jungians name this archetypal factor that skews the love map toward a particular person, the anima and animus.[26]

These figures may bear surface traits of the love map, but can't be reduced to it.

"Anima" and "animus" originate in the Latin words for "soul" and "spirit"; so your heart may fall for a composite childhood image but always an unknown configuration is structuring your map, and permeating it with experiences of miracle and mystery.[27] That's why, Jungians would say, love is so overwhelming. It knocks your socks off as it lifts you right out of your shoes, and out of this world.

The experience of romantic love is beyond all conditions, claiming devotion beyond all bounds. For Plato, mania was an intervention of the gods, specifically Aphrodite and Eros.[28] Little else in life feels more exclusively meant for me, more personally directed at you, than the manic moment of romance. Romance feels fateful, feels like kismet, karma, destiny. "It had to be you." "Nobody else would do." "Only you." "I wandered around, finally found . . ." "You are my lucky star." This fatal attraction, impersonally called chemistry and attached to subliminal pheromones, has its autonomy of force apart from both genetics and environment.

Whether this feeling be delusional or not, it provides convincing witness to what the Jungians are claiming with their interpretation of romantic love. Something "meant," something else that is particularly "romantic," accompanies the phenomenon. Of course, identical twins lose some of their sameness by falling differently.

So we have seen two ways of imagining the love map—the Jungian anima/animus and the nature-or-nurture model. According to the latter, "romantic love styles are not strongly influenced by heritable factors." The only possible alternative is the environment. You learned your style of love during early years. How? "Unique experiences," on the one hand and, on the other, "perhaps sharing parents and making similar observations of parents' relational styles."[29] Perhaps. The thesis assumes that you fall in love, if not directly with your parents, as Freudianism implies, then with surrogates for them or at least following their patterns. Again the parental fallacy is brought in to account for what is not understood. Whether "I want a girl just like the girl who married dear old Dad," or a girl as different from her as possible, it is a great leap of faith and an insult to the person for whom my heart has fallen to believe that my fantasies and styles of love replicate Mom and Dad, except on the collective socialized level of the map.

For Jungians, Mom and Dad are preview images of the anima and animus. Even if we do imitate Mom and Dad and their style of loving, we're not photocopies.

Fantasy embellishes the map, or more likely designs it. Empirical studies of romantic love declare "that romantic love is inexorably tied up with fantasy."[30] Idealization is essential to it, not imitation; not replication of the known, expectation of the unknown. Some details of parental manners of relating suit, others are never reproduced, and the factors that spin the fantasy and select the details are anima and animus. The archetypal fantasies integrate whatever maps we pick up from Mom and Dad, and not the other way around.

There can be other "causes" than family styles for similarities between twins. Twins may seek to replicate the relationship they have with each other—that stability, that friendship, that practicality and caring, and unconscious egg-given physical closeness, transferring to a mate what has been their lifestyle so far. Kissing and fighting go on in the womb.[31] Replication alone might give them similar love maps. But the object of our search is less the reason for their similarity than their difference regarding manic romantic love, that condition of torment and desperate need, of highs and lows, of obsessive dependency, a condition you seem never able to get over.

Another reason for dissimilarity in romantic styles of twins is the need for "a psychological mirror," which romantic love provides.[32] In the mirror of similarity we see only our twin face; in the mirror of mania we see something altogether other, the face that we cannot find, do not know, and that seems to require a romantic agony. If monozygotic identity is laid down in your DNA and reinforced with every shared environmental breath, it takes wrenching distortion to bring about difference.

The love map may account for visibilities like those fluid hips, those cars or camels, but love falls also for "something else," invisible. We say, "There's something about her"; "The whole world changes in his presence." As Flaubert supposedly said: "[She] was the focal point of light at which the totality of things converged."

This is off the map altogether. We are in the terrain of transcendence, where usual realities hold less conviction than invisibilities. If ever we wanted obvious proof of the daimon and its calling, we need but fall once in love. The rational sources of heredity and environment are not enough to give rise to the torrents of romantic agony. It's all you, and never do you feel more flooded with importance and more destined; nor can what you do turn out to be more demonic.

This intoxication with self-importance suggests that romantic love "has in fact promoted the growth of individuality."[33] According to Susan and Clyde Hendrick, it can be well argued that the Western sense of person parallels the place given to romantic love in the culture, as shown first by courtly romance and the troubadours, and then in the Renaissance. Ideals of individualism and individual destiny reached an apogee in the nineteenth century, as did the delirious exaggerations of romantic love, so that, as the Hendricks say, romantic love may "be construed as a force or device to help create or enhance self and individuality." These psychodynamics must locate the call of love within the personal "self." My psychodaimonics imagines this call more phenomenologically, using the language that love itself uses—myth, poetry, story, and song—and that places the call beyond the "self," as if it comes from a divine or demonic being.

That's why the manic style of romantic love doesn't converge with the other maps of loving. Calling crystallizes in that person whose face calls you to what feels like your fate.

That person becomes a divinity exteriorized, master of my fate, mistress of my soul, as the Romantics say, both demonic and angelic, the one I must cling to and cannot part from, not because I am so weak, but because it, the call, the destiny, is so strong. Of course I am tormented, possessive, dependent, in pain. The daimon is shredding my love map.

Identical twins may choose the same aftershave and toothpaste, but "the most important choice of all—that of a mate—seems to be an exception." "Romantic infatuation . . . forms . . . almost adventitiously." Behavioral science concludes "that human pairing is inherently random."[34] It retreats to the statistical luck of the draw to account for the most important choice of all, because psychology as a science dares not imagine what it cannot measure.

We can, however, read the recent research as support for the autonomy of the genius. Its fire lights up precisely the companion required, for better or worse, for long term or short, convincing me that this other is a one-and-only and this event is unique. The other styles of loving charted in the research—sharing, caring, practical commitments, and libidinal intimacy—are less selective, less personal. They do not insist upon this particular partner who embodies the image I carry in my heart. Romantic mania sees what is already there in the acorn before you even came along.

The Spanish philosopher Ortega y Gasset says we fall in love on few occasions in a long life.[35] It is a rare and fortuitous event, and it strikes incredibly deeply. When such love happens, it is for no other reason than the singularity of the object. Only *this person.* Not attributes and virtues, not voice or hips or bank account, not projections left over from earlier flames or hand-me-down family patterns, simply the uniqueness of this person whom the heart's eye selected. Without that sense of fate in the choice, the romance of the love doesn't work. For this sort of love is not a personal relationship or a genetic epistasis, but more likely a daimonic inheritance, a gift and curse from the invisible ancestors.

A similar sense of destiny, if less sudden and less heated, and a similar devotion can mark falling for a place and even for a work, as well as for a person. You can't leave it, you must stay with it until it's over, you perform ritual magic devotions to keep it going. The same enchantments occur, the same sense arises that I could live the rest of my life with you, whether "you" is a person, a place, a work. And the similar feeling exists that not only is my life called here, but my death.

Death is a ponderous and repugnant term to connect with the intense vibrations of romantic love; but romantic love especially reverberates with feelings of both the eternal and the shortness and fragility of life, as if death's call to a limitless "beyond" elsewhere were always shadowing and inspiring romantic passion. One takes the most extraordinary risks. And when literature joins romantic lovers it also joins their love with death.

The eye of the heart that "sees" is also the eye of death that sees through visible presentation to an invisible core. When Michelangelo sculpted portraits of his contemporaries or of the figures of religion and myth, he attempted to see what he called the *immagine del cuor,* the heart's image, "a prefiguration" of what he was sculpting, as if the chisel that cut the rock followed the eye that penetrated his subject into its heart.[36] The portrait aimed to reveal the inner soul of what he was carving.

A heart's image lies within each person. It is what we truly reveal when we fall helplessly in love, for then we are opened to display who we most truly are, giving a glimpse of our soul's genius. People say: "He looks so different—he must be in love." "She's fallen in love; she's utterly changed." When love moves the heart, something else is perceived in the idolized object, which poetic language tries to capture.[37] Michelangelo tried to express this image in the sculpted form. The categories of nature and nurture do not reach into the heart or see through its eye. That is why we have had to add to our examination of genetics and environment this coda on love.

The meeting between lover and beloved is heart to heart, like that between sculptor and model, between hand and stone. It is a meeting of images, an exchange of imaginations. When we fall in love we begin to imagine romantically, fiercely, wildly, madly, jealously, with possessive, paranoid intensity. And when we imagine strongly, we begin to fall in love with the images conjured before the heart's eye—as when starting a project, preparing a vacation trip, planning a new house in a different city, swelling with pregnancy. . . . Our imaginations draw us ever more fully into the venture. You can't leave the lab, can't stop buying equipment, reading brochures, imagining names. You are in love because of imagination. By freeing imagination, even identical twins are freed of their sameness.

ENVIRONMENT

Before we leave this chapter we must go back again to our own set of twins, Nature and Nurture aka Environment. Since environment is the concept that the two major themes of this chapter, genetics and love, employ to explain the obscure grounds of difference, we can't allow the term to go unexamined.

The unusual and little-used verb "to environ" means surround, enclose, envelop; literally, to form a ring around. "Environment," the noun, means a set of circumstances (*circum* = around); the context, the physical conditions and external situations, that "surround" our persons and our lives.

The research on twins divides environment into two main kinds: shared and unshared. To have a shared environment, in general, means to have been raised in the same family around the clock for some years, partaking in the family's activities, values, conversations, habits; to have sat in the same classrooms with the same teachers; to have struggled with the same coaches and teammates. The image of a shared environment is, of course, idealized and rather resembles a fifties white-world movie.

"Unshared environment" refers to the singular experiences of each twin alone. What is unshared must include chance occurrences and illnesses, and the feelings, dreams, thoughts, and relationships that are personal and private.

Can we draw a line sharply between shared and unshared? The actual shared environment is jam-packed with differences: how the mother differentiates each of an identical pair of twins; how each develops its own parental relationships; differences in care during postnatal hospitalization (which is often necessary in twin births); health complications in infancy, physical positions in cradle and crib, and at the breast; and so on.

Especially important is the difference between members of the identical pair in their relations with each other, where they are governed by an archetypal logic of complementarity (weaker/stronger, smarter/dumber, first/last, extravert/introvert, earthly/heavenly, mortal/immortal, and so on). Besides, researchers note that between twins within a shared competitive environment a rivalry develops that yields unshared individualized responses in each.[38]

Rivalry results not only from the competitive ethos of our culture. It reflects the innate urge of "sames" to differentiate their identities. Each person seeks to be an "each" in conformity with his or her heart's image and the path of its destiny, despite genetics, despite environment. Every family is a hearth of similarities *and* a centrifugal force whirling each member to competitively assert his or her differences. In the case of identical twins, the very pull for closeness pushes them apart. Magnets that cling together at one pole mutually repel at the other. Let's attribute differences not merely to competitive rivalry, but also to the angel's call to a unique fate.

The idea of environment needs even further analysis. It surely goes beyond images of the family network—a simple sitcom set of similar jokes and squabbles, similar snacks from the fridge, similar bedtimes. The environment is also the furniture and the pickup, the pets and the plants on the windowsill. It extends outside the walls to the yard and the neighbors, to the action in the street, to what is produced thousands of miles away and comes in via TV, Internet, and Walkman. It must also include the supermarket which packages and shelves the world: bananas from Ecuador and fish from Newfoundland, and also the chemical coatings on the bananas and the traces of mercury washed from pulp mills into the cells of the fish.

Once we have opened the ecological eye, where does environment—even immediate, unshared, private, individual environment—stop?

Can in fact there be an "unshared environment"? Can I truly possess a shut-off moment that is all mine alone? Even the pillow on which I lie breathing as I float into my private midnight dream bears traces of duck down, polyester, and cotton and the environments from which this pillow was manufactured, as well as of the traffic of mites sharing the pillow with me.

I have come to believe that the concept of a walled garden of isolation refers to no actual reality; it is a necessary fantasy for intensifying communication with invisibles whose omens and hints are so dimly perceived. The idea of "unshared" provides a gate into the garden of individuality. We need the idea to confirm our private sense of uniqueness and to hear its call.

The category "unshared environment" is an invention of the hard sciences to locate the cause of individual differences. It is used to explain what cannot be accounted for by their other categories, heritability and shared environment. But the idea "unshared" rests on an image of enclosure, of a private surrounding that affects me alone in a particular way. The only possible unshared and unsharable phenomenon that is always around and impinging on my life is the uniqueness of the daimon and the individuality of my relation with it, and it with me. By using the language of behavioral science, disguised in the circumlocutions of "unshared environment," the daimon shows itself to be a determinant on equal footing with nature and nurture. How else enter the secured strictures of the lab except in the language of the lab and by means of the password "unshared"?

Unshared does not mean isolated, for there is no way out of the shared environment which is this planet. And although there is no isolation, there is indeed uniqueness. The first is not necessary for the second.

You don't have to be literally sealed away in order to be different. Your difference from every other person, the "unshared experience," occurs every moment within the shared because of the uniqueness of your individual identity. Your difference doesn't require walls for its guarantee; this guarantee was given from the beginning by the image in your heart that accompanies you through your life. A *fantasy* of isolation, however, may be useful for attending to the daimon. Hence people take retreats, go on vision quests, fast and purge, or simply stay in bed in the dark for a few days to recover their particular unshared calling.

—

The upshot of genetic studies leads in two (!) directions: a narrow path and a broad one. The narrow road heads toward simplistic, monogenic causes. It wants to pinpoint bits of tissue and correlate them with the vast complexity of psychic meanings. The folly of reducing mind to brain never seems to leave the Western scene. We can never give it up because it is so basic to our Western rationalist and positivist mind-set. The rationalist in the psyche wants to locate causes you can put your hands on and fix.

Machines provide the best models for meeting this desire. Take them apart, find their inner mechanisms, and then adjust their functioning by modifying their ratchets, enriching their fuel, greasing their connections. Henry Ford as father of American mental health. Result: Ritalin, Prozac, Zoloft, and dozens of other effective products for internal adjustment that we consume in abundance, millions of us, daily or twice daily. The simplistics of monogenic causes eventually leads to the control of behavior by drugs—that is, to drugged behavior.

Robert Plomin, on whose passionate, prolific, and perceptive writings this chapter has frequently relied, urgently warns against using genetics in a simplistic manner. He states: "Genetic effects on behavior are polygenic and probabilistic, not single gene and deterministic."[39] I gather from him a warning to psychiatry: Do not capsize your noble vessel under the weight of pharmaceutical, insurance company, and government gold, and do not set your compass toward Fantasy Island, where genetics will define "disease entities in psychiatry."[40] "We have learned little about the genetics of development [how genes act and interact over time] except to appreciate its complexity."[41] Therefore we can never arrive at that equation where one defective gene equals one clinical picture (except for true anomalies like Huntington's chorea).

These warnings have little effect; simplistic thinking fulfills too many wishes. The heads of Henry Ford and Thomas Edison are carved into the Mount Rushmore of the mind. The monster of mechanism appears in every century of modern Western history and must be watched for by each generation—especially ours, when to hold out for "something else" besides nature or nurture means believing in ghosts or magic.

Ever since French rationalism of the seventeenth (Marin Mersenne, Nicolas de Malebranche) and eighteenth (Étienne de Condillac, Julien Offroy de La Mettrie) centuries and right through to the positivism of the nineteenth (Antoine Destutt de Tracy, Auguste Comte) in which all mental events were reduced to biology, a piece of the collective Western mind has been yoked like a dumb ox to the heavy tumbrel of French mechanistic materialism. It is astounding how a people with such subtle taste as the French and with such erotic sensibility can go on and on contributing so much rationalist rigor mortis to psychology. Every import that arrives from France must be inspected for this French disease, even though it carries the fashionable label of Lacanism, Structuralism, Deconstruction, or whatever.

Today rationalism is global, computer-compatible everywhere. It is the international style of the mind's architecture. We cannot pin it to a particular flag, unless to the banners of the multinational corporation that can spend big bucks turning psychiatry, and eventually psychological thinking, and therefore soul control, toward monogenetic monotheism. One gene for one disorder: Splice the gene, teach it tricks, combine it, and the disorder is gone, or at least you don't know you have it. The narrow path leads back to the thirties and forties of psychiatric history, though in a more refined manner and with better press releases. From 1930 into the 1950s, correlating specific brain areas with large emotional and functional concepts provided the rationale for the violence of psychosurgery and the lobotomizing of many a troubled soul at odds with circumstance.

The narrow path is yet more retro, going back to the skull analysis of Franz Josef Gall (M.D., Vienna, 1795), who settled in Paris and was much appreciated by the French. From him came the "evidence" that skull bumps and declivities could be correlated with psychological faculties (a system later called phrenology). Much as they are today, the faculties were given big names, such as memory, judgment, emotionalism, musical and mathematical talent, criminality, and so on. Refinement in methods over the years does not necessarily lead to progress in theorizing: 1795 or 1995—material location, and then reduction of psyche to location, prompts the enterprise.

The contrary direction to narrowing nature to brain simplistics is expanding nurture to a far more embracing notion of environment. If environment means literally what's around, it must also mean whatever is around. This because the unconscious psyche selects quite arbitrarily among the stuff encountered every day in the environment. Tiny and trivial bits of information may have huge subliminal psychic effects, as the days' residues in dreams show. We do dream of the damnedest things! Much of each day is never noticed or recalled, but the psyche picks up the environmental flotsam and delivers it to the dream. The dream—a processing plant recycling the environment, finding soul values in junk. The dream—an artist, appropriating images from the environment for recollection in tranquility.

Because we walk about in fields of psychic realities that influence our lives, we have to broaden the notion of environment in terms of "deep ecology," the hypothesis that the planet is a living, breathing, and self-regulating organism. Since anything around can nourish our souls by feeding imagination, there is soul stuff out there. So why not admit, as does deep ecology, that the environment itself is ensouled, animated, inextricably meshed with us and not fundamentally separate from us?

The ecological vision restores to environment also the classical idea of *providentia*—that the world provides for us, looks out for us, even looks after us. It wants us around, too. Predators, tornadoes, and blackflies in June are only pieces of the picture. Just think of all that's delicious and sweet-smelling. Do birds sing but for each other? This breathable, edible, and pleasant planet, invisibly serviced and maintained, keeps us all by means of its life-support system. Such would be an idea of nurture that is truly nurturing.

"Environment," then, would be imagined well beyond social and economic conditions, beyond the entire cultural setting, to include every item that takes care of us every day: our tires and coffee cups and door handles and the book you are holding in your hands. It becomes impossible to exclude this bit of environment as irrelevant in favor of that bit as significant, as if we could rank world phenomena in order of importance. Important for whom? Our understanding of importance itself has to change; instead of "important to me," think of "important to other aspects of the environment." Does this item nurture what else is around, not merely *us* who are around? Does it contribute to the intentions of the field of which we are only one short-lived part?

As notions of environment shift, we notice environment differently. It becomes more and more difficult to make a cut between psyche and world, subject and object, in here and out there. I can no longer be sure whether the psyche is in me or whether I am in the psyche as I am in my dreams, as I am in the moods of the landscapes and the city streets, as I am in "music heard so deeply / That it is not heard at all, but you are the music / While the music lasts" (T. S. Eliot).[42] Where does the environment stop and I begin, and can I begin at all without being in some place, deeply involved in, nurtured by the nature of the world?

— 🦌 —

CHAPTER 7

PENNY DREADFULS
AND PURE FANTASY

How do we select the right nutrients for the acorn? How can we judge what is a waste of time? Is there health food for the soul?

In the good old days, values were established and directions from them clear. There was standard stuff to study, a canon (today renamed the core curriculum)—not only in the basic three R's, but also in drawing, elocution, music appreciation, nature studies. The minds of very small children were guided, or drilled, whether in the direction of reason or of aesthetic imagination. John Stuart Mill, the nineteenth-century philosopher whom we know today mainly for his utilitarianism and his ideas of liberty, never attended school. Educated at home by his father, he began learning Greek at three and Latin at eight, and by fourteen had read most of the major ancient texts in the original. Another wondrous example of nineteenth-century education was the Anglo-Irish mathematician William Rowan Hamilton:

At three he was a superior reader of English and considerably advanced in arithmetic . . . at five . . . he loved to recite yards of Homer in Greek; at eight he added a mastery of Italian and French . . . and extemporized fluently in Latin. . . . By thirteen William was able to brag that he had mastered one language for each year he had lived.

This demonic appetite for language took him through Persian, Arabic, Sanskrit, Chaldee, Malay, Bengali . . . "and he is about to commence the Chinese" wrote his uncle, complaining of the cost of providing the books for his ravenous nephew.[1]

Francis Galton, who pioneered the study of genius and was yet another of these freak Victorian masterminds, could read by the time he was two and a half, sign his name before three, and wrote this letter to his sister before he was five:

> My dear Adele,
>   I am four years old and can read any English book. I can say all the Latin substantives and adjectives and active verbs besides 52 lines of Latin poetry. I can cast up any sum in addition and multiply by
>   2, 3, 4, 5, 6, 7, 8, 10
>   I can also say the pence table, I read French a little and I know the clock.
>   Francis Galton
>   February-15-1827[2]

Nearer to our day—in time only, but just as distant in spirit as Galton and Mill—is the punishment meted out to Dorothy Thompson by her Methodist minister father. Thompson, born a century ago, was once named by *Time* magazine the most influential woman in America next to Eleanor Roosevelt. She was a persuasive liberal journalist, the first American woman to head a foreign news bureau, and the first correspondent to be expelled from Germany by personal order of Hitler. In her columns and broadcasts she reached millions for years, taking on the right wing, the Republicans, the anti-Semites, the fascists, and Clare Booth Luce with courage, skill, and much learning.

Once, when she slapped her little sister

> her father locked her in a closet and would not let her out until she could recite Shelley's "Adonais" from beginning to end. By the time she was grown, Dorothy could deliver without pause whole chapters of the Bible, the sonnets of Shakespeare, great chunks of *Leaves of Grass,* Chesterton's "Lepanto," dozens of the Psalms, and the entire Constitution of the United States.[3]

The kind of punishment, though decreed by her father and decidedly cruel and unusual by today's educational standards, seems to have been chosen by her own protective daimon, who had, of course, anyway selected that particularly literary father. The memorizing of texts fit the pattern of her life of writing among such colleagues as Alexander Woollcott, Rebecca West, H. L. Mencken, and Thompson's own husband, the Nobel Prize–winning writer Sinclair Lewis.

Mill, Hamilton, Galton, and Thompson are exceptions only in their early mastery, not with respect to the materials mastered. From Plato (who insisted upon music as essential to the canon) through the Stoics and Sophists; from the Catholics (especially the Jesuits), the Orthodox Jews, and Philipp Melanchthon (whose ambition it was to educate Protestant Germany) to Rousseau and Froebel with their Romantic programs; and on up to Rudolf Steiner and Maria Montessori, there have always been strong recommendations in the European tradition for an authorized program to prevent the young mind from wasting itself on trivia. The inner life of the mind, whether endowed innately or merely a tabula rasa, needed to be correctly nourished in its full range, not only by means of logic and mathematics but also by addressing its ethical character and imaginative powers.

Therefore many recommendations have been less strictly mental and less literate, but just as dogmatically enforced. Hands to be kept busy; play restricted or supervised; no idleness; chores finished. Construction: Make things, tinker, sew, learn crafts, do repairs and maintenance. Manners at table, in dress, in hygiene, with neighbors. Language was disciplined so the child would be well-spoken. Moral instruction from the religious, who ministered to the soul with Bible, hymns, and homilies. And certainly not least, especially for the Romantics from Rousseau through Steiner, was the instruction of nature, the soul's primordial nutrient drawn from fields, flowers, and farmyards, and from the coasts and headlands of rocks and tidal pools, sea sounds and the winds.

Edith Cobb's *The Ecology of Imagination in Childhood*[4] makes it clear that the poetic basis of mind needs the nourishment given by the phenomena of nature. Imagination cannot come into its own without immersion in the natural world, or at least without occasional contact with its wonders. John Lennon, for instance, a city boy, visited Scotland at the very beginning of adolescence, and while out for a walk one day he lapsed into "a trance . . . the ground starts going beneath you and the heather, and I could see this mountain in the distance. And this kind of *feeling* came over me: I thought . . . this is that one they're always talking about, the one that makes you paint or write because it's so overwhelming that you have to tell somebody . . . so you put it into poetry."[5]

Conservative thinkers from Plato through Steiner to scornful Allan Bloom and that thug of virtue, William Bennett, with their various notions of back-to-basics, disciplined education that supposedly brings out the best in the child by giving it the best, would at the same time suppress vulgarities like porn and pulp (and even wine, according to Plato), insisting that imagination must be fed good stuff of cultural quality, natural reality, inventive challenge, and moral example. The soul, they say, needs models for its mimesis in order to recollect eternal verities and primordial images. If in its life on earth it does not meet these as mirrors of the soul's core, mirrors in which the soul can recognize its truths, then its flame will die and its genius wither. Ideal heroes and heroines provide the ectypes on earth that release the guiding archetypes of the soul.

But please now look at these stories of those whose flame blazed and whose genius flowered, and try to swallow the kinds of "soul food" their imaginations relished. Cole Porter, debonair songwriter of sophisticated word-rich lyrics, en route to and from his music lessons while a small-town Indiana schoolboy, became an "insatiable consumer" of spicy books—penny dreadfuls—hiding them away in his music bag. No sooner was the lesson done than he sped off to spend the day plunged into cheap adventure tales. Frank Lloyd Wright played viola as a boy; he read Goethe, *Hans Brinker,* Jules Verne—but also "tattered thrillers from the Nickel Library." "Blood-and-thunder penny pulps . . . exerted great fascination [on James Barrie] with their garish covers and manly oaths issuing in balloons from sneering faces." Richard Wright, Mississippi poor and without enough to eat was "forbidden to read anything except church literature and the Bible at home." He managed to get hold of "pulps and dime novels . . . with money he earned as a delivery boy." He loved murder mysteries and read "Flynn's *Detective Weekly* and *Argosy,* both popular magazines of the 1920's." Havelock Ellis read his Milton and Walter Scott and Defoe; but also he fell prey to a "hypnotic concentration" on *The Boys of England,* a penny weekly which printed dramas "as high and remote from reality as were some of its settings." Ellis read "while he was eating, while stomping the streets alone, and even something while ostensibly sleeping."[6]

Sir Edmund Hillary, the first European to scale Everest, read, before his teen years, the Tarzan tales of Edgar Rice

Burroughs, and also H. Rider Haggard, and others like them. "In my imagination I constantly reenacted heroic episodes, and I was always the hero."[7] Another reader of Rider Haggard was John Lennon.

Then there is the high school dropout guy who "dressed mostly in black, drove a silver Civic, dined at Denny's and Jack in the Box, read crime novels and comics voraciously, loved Elvis and the Three Stooges, always celebrated his birthday at the movies, and—legend has it—amassed $7,000 in parking tickets."[8] The movies he particularly liked portrayed women in prison and Asian martial arts. The person? Quentin Tarantino, scriptwriter and film director. His major film to date: *Pulp Fiction*.

We need to remember that as the bodies of sports giants have often been raised on junk food, the imagination may be fed by cheap, popular, and "unhealthy" equivalents. What matters is passion, which may be more predictive of capacity and productive of motivation than other usual benchmarks. Cole Porter said: "I suppose some of my lyrics owe a debt to those naughty books."[9] There is no right food and no wrong food; the food must only meet the appetite, the appetite find its kind of food.

As for the "acornic" significance of "extra-curricular books," consider Coleridge. He read of " 'the Sufferings and Surprising Adventures of Mr. Philip Quarli' one of whose deeds was the shooting of a large and beautiful sea-bird . . . an action he immediately regrets."[10] *The Rime of the Ancient Mariner,* to which this dead seabird is central, is perhaps Coleridge's best-known longer work.

There are, I believe, certain necessary nutrients besides the occasions of chance that evoke the early imagination, as they did for Lennon on the heath and for Havelock Ellis immersed in his penny dreadful. Among the many prerequisites for furthering imagination I would single out at least these three: first, that the parents or intimate caretakers of a child have a fantasy about that child; second, that there be odd fellows and peculiar ladies within the child's perimeter; and third, that obsessions be given courtesy.

Biographers usually look to the mother. Lyndon Johnson was called a mama's boy; so was Franklin Roosevelt; Harry Truman handwrote letters to his mother while at the Potsdam Conference ordering world history. So it is customary to see in a mother's ideals and intensity of ambition what is carried out by one or another of her children. According to biographers, the source of success appears to lie in a mother's doting—or in her neglectful selfishness, which forces an offspring out on its own.

This piece of the parental fallacy, with all its accompanying jargon about bad double-binding mothers or seductive smothering mothers, and also about absent or possessive and punitive fathers, so rules the explanations of eminence that its jargon determines the way we tell the stories of our own lives. Notice that these psychologisms draw attention away from the child and back to the parent, who asks: "How am I doing?" They raise doubts and anxieties, not about the nature of the child, but about the parents' own problems: Have I the right attitude? Am I too strict? Too lenient? Am I good enough?—all of which reveal the inherent and almost inescapable self-referential narcissism in the parental fallacy. Of this we have already said enough in the chapter devoted to this theme. Here we need only recover one decisive influence from our global condemnation of the parental fallacy, and that is the parental *fantasy*.

PARENTAL FANTASY

What is the connection, if any, between the parental imagination—by "parent" I always mean the immediate, intimate caretaker of a child—and the child's acorn? How do the parents imagine the child? What do they see in this little person who has been dropped in their laps; what is it bearing on those frail and bony shoulders, what is it looking for with those eyes? Have the parents a fantasy of an invisible fate in the visible traits displayed every day?

Justus Bergman certainly looked for, and recorded, the visible traits displayed every day in his daughter, Ingrid. He was a man filled with fantasy. Ingrid was named after the Swedish princess born two years prior. On Ingrid's first birthday, Justus filmed her in a white dress; on her second birthday he filmed her again. His third film shows her laying flowers on her mother's grave. Justus had a photography shop and studio on Stockholm's elegant Strandvägen, a hundred yards from the Royal Dramatic Theater, and Ingrid was a favorite subject of his camera, dressing in various roles and loving to act in front of her father. At age eleven, during an interval at the theater, she announced her vocation: "Papa, Papa, that's what I'm going to do."[11]

The parental fallacy here sees sublimated incest, a father's daughter who lived out his controlling fantasy, as so many sons live out their mother's dreams. The Platonic fantasy, however, says Ingrid's soul selected exactly the right place and the right father to foster her acorn's desire. She even selected the right mother, who, by dying early, allowed the intertwining of Ingrid's calling and Justus's fantasy to proceed unimpeded by triangles of jealousy.

The parental fantasy may not come as directly as in the example of Justus Bergman. It may instead show itself via dreams, or in overanxiousness, or in parental fights over school, over discipline, over sickliness—and over odd obsessions such as reading pulp fiction and watching midnight movies. The way the child's behavior is interpreted accords with the fantasy of the caretaker's vision. Does the mother kick her boy out of the house to play rough with other kids in the street because it's her fantasy that this boy needs to toughen up and be the man about the house (counterphobic to his weaknesses, and hers), or because of her fear of sissies and "queers," or because in her mind's eye she sees her son as a raider, with dash and good looks? The behaviors her instructions ordain or prohibit affect the child less than does the fantasy guiding her instructions.

To expect primary caretakers, for example, parents, to see through the child into the acorn, to know who is there *in nuce,* and to tend to its concerns—is far too much. That is why teachers and mentors come into the world. He or she is another special person, often someone whom we fall in love with early, or who falls for us; we are two acorns on the same branch, echoing similar ideals. What heartsease and bliss in finding a corresponding soul who singles us out! How long we move about, desperate to discover someone who can really see us, tell us who we are. One of the main seductions of early love, and early therapy, arises from the desire to meet a person who can (or who you believe can, or who can at least pretend to) see you.

Greg LeMond, the remarkable American cyclist who won the Tour de France, received from his father money for equipment, clothing, and bicycling magazines. In addition to that encouragement, LeMond had a mentor: Roland Della Santa, a master bicycle-frame builder. "Once or twice a week," said LeMond, "I went to Roland's shop and hung out while he worked. He'd tell me stories about the great European stars, thousands of screaming fans and legendary races . . ."[12] The mentor provides specialized knowledge as well as the lore, the atmosphere of a tradition.

As caretakers, parents cannot also be mentors. The roles and duties differ. It is enough for a parent to keep a roof over your head and food on the table, and to get you up and off to school. Providing a cave of security, a place for regressions is no small job. Freed of these tasks, the mentor has only one: to recognize the invisible load you carry and to have a fantasy about it that corresponds with the image in the heart. One of the most painful errors we make is to expect from a parent a mentor's vision and blessing and strict teaching, or expecting from a mentor shelter and concern for our human life. Van

Cliburn's mother, who taught him piano for years, set a sharp border between her two natures: "When I'm teaching you, I'm not your mother."[13]

The failure to distinguish sufficiently between the rather ruthless limits of mentoring and the rather broadly mundane responsibilities of parenting—as when parents try to be guiding instructors, and mentors make a family of their following—leads to bitter breakups between apprentices and mentors. The younger person's wish to be fathered or mothered in a caring personal way (according to the Yale study by Daniel J. Levinson and his team) is the main reason for a failed end to the mentor relationship.[14] The confusion of expectations results also in the common resentment of "adult children" who complain that their parents never accurately assessed them, never recognized their inner nature.

The complaint may refer to more than absent parenting or mentoring. There may have been no access to fictional or historical figures, those imaginary mentors who can continue as guides even into older age. When Truman was about to fire MacArthur for insubordination and incompetence, he went back to the image of Abraham Lincoln, who had to fire General George McClellan despite all the political consequences of alienating McClellan (who later entered politics and tried for the presidency). The parallels and threats were clear, but Lincoln provided the mentoring image.[15] Diane Arbus had *Jane Eyre;* J. P. Morgan, Washington and Napoleon; John Lennon, *Alice in Wonderland.* Gary Gilmore, executed for murders, had "studied the legends of violence . . . the stories of John Dillinger, Bonnie and Clyde, and Leopold and Loeb . . . Barbara Graham, Bruno Hauptmann, Sacco and Vanzetti, the Rosenbergs. . . . [He] brought home books about condemned men and women, and read them avidly."[16]

Books too can be mentors, even providing a moment of initiation. R. D. Laing, writer, philosopher, and revolutionary psychiatrist, tells of this discovery in a small public library, while he was still an adolescent in the 1940s. He came upon Kierkegaard while

> eating my way through the library, I mean I was looking at all the books . . . working my way from A to Z. . . . The first major thing of Kierkegaard that I read . . . was one of the peak experiences of my life. I read that through, without sleeping, over a period of about 34 hours just continually. . . . I'd never seen any reference to him . . . that directed me to it. It was just this complete vista. . . . It just absolutely fitted my mind like a glove . . . here was a guy who had *done* it. I felt somehow or another within me, the flowering of one's life.[17]

This moment of initiation is also like a ritual of adoption. Kierkegaard—along with Marx, Freud, and Nietzsche—became one of Laing's spiritual parents, a member of the family tree that nourished his acorn and fed his intellectual fantasy. You expect less from your natural parents, and they become easier to bear once you have discovered the other family tree on which the life of your soul depends.

Perhaps the worst of all atmospheres for your daimon, trying to live with your parents in their place and circumstances, arises when these parents have *no fantasy whatsoever* about you. This objective, neutral environment, this normative, rational life is a vacuum with nothing blowing through. So-called good parents abstain from fantasies for their children. Each person has his own life and her own decisions to make. "Good parents" don't interject their prejudices, their values and judgments. Unconditional positive regard is all a young person needs: "I'm sure you'll succeed at whatever you decide to do." "I'm with you, whatever it is, all the way." The fantasy that governs these parental stupidities is distancing, euphemistically called independence: You have your own room, with your own TV and your own phone line. Independence as distancing finds its daily (or evening) expression in the great American long distance addiction and the phrase "I love you" spoken over the phone. No ideas, no indignation, no anxiety, and no fantasy; love as anesthetic. This sentence, "I love you," parroted back and forth by child and parent may have a subtext that means many things, but it definitely does not mean love, for when you love someone you are filled with fantasies, ideas, and anxieties.

For a documentary of this void, watch the twelve-part television series *An American Family,* which chronicles the day-to-day "life" of the Louds, a Santa Barbara, California, household of Mom and Dad and five kids during the early 1970s. Marriage, family, and individual personality gradually collapse before your eyes, and the reason unfolds as you watch: The home has no living fantasy.

The great difference between these people in California and the ones portrayed in Chekhov or in novels of family decay—*Buddenbrooks,* say—lies in a family life enriched by class commitments, cultural concerns, probing conversations into the imagination, wild longings, regrets, and especially despairs. Literature gives to the despairs the complex flavors of irony and the beauty of tragedy. These fictional people are not only living family, they are living fantasy. The fictions of these families are more vivid than the family-fiction lived by the Louds, which has no stretch to its imagination.

> If there is such a thing as negative culture or culture minus, the Louds have it. The blaring sound of rock is the high point of the creativity in the family. . . . There is no religion, no threatening Jehovah, no merciful Mary, no sense of the beyond of the Talmud, the catechism, the myths of Jupiter and Hera; there is no avenging sensibility, no real moral right or wrong, no sense of judgement of good or bad weighing over the family.

Husband and wife "sit in their living room afraid, it seems, of nothing—no demons give them bad dreams, no wild animals haunt their steps. A brush fire comes within inches of their house. . . . They comment about the fire casually. If the house burns it's insured; nothing really has the power to hurt them." They belong to no clubs or organizations and have no real hobbies. . . . "no passions, such as movies, painting, reading, sewing. When they're in the house they lie by the pool."

Anne Roiphe, whose introduction to the published text of the documentary I am quoting, claims that "culture, if it means anything, must mean the binding of the individual into the social fabric."[18] But the Louds were woven into the consumer–rock music–alcohol–TV–automobile–health–school–apparel–business fabric. Anyway, the social fabric is only a part, and an insufficient part if that social fabric impoverishes individual fantasy. What came into that household left the Louds unsatisfied and numb to that dissatisfaction.

More important to culture than social fabric is the necessity of imagination. And the Loud family are extraordinary people for its lack. They have no fears, no desires, no strong angers or ambitions, no pity and no terror, and no images or language for their expression. Their emotions and their imaginations have not been fed by fantasy. It is as if they have been insured against its risks. Or, more likely, they do share one major fantasy: denial. "I think we're a very well-adjusted family," Mrs. Loud says after the falling-apart and divorce. She is absolutely right, for the Louds are indeed well adjusted to the American dream, with their own blue lagoon in their own sunny yard, sharing their hyperactive passivity. Denial as fantasy; innocence as ideal; happiness as pursuit.

Was the virus that led to the family's disintegration brought by the camera that intruded into their intimacy for seven long months? Or was there no intimacy to begin with, despite the sharing? Did the Louds fall apart because their real life was transposed to TV—or was there no real life? Perhaps the camera was merely a lens that magnified the virus already latent in the home. Despite the limits of this series as an anthropological study, it does display the present fault in the

American family: the want of stimulating fantasy, which, I am claiming is the principal fun and agony of parenting.

In the old days, the agon in the family had to do with major struggles between the fantasies of different characters and generations, such as following in the father's business versus getting an education, staying on the land versus moving to the city, marrying the one chosen for you versus marrying whom you chose. And the heart's image of those old days could announce itself only as stubborn refusal to follow or by open rebellion against the parental fantasy that was engraved in a collective social code. The codes have changed, the collective pressures differ, but the heart must still find the courage to make its choices.

The minor gesture toward the unapproved, the half step into rebellion, says "I am not Mother's little helper," "I am not a bookworm nerd," "I am not a lazy layabout," "I am not a bright little career girl." The family fantasy that has a child typed and pinned and wriggling on the wall forces fateful choices on the heart, choices to find another kind of fantasy, anywhere. In the Loud family one son took more than a half step, and he was diagnosed and medicated. The repression of fantasy in them returned full flood into him, into his music, his language, his habits, including cross-dressing.

For it is not ultimately parental control or parental chaos that children run away from; they run from the void of living in a family without any fantasy beyond shopping, keeping up the car, and routines of niceness. The value of the parental fantasy for the child is that it does force it into opposition and into a beginning recognition that its heart is odd, different, and unsatisfied by the shadow cast upon it by the family's view. Far better for parents to wish the new baby were a boy, call her Harry, Sidney, or Clark, and cut her hair short, than for them not to have any wish at all. At least the acorn is challenged and has a reality to contend with, the reality of the parental fantasy, which can result in seeing through the parental fallacy itself—seeing that I am not conditioned by and the result of my parents.

As a parent is not a mentor, so a parent is also not a nut—which brings us to the second necessary nutrient for the acorn: odd fellows and peculiar ladies. The acorn needs living personifications of fantasy, actual people whose lives seem pulp fiction, whose behaviors, speech, dress carry a whiff of pure fantasy. For me, an "extended family" means not simply more interchangeable caretakers among the many relations; it means extending relations beyond the perimeter of what is customary, an extension of imagination from the familiar to the fictional, to those figures talked about, told about, but rarely seen—in jail, in a foreign land, disappeared years ago. Fictions of faraway folk conjure up images of possibilities for the potentials in the acorn. Sometimes these possibilities are directed straight at the child, as if in indirect recognition of latent character: the wayward drunken uncle whom you "take after"; those look-alike cousins from Texas who never went anywhere and never married, who wear strange dresses and shoes and quote Scripture—"so if you don't watch out, you'll grow up to be just like them."

From Mr. Magoo to Big Bird, the peculiar figures of pure fantasy play on this desire for the extraordinary personage. If Dr. Spock for the parents, then Dr. Seuss for the child. Every evening's prime time brings in odd neighbors with strange behaviors that come in and out of the sitcom family set, extending the family with far-out fantasy people. How strongly the child longs for parents to break their roles, dress up for Halloween, put on something wild. What is the attraction to theater, to the costume trunk, to make-believe with false faces and greasepaint kits in front of the mirror? Is the point to escape the form I have been put in and by magic disclose the image in the heart? Can I release the genie from its entombment in adaptation by a sudden vision of who might also be here? Is the camcorder in the hand of the child an attempt to restructure the usual into the fantastic?

Primary caretakers who cannot be mentors on the one hand or crazies on the other can at least keep the door unlocked for invasions from the other side, for abduction by the

alien imagination, for reminding a child of its essential belonging to the call of the angels.

For the third necessity—that a child's obsessions be given
courtesy—I want to draw upon Mary Watkins's intelligent
observations of imagination in dreams, in fantasy, in madness,
in creative writing, and in children.[19] While imagining is
going on, you are somewhat out of yourself, in another zone.
Sometimes the state is no more than a daydream, a staring, an
absence; sometimes the unfolding of an entire future project;
sometimes a hallucinatory terror at night; sometimes an ec-
static vision such as saints enjoyed. There are various intensities—but the more thoroughly engaged you are, the more
real the imaginative fantasy, its scenes, its voices, its beings, its
feelings and insights. Its reality possesses you and the words
"fantasy," "imagination," "vision" do not really apply. It feels
all too real and too important. Children under ten, and adolescents too, and of course the very old, find themselves again
and again drawn away from the usual into this condition.

Imagining demands absolute attention. The mind in the
imagining zone cannot tolerate interruption any more than
you can when trying to rewire a circuit breaker or prevent a
sauce from curdling, or while preparing notes for tomorrow
morning's meeting. Yet when a child sits on the floor in the
middle of a mess with three dolls and a slopped pan of water,
or runs wild around the yard, in and out of bushes, it is just as
thoroughly engaged in its task as you are. Probably more. Its
play is its work. Play is a child's job. To pick the little worker
up and carry it off, to call the child away to get dressed or
clear up before the task is over, breaks right into the middle
of its work. Can your obedience to the fantasy of the clock
and its kind of reality accommodate the child's reality of
fantasy?

The acorn is obsessive. It is all and only concentration,
undiluted, like a drop of essence. A child's behaviors elaborate this condensity. The child puts into play the germinal
code that pushes it into these obsessive activities. By means of

its concentration, a child gains breathing space and practice for the homunculus of its innate truth, allowing this truth to articulate itself into styles and forms and facilities which it can perform only obsessively, repetitively, exhaustively. Courtesy is called for. Knock before entering.

— 🦗 —

CHAPTER 8

DISGUISE

Mark Twain supposedly observed that the older he got the more vividly he remembered things that had not happened. But cover-ups and peculiar pseudologias may begin at any age. They seem part of autobiography, maybe necessary to it. There seems, indeed, a curious need to falsify, disguise, or destroy the story of your life.

We rearrange the details and embroider them; we even appropriate events from others' lives into our own. Or we censor, as Josephine Baker destroyed masses of old photographs.[1] Twain suggests that the story of your life tends to take over its history. But who is the storyteller creating your biography by these inventions and suppressions? Who is the editor wanting to cut so much out and to compose a fiction of the facts?

Eugène Delacroix spread the story that his unknown father may well have been the great French statesman Talleyrand.[2] Jung's legend was that he descended from one of Goethe's illegitimate liaisons. John Wayne said his father owned a drugstore in Glendale, and an ice cream and paint business; this was coolly, cruelly, denied by a longtime resident who knew the family and town well.[3]

When Lyndon's brother, Sam Houston Johnson, was asked to fill out some of the President's tales of boyhood, his brother refused. He couldn't, he said, because they "never happened."[4]

Fidel Castro had two report cards—one from school and one in which he put his own grades for his parents' signatures.[5] Georges Simenon, who wrote probably more good, readable books—mainly mystery novels—than anyone this century, rewrote his autobiography as fiction and then recast it again in further disguise. Disguise began for him on day one when his mother, spooked by the sinister implication of his birthday—it was Friday the thirteenth—had her husband make the false declaration at the registry of February 12.[6] "The origin of [Isadora Duncan's] first name has never been established. At her birth she was named Dora Angela."[7] She was billed in a theater production as Sara. Besides, she mislaid and lost her passports again and again, and her age changed with circumstances.

Leonard Bernstein had two different first names: Louis, legally and all through childhood, until at sixteen he officially took the name Leonard, by which he had been called all along. Bernstein also said his father blocked him all the way, and that "My childhood was one of complete poverty." He insisted that the Boston Latin School, which he attended from seventh to twelfth grade, offered "absolutely no music at all." In fact, Bernstein was piano soloist with that school's orchestra and sang in its glee club. As for the poverty: Leonard grew up with maids, at times a chauffeur-butler, and two family cars; his father owned two houses and was able to pay for his son's years at Harvard.[8]

Henry Ford took apart his first watch at age seven.

To judge from his own recollections in notebooks, and in the numerous second-hand accounts based on interviews in which the anecdotes had obviously flowed free, the infant Henry Ford was forever dismantling, investigating, and generally displaying his mechanical genius in all directions.

Henry told an oft-repeated tale that he would slip out of the house after dark to collect neighbours' watches, and then bring them home to repair them.

Other similar tales abound. Ford's sister Margaret, however, says:

"I never knew of him going out at night to get watches." She protested for years at Henry's later restoration of their farm home. He had put into the re-done bedroom a little watchmaker's bench and tools.

There was never any such bench up there, she insisted.[9]

Henry Kissinger, whose father lost his teaching job in Furth, Germany, because he was Jewish, claimed in 1958, "My life in Furth seems to have passed without leaving any lasting impressions." In 1971, Kissinger said again: "That part of my childhood is not a key to anything. I was not acutely aware of what was going on. For children, these things are not that serious." Yet these were the years of persecutions and beatings, exclusions from schools and playgrounds, forbidding of relations between Jews and non-Jews, and the abrogation of citizenship rights. Family and friends who lived side by side with young Henry report that Jewish children were not allowed to play with others and had to stay shut up in the garden. They couldn't attend dances, go to the public swimming pool, even the tearoom. "Every day there were slurs in the street, anti-Semitic remarks, calling you filthy names." Henry's mother "especially remembered her children's pitiful fright and puzzlement when the Nazi youths would march by taunting the Jews."[10] But Henry Kissinger says: "For children, these things are not that serious." "That part of my childhood is not a key to anything."

BIOGRAPHY

Writers especially resist biographies. Henry James burned his papers in a garden bonfire. Charles Dickens did, too. At twenty-nine(!) Sigmund Freud had already burned his papers; he is quoted as saying: "As for biographers, let them worry. . . . I am already looking forward to seeing them go astray." And he destroyed, and tried to purchase from recipients, other of his papers, as he got older.[11] Lyndon Johnson wrote "Burn this" on the top of inconsequential letters he wrote from Washington to former students and friends back home. William Makepeace Thackeray, T. S. Eliot, and Matthew Arnold wanted no biographies written of them. Leon Edel, a philosopher of biography and master of its art, reports:

> Some feel it [biography] to be a prying, peeping and even predatory process. Biography has been called "a disease of English literature" (George Eliot); professional biographers have been called "hyenas" (Edward Sackville-West). They also have been called "psycho-plagiarists" (Nabokov) and biography has been said to be "always superfluous" and "usually in bad taste" (Auden).[12]

Some writers—for example, J. D. Salinger—will not even give interviews, and may threaten or pursue lawsuits to deter biographers. Willa Cather wanted no one to examine her life, and Eudora Welty is "extremely private and won't answer anything personal about herself or about friends."[13] Another philosopher of biography, Carolyn Heilbrun, accuses Welty of having "camouflaged herself" in her memoirs, *One Writer's Beginnings,* because "to have written a truthful autobiography would have defied every one of her [Welty's] instincts for loyalty and privacy." (Heilbrun herself has published under the disguise of "Amanda Cross.") Heilbrun's notions of truth and camouflage differ from Welty's, whose truth is consistent with the tradition of writers against biography. These writers seem to be saying that whatever is personal about me, about my very life, shall be closeted, even burned in a sacrificial conflagration, in order to sustain the truth of my work. My life, as Auden says, is "superfluous." The reason you want a biography of me is because of my work, so the "I" you are searching for is in my work.

In the light of previous chapters, we can make good sense of all this autobiographical subterfuge. Something in us doesn't want to lay out the facts for fear they will be taken to be the truth, and the only truth. Something in us doesn't want biographers to pry too closely, to grasp too keenly the inspiration of a life's work. Legends emerge and spin a veil. Something wants to protect the work from the life, to shield the accomplishments, in whatever realm they may occur, from the contexts in which they occurred. Ford's sister and Johnson's brother provide the context (unless they themselves have debunking, spiteful legends to fulfill), and many biographers feel obliged to counter the very autobiographies that are their first sources.

What is this "something"? The acorn, of course. It will not be reduced to human relationships, to influences, to fortuitous events, or to the domination of time, to "This followed that in the course of development," as if life could be encompassed by the formula "One thing led to another." Nor will it be reduced to the sudden intervention of fortune. Hence the constructions, reconstructions (and deconstructions of what is already familiar), disguises, and denials by the subjects under scrutiny; these preserve the romantic vision by romancing the facts.

Biographical "falsifications" belong as much to the narrative as do the "facts." Who knows most—Henry Ford, or his sister Margaret, or other contemporaries—about what "really happened"? What is *real* is the legend of Henry Ford, which exemplifies the power of invention at work in this inventor's own story. As we live we are being invented, though the haphazard events of the day seem to hang on no coherent thread. Biographical recollection provides the thread. Childhood makes sense in retrospect. Then we see the acorn from retrospective perches in the many-branched oak. Is this "recollection of things that had not happened" (Twain) falsification or revelation?

Furthermore, why grant the biographer of Kissinger more authority than Kissinger himself? Who, after all, is the author of this life? The biographer Walter Isaacson sees "denial" in Kissinger's statement that the rampant anti-Semitism surrounding his early years did not bear significantly on his life.[14] Isaacson also utters a causal innuendo linking Kissinger's later political character to his early environment. This is standard biographical detective work, standard benchmark developmental theory, standard psychohistory. Whether you like Kissinger or not, at least as the subject of the biography he is more compelling than his biographer.

Mrs. Paula Kissinger, Henry's mother, saw in her children "pitiful fright and puzzlement when the Nazi youths would march by." But Henry Kissinger, national security adviser and secretary of state, geopolitical power man extraordinaire, who could face down Senate inquiries, White House intrigue, Brezhnev, and Mao, meet Nixon eyeball to eyeball, order wiretaps, and propose the massive bombing of "the enemy" in Southeast Asia, would hardly be menaced by a bunch of parading blond kids in short pants. "For children these things are not that serious," because, owing to the acorn, Henry was never only the child his mother saw.

The truth of the Kissinger "case" is not whether Nazism affected his personality, or to what degree and in which ways this childhood persecution then influenced his political thought and action. The truth is Kissinger's resistance to reduction. His resistance to being biographized is the reason for his "denial." The genius of his plots and ploys of power resists reduction to the paranoia of persecution. When we imagine Henry Kissinger's life as an exhibition of the acorn theory, then the world of Furth in which his life began becomes a mere practice ground for the later career. Both are parts of the same agility, machinations, and implacable mastery of political power that stays on top of circumstances by not yielding to them ("stonewalling"; denial as policy), by denying their ability to win out over him.

Not Kissinger, but autobiography itself, is essentially duplicitous because the *auto* and the *bio* may represent two distinct tales, that of the acorn and that of the life. There may even be a third person in the complot: the act of writing, the *graph*.

Writing, too, is a performance art. Somewhere down the line a public waits, if not always in the mind of the writer, at least in the eye of the publisher. Isadora Duncan, says her biographer and longtime friend Victor Seroff,

> told me that her publisher [of her memoir, *My Life*] was insisting that she describe in detail how she had felt while losing her virginity. Faced at that time with a truly desperate economic situation, Isadora felt that she had to comply. And since the episode had occurred many years earlier in Budapest, Isadora asked me to play one of Liszt's Hungarian rhapsodies to suggest the proper "Hungarian atmosphere."
>
> . . . Perhaps better still, [the Liszt suggested] "an aphrodisiac atmosphere," while, reclining on the sofa, she wrote the details. . . . She was merely pretending. . . . it must have been too spicy even for her publishers, for the chapter was rewritten before publication.[15]

The scene may have been invented, the "memory" conjured by Liszt, but the passionate erotics are true to the pattern of Duncan's all-for-love life and belong to the authenticity of her character.

If we are following a *pattern* of disguises and inventions, then we can't pin the pattern on quirks in each of the individual personalities. Rather we need to discern the purpose of the pattern itself, which iterates in a variety of cases.

—

Psychiatry has an old and still appropriate term, *pseudologia fantastica,* for the invention of tales that never happened in fact (Twain) "in a manner intriguing to the listener."[16] These belong to the category of factitious disorders, that is, behaviors not "real, genuine, or natural." In extreme form they show "uncontrollable pathological lying." When the disguises and inventions take on a predominantly physical form of faked illnesses leading to unnecessary hospitalizations, then the disorder is named Munchausen's syndrome after the fictional baron, who told marvelous tales and appeared in many disguises with great dramatic flair. More familiar in everyone's circle of acquaintances are longtime ordinary drunks, who, when suffering from Korsakoff's syndrome, fill the gaps in their memories with meandering confabulations. But even children with unfuzzed brains confabulate, so that they are notoriously unserviceable witnesses in courts of law. All these phenomena belong to a psychological shadowland where two worlds collide: fact and fable. Psychiatry reads the fable as fictitious, factitious, pathological lying.

Fable clearly wants to dominate in these exemplary figures who tell tall tales, as if the biographical fictions, disguises, and denials want to say: "I am not your facts. I will not let what is strange in me, about me, my mystery, be put in a world of fact. I must invent a world that presents a truer illusion of who I am than the social, environmental, 'realities.' Besides, I do not lie or invent: Confabulations occur spontaneously. I cannot be accused of lying, for the stories that come out of me about myself are not quite me speaking."

From the Germans, English has obtained a word for it: doppelgänger. Someone walks the earth who is your twin, your alter ego, your shadow, another you, another likeness, who sometimes seems to be close by your side and is your other self. When you talk to yourself, scold yourself, stop yourself up, perhaps you are addressing your doppelgänger, not out there like a twin in another city but within your own room.

The Inuits have another way of speaking of another soul, whether internal and in the same body or an external one that comes and goes, alights and leaves, inhabits things and places and animals.[17] Anthropologists who walk with Australian aborigines call this second soul a bush-soul.

Fairy tales, the poems of Rumi, and Zen stories say something about this doubleness, this strange duplicity of life. There are two birds in the tree, a mortal one and an immortal one, side by side. The first chirps and nests and flies about; the other watches.

The placenta must be carefully disposed of in many cultures, for it is born with you and must not be allowed to enter the life you live. It must remain stillborn and return to the other world, or else your congenital twin may form a monstrous ghost.

Twins themselves are often considered ominous, as if a mistake had occurred; the two birds, the human and ghost, this world and that, both present in this world. Twins literalize the doppelgänger, visible and invisible both displayed. So tales tell of the murder (sacrifice) of one twin for the sake of the other: Cain and Abel, Romulus and Remus. The shadow, immortal, otherworldly one gives way so that the mortal one can fully enter this life.

NAMES AND NICKNAMES

An attenuated form of the imaginary twin appears in the conventions of naming—in middle names and double names; in naming after a dead namesake, after a biblical hero or heroine, a saint, a celebrity to catch the blessing of that invisible manna.

How many of us hate our names? Hate our parents because they named us as they did? "Who" feels this insult—only my egocentric idea of myself, or the acorn?

Kids have nicknames. So do ball players, jazz musicians, mobsters, and gang members. Does the genius have one name and the person another? Is nicknaming a subtle recognition of the doppelgänger, a mode of remembering that it is Fats who sits at the keyboard and Dizzy who blows the horn, not Mr. Waller and Mr. Gillespie, who tie their shoes and eat their breakfasts.

The nickname contains some inner truth that may stick through life and be perceived before the genius shows in larger style. Nicknames are not mere tokens of affection to humanize shortcomings. This feeling interpretation likes to understand the nickname as a way of bringing the star down to human dimension, so that we can relate and not be overawed by genius. Feeling interpretations always want to make us comfortable, and so a nickname levels the ground. Herman Ruth is just the "Babe"; those Most Wanted killers Mr. Nelson and Mr. Floyd are "Baby Face" and "Pretty Boy"; and the superpowerful five-star general and two-term president is just plain "Ike."

Suppose instead of this humanizing comfort that reduces the genius to pet turtles and pet rocks, we consider personality "Number Two," as Jung called it, or the daimon, as Socrates called it, to be a distinct image, which, having a life, also has or needs a name. And this figure appears diminutive as part of its disguise, in order to be sheltered from humanization and to protect its magic power from those "prying, peeping and predatory" biographers. Diminutive nicknames, these euphemisms surrounding the magical potency of accomplishment and the fear potency arouses, follow a pattern in myth and fairy tale. There "the little one," with a diminutive ending in Russian, French, German, or whatever becomes the clever and magical savior. The little elf by the side of the path, the little cucullus under a hood, the smallest sister of twelve—these have the moxie to make things happen because they represent the otherworld in this one.

When we read in *The World Almanac*[18] the name changes of the stars—Madonna Louise Ciccone to Madonna; Diana Fluck to Diana Dors; Cheryl Stoppelmoor to Cheryl Ladd; Roy Scherer, Jr., to Rock Hudson; Borge Rosenbaum to Victor Borge; Sophia Scicoloni to Sophia Loren; Thomas Mapother to Tom Cruise; James Stewart to Stewart Granger; Albert Einstein to Albert Brooks; Anna Maria Italiano to Anne Bancroft; George Alan O'Dowd to Boy George; Ramon Estevez to Martin Sheen; Annie Mae Bullock to Tina Turner—and are told the changes are made for public acceptance and commercial success, we are being fed only the human side of the reason. The other side is that you can't be both mortal and an immortal star. You need two names because they reflect the two persons, an inherent duplicity operating between the acorn and its bearer.

Does each have its own name? When Barbara McClintock, who was awarded a Nobel Prize in 1983 for her work in genetics, sat for a final exam in geology at Cornell, a strange thing happened.

> They gave out these blue books, to write the exam in, and on the front page you put your own name. Well, I couldn't be bothered with putting my name down; I wanted to see those questions. I started writing right away—I was delighted, I just enjoyed it immensely. Everything was fine, but when I got to write my name down, I couldn't remember it. I couldn't remember to save me, and I waited there. I was much too embarrassed to ask anybody what my name was, because I know they would think I was a screwball. I got more and more nervous, until finally (it took about twenty minutes) my name came to me. I think it had to do with the body being a nuisance. What was going on, what I saw, what I was thinking about and what I enjoyed seeing and hearing was so much more important.[19]

To forget your own name! Could this incident be testimony to the genius? Could McClintock's invisible *genius* have come through and done the job, and so the body of a college girl sitting there could not sign for what she had not done herself? McClintock attributes the strange lapse to her distance from the body, to her being in the mind. "The body was something you dragged around. . . . I always wished that I could be an objective observer and not what is known as 'me.' "

If the "other name," other than the one in the civil records, indicates the "other one," then about whom is the biography? Is this the appeal of biography, that it is *the* genre for connecting the two souls, called by biographers the life and the work, the human and the genius? Is that why we are fascinated by biographies? They expose the intricacies of the relation between the two names, and we, reading, might gain an insight into our own genius and how to live it by studying how others did so notoriously, successfully, and also seeing their pitfalls, their tragedies.

Not for heroes and models or for escapes into lives not our own, but to solve the fundamental mystery that we are each twice-born, born with a doppelgänger, and if we cannot find this estranged angel by ourselves, we turn to biography for clues. These sorts of superstitious and to us obscure practices regarding the placenta and the elf, the doppelgänger and a variety of souls and soul-names, seem to collect around a central theme: that we are not alone at the beginning. We come to the world with a magical or otherworldly counterpart that is not supposed to be around when and where we are.

For Barbara McClintock, in about twenty minutes her name came to her. Her different souls appeared as a "body me" and an "observer me." She was already a twice-born person in the sense that the name given her at birth was Eleanor. But "they soon decided that 'Barbara' would be more appropriate for a girl of such unusual fortitude." When she was four months old, her name was changed.

Among the Inuits, when you fall ill, your usual name leaves you, is "gone." And you have another name. If you die, then it is the one with that death-soul name who has died and is the dead one; if you recover, then your former name returns and the death-soul one "is gone." We say: "He's his old self again." The status quo ante has been restored.

This "other" may visit when we sleep or are in altered states, while fasting or in solitary confinement, or at crisis times when death seems certainly imminent ("As I was falling from the rock face, my whole life passed in review"). The eternal twin holds all at once because its life is not in time.

How else do these phenomena appear in our psychological culture? In several ways, mainly peripheral if not distorted. Pathologically, as drug-induced dissociations and multiple personality disorders; in illness as an autonomous visitor, "the sense of another presence co-occupying your body," as John Updike describes his psoriasis in his memoir, *Self-Consciousness,* and as others have spoken of their depressions, anxiety states, intrusive thoughts, and obsessive-compulsive pressures. And then, more acceptably: in childhood as imaginary friends, in "para"-psychological phenomena, in therapeutic techniques as active imagination, in artistic productions as characters, personae. Also in unexplained hypnagogic visions during surgery, seeing oneself from above the table.

These peculiar encounters say something about a culture that marginalizes the invisibles. If a culture's philosophy does not allow enough place for the other, give credit to the invisible, then the other must squeeze itself into our psychic system in distorted form. This suggests that some psychic dysfunctions would be better located in the dysfunctional worldview by which they are judged.

—

As my last witness to autobiographical duplicity I call on Leopold Stokowski, the most controversial, original, popular, and "difficult" orchestra conductor of the twentieth century. A stream of writers with serious intent, goodwill, and records of accomplishment tried to get Stokowski's co-operation for biographies. One after another he threw them out.

Of course, biographies have nevertheless been printed, and they tell that Stokowski was not a native Pole, having been born in England of an English mother whose lineage was English and Protestant on both sides, and a father, born in London, whose mother, too, was English Protestant. Only Stokowski's paternal grandfather was Polish born. Yet Stokowski, who did not go to Poland until late in his life, spoke with an Eastern European accent.

The accent was only one disguise. "Anyone who tried to delve into his past had a hard time, for Stokowski thoroughly delighted in inventing. . . . Interviewers asking about his past invariably ended up with fiction." The disguises and inventions then became contagious. The *Oxford Companion to Music* and *Time* magazine reported he was probably Jewish or partly Jewish. The authoritative *Grove Dictionary of Music and Musicians* stated his real name was Leo Stokes. As for written documents: Stokowski's daughter said her father and mother had a "very definite agreement" that no letters or writings about him were to be released. Her mother "destroyed all their letters."[20] Implausible inconsistencies abound. Stokowski claimed Sir Charles Hubert Parry as one of his composition teachers. Parry stopped teaching two years before Stokowski entered the school in question.

One of the many marvelous tales told by the maestro explains how he got his first violin:

> "I know how old I was because one night a man walked into that [Polish] club with a little something in his hand. . . . I said to my father, 'What's that?' He said, 'It's a violin.' And I said to my grandfather, 'I want a violin.' . . . He did buy me—what's it called—a quarter-size violin—and so I began at the age of seven playing the violin and that is still my favorite instrument. . . ."

The first problem we encounter here is that his grand-father had died three years before Leopold was born. Sec-ondly, his brother wrote, "Leo never went to Pomerania or Lublin [where the event supposedly took place] or anywhere else out of England until he was of age. He did not learn the violin when young, and not at all as far as I know."

Though Stokowski's story of playing the violin reappears, and he listed the violin as his instrument when joining the musicians' union in 1909, his biographer Oliver Daniel says he never encountered a single person who ever saw Stokow-ski play a violin.

Recollections, suppressions, confabulations. Stokowski was called an enigma and *misterioso,* despite his extravagant display of himself all through life. His own reasoning seems clear: "I think that one should cultivate memory. . . . I think that one should also cultivate forgetfulness." Stokowski's entire life re-quired a counterlife (Philip Roth's term), the creation of a fan-tasy biography.

Stokowski lived actively into his ninety-sixth year. "In his last days he burned most of the letters he had received from the great people, like Stravinsky. He didn't want any record of himself."[21] (Except, of course, the extraordinary recordings of his conducting which he was making until his death.) This pattern that Stokowski fought so hard to preserve—inventing his origins, disguising his youth, falsifying dates, losing his memories—the gods themselves seemed to favor and even continue. For after his death in England,

> paintings of Stoki . . . many drawings and paintings that Stokowski himself had done, notebooks, talismans, me-mentos, and many personal items that he had acquired during his long life were loaded into a huge container and sent to America. During a severe Atlantic storm, the con-tainer was washed overboard.[22]

The intense resistance to biography has been described by Michael Holroyd, a biographer of, among others, George Bernard Shaw. He draws a distinction between life and work and succinctly expresses the popular feeling:

> Whenever . . . any man of imagination is made the subject of biography, his light may be extinguished. For, the argument goes, life is simply a shell, the kernel of which is creative work. . . . [The biographer] has the Midas touch—but in reverse. Each piece of gold he touches turns to dross. If you value your work you must not let a biographer near you—that's the popular feeling.[23]

Holroyd defends the biographer's trade against the antibiographical tirade, but he stops short. He neglects the emotional truth of the antibiographers' view. He seems to miss the archetypal conflict between work and life and the archetypal necessity of concealment. For it is the genius who is the antibiographical factor, the genius who may be offended by life on earth, even though all its efforts seem expended down to touch earth and expanded out to reach widely into the world. Still, it never quite humanizes.

The enemies of the biographer are not only the subject and the family of the subject, the loyal friends with their private caches of letters and memories, the anal archivist, the sealed-away documents like state secrets. The genius, too, is the enemy of rational accounts that ipso facto explain it away. The great disguiser is the daimon. Somehow the descendants of the eminent continue to feel its hovering presence, monitoring their protectionism years after the person in question has given up the ghost.

Writing biography becomes another "impossible profession," Janet Malcolm's characterization of psychoanalysis. Impossible, because the person whom biography purports to be about is not altogether a person, as the case an analyst works with is the invisible psyche, brought in by a person. Biographers are ghost writers, even ghost busters, trying to seize the invisible ghosts in the visibilities of a life. A biography that sticks to the facts as closely as it can finds ever clearer traces of the invisible, those symptoms, serendipities, and intrusive inventions that have led, or pursued, the life the biography recounts. Jung tried to make this apparent by presenting two personalities as the subjects of his autobiography. Like an old Eskimo, he included the dream-soul even in its title.

A recent thinker about biography states that "Biography has never really had a generally accepted terminology and protocol, a poetics that could be upheld and resisted."[24] This uncertainty about what it is doing comes with the duplicity of the territory; and disillusionment is the biographer's best reward. Not the biographer's disillusionment with his or her subject, that disillusionment so often expressed in fits of pique over dishonesties and concealments. Rather, a bracing disillusion with the world of straight fact, a disillusion that can convert the biographer to a more happy illusion: the reality of the daimon who prompts the life and the work—his or hers, too. This would then be the acorn theory's contribution to biographical theory.

The relative weight of work and life, genius and person, haunts one's life with the feeling of never being able to size oneself up. There is a constant play between importance and humility, reflected in those states called mania and depression. Galleries hold retrospectives; academies stage awards ceremonies, offer testimonials, grant honorary degrees; critics estimate and evaluate, attempting to strike the right balance. This uncertainty about "size" is formulated by the Bella Coola people who say the soul-image is "small but of great power." "The heart-soul is likened to a kernel of corn" by the San Juan people.[25] The smallness of the kernel and the kernel's power are both felt by the subject, and they appear also as one of the major conflicts in biographers, who inflate their subjects and detract from them at the same time, filling in the genius with human shadow. One biography of D. H. Lawrence is called *Portrait of a Genius, But.* But what draws biographers to write in the first place, and us to read? The wish to catch sight of the genius—not Mr. Gillespie and Mr. Waller, but Dizzy and Fats.

When the daimon speaks it says: The stories I tell about tinkering with watches (Ford) or about rising from poverty all on my own (Bernstein) *are* the facts. The fables I tell more truly tell who I am. I am telling the story that gives backing to what has happened. I am reading life backward. I am telling the story of genius, not of little Lyndon, little Lenny, little Leopold. They are the figures whose image in the heart forced them forward, distorting their childhoods from the usual, and so I must tell a story of distortions to really tell the truth. The story must be adequate to the exceptionality of the genius. The ordinary lot of suburban Jewish meals (Lenny B.), of haying on father's farm (Henry F.), of hill-country squabbles and prayers (Lyndon J.) are simply not adequate, and probably cause the angel great discomfort.

Stokowski was protecting his angel all through his life, preventing it from being written into the wrong tale, which might have killed it. And Freud, at twenty-nine, before he had made a single mark or hit upon a single one of his lasting ideas, already knew the art of disguise. What prompted that protective/destructive fire but prescience of what was to come? To protect the genius we must protect the story in which the genius can live, else it might take its invisibility literally, grow silent, and disappear for fear of being reduced to mediocrity.

We need this same imagination, which seeks the small kernel, when we are annoyed by the confabulations of later childhood and adolescence. The disguises and boastings are not mere cover-ups, daydreams, and grandiose fantasies. They are fears of loss, fears of colonization, fears of slavery to a normalizing system that, by capturing my image in biography, might take over and walk away with my soul.

Of course the biographer must pry and peep, since what is searched for is the invisible—but it is invisible not because of my concealment but because of the archetypal nature of the kernel itself. "Nature loves to hide," said Heraclitus. The acorn of a human nature does, too. It hides all through the visible, displaying itself in the very disguises in which it hides. Biographers get to the invisible by sorting through the disguises, but only if the eye that seeks is intent upon the invisible, bringing to its task the same love that nature has for hiding. Maybe it takes genius to see genius.

CHAPTER 9

FATE

FATE AND FATALISM

"But if the soul chooses its daimon and chooses its life, how have we still any power of decision?" asks Plotinus.[1] Where is our freedom? All that we live and believe to be ours, all our arduously-arrived-at decisions, must in truth be predetermined. We are snared in a delusional veil, believing that we are the agents of our own lives while all along each life has been laid down in the acorn and we are but fulfilling a secret plan in the heart. Our freedom, it seems, consists only in opting for what the acorn intends.

To cast off this erroneous conclusion, let's make clearer what the genius does and does not do. Let's become more precise about the range of the acorn's powers. In what ways is it effective, and how is it limited? If it *causes* behaviors in childhood, what do we mean by "cause"? If it *intends* a specific way of life, such as theatrical performance, mathematical invention, or public politics, what do we mean by "intention"? Has it a final end in view, even an image of fulfillment and a date of death? If it is so powerful as to fatefully *determine* school expulsion and childhood illnesses, what do we mean by "determinism"? And, finally, if it is the acorn that gives the feeling that things could not be otherwise, that even the wrongs have been *necessary,* what do we mean by "necessity"?

Answers to these questions are at the heart of this book. For if these concerns are not laid out clearly and dealt with, we are likely either to abandon ourselves to fatalism or to abandon the book to fantasy.

Fatalism is the seductive other side to the heroic ego, which shoulders so much in a do-it-yourself, winner-take-all civilization. The bigger the load, the more you want to put it down or pass it off to a larger, stronger carrier, like Fate. The hero is America personified. The heroic ego landed on Plymouth Rock, went with Daniel Boone into the wilds with gun, Bible, and dog, stands tall in Tombstone with John Wayne, and stonewalls his corporation against the whole bloody planet. This ego cut its way through the forest and made its own path despite competitors and predators.

Even she, Little Red Riding Hood, has to cope with harassment by the predator wolf on her lonely path. This burden of being alone with your own self-made destiny in a world lurking with figures that want to do you in makes life one helluva struggle. If I do not beat back the obstacles and push my way forward, I could be "left back" in school, or become an "underachiever" and sent for counseling to get me through psychological "blocks" and "fixations." I have to advance from preschool onward. I have to develop, climb, defend, secure simply to exist, for that is the heroic definition of existence. Not much fun here—and when Little Red Riding Hood does pause to pick flowers to put in her generous basket of goodies for Grandmother, up pops the toothy wolf.

In this paranoid definition of life—life as struggle, competition for survival, the other as either ally or enemy—fatalism offers surcease. It's all in the stars; there is a divine plan; whatever happens, happens for the best in the best of possible worlds (Voltaire's *Candide*). The world is off my shoulders, for it is really carried by Fate and I am really in the lap of the gods, just as Plato's myth says. I am living the particular fate that has come straight from the lap of Necessity. So it doesn't matter what I choose. I'm not really choosing, anyway; choice is a delusion. Life is all predetermined.

This way of thinking is fatalism, and it is not what is meant by fate. This way of thinking reflects a belief system, a fatalistic ideology, not the goddesses Moirai, whom we call in English the Fates and who appear in Plato's myth arranging the lots and leading the daimon toward our birth. They do not predetermine each and every event as if life were set up by them.

Rather, the Greek idea of fate would be more like this: Events happen to people. "They cannot understand why it happened, but since it has happened, evidently 'it had to be.' "[2] *Post hoc, ergo propter hoc.* After the event (*post hoc*), we give an account of what made it happen (*ergo propter hoc*). It is not written in the stars that the stock market must crash in October 1987. But after it has crashed, we find "reasons" that clearly made it necessary for it to have crashed right then.

For the Greeks, the cause of these untoward events would be fate. But fate causes only events that are unusual, that oddly don't fit in. Not each and every thing is laid out in a superior divine plan. That sort of comprehensive explanation is fatal*ism,* which makes for paranoia, occultist Ouija board prognostics, and passive-aggressive behavior combining meek submission to fate with bitter anger against it.

So it is better to imagine fate as a momentary "intervening variable." The Germans use the term *Augenblicksgott* for a minor divinity that passes in the blink of an eye and has a momentary effect. The religious might speak of an intercessionary angel. Rather than a constant companion who walks with you and talks with you and holds your hand through all the crises of the day, fate intervenes at odd and unexpected junctions, gives a sly wink or big shove.

You sell your shares after studying the market. The very next day, a corporate takeover is announced and what you sold goes up 30 percent. Just at the finish line, the wind dies down—and the rival boat glides past to win by one second. But if you get out of the market altogether and stuff your gold in your mattress because it is not your fate to invest, or if you decide you were not meant to win the sailing cup, perhaps not meant to win at all, or even to sail, and that the sudden dying wind is an omen indicating that you are out of touch with the elements, and so you sell your boat and shift your sport to rock climbing or lapse into melancholy—these are *your* choices, resulting from the meaning *you* find in the wind. To see the Hand of Fate in these untoward events raises their importance and gives pause for reflection. To believe, however, that your market timing and the one-second loss are deciding your life for you—this is fatalism. Fatalism would give all over to fate. No need to vote, no need to fight for gun control or join Mothers Against Drunk Driving, no need even to have a fire department, since shit happens and it's all meant to fall just as it falls. Cast the I Ching; the little sticks will tell you what fate wants you to do. That's fatalism.

Catching the sly winks of fate is a reflective act. It is an act of thought, while fatalism is a state of feeling, abandoning thoughtfulness, specific details, and careful reasoning. Instead of thinking things through, you give up to the larger mood of fatality. Fatalism accounts for life as a whole. Whatever happens can be fit within the large generality of individuation, or my journey, or growth. Fatalism comforts, for it raises no questions. There's no need to examine just how events fit in.

The Greek word for fate, *moira,* means a share, a portion. As fate has only a portion in what happens, so the daimon, the personal, internalized aspect of *moira,* has only a portion in our lives, calling them but not owning them.[3]

Moira derives from the root *smer* or *mer,* meaning to ponder, to think, meditate, consider, care.[4] It is a deeply psychological term, requiring us to scrutinize events with respect to the portion that comes from elsewhere and is unaccountable, and the portion that belongs to me, what I did, could have done, can do. *Moira* is not in my hands, but *moira* is only a portion. I can't abandon my actions or my abilities and their realization—and their frustrations and failures—to *them,* the gods and goddesses, or to the will of the daimonic acorn. Fate does not relieve me of responsibility; in fact, it calls for more. Particularly, it calls for the responsibility of analysis.

By analysis I do not mean a reductive psychoanalysis. I do not mean pinning blame on a cause, saying, "The daimon made it happen. It's my fate. I can't help making mistakes in the stock market. I was never taught by my father; my mother spent money like water; as a child I never had an allowance and so never learned to manage money. I am self-destructive. . . ." And so on and so forth, pinning blame on a chain of causes, leading back to the parental fallacy.

When the Greeks analyzed an untoward and obscure event, they went to the oracle to ask to which god or goddess they should sacrifice regarding this trouble, this desire, this piece of business.[5] First, to become more specific; second, to propitiate more accurately. Analysis in this model tries to discover which Fate, which archetypal hand asks to be noticed and remembered.

We remember fate's portion when adding *"Deo concedente,"* or "God willing," as the Irish put it, after any little plan, such as one to take the train tomorrow. "I'll see you at the station then, God willing." I intend to go there. I will make arrangements. But the untoward can happen—so I remember the fates' portion with *"Deo concedente."* Or I touch wood. Pious old Jews hardly said a sentence without invoking the possibility that something untoward could intervene and counter their intentions.

This recollection, by touching wood, of the unpredictable interventions of fate brings us back to the daimon. For the daimon surprises. It crosses my intentions with its interventions, sometimes with a little twinge of hesitation, sometimes

with a quick crush on someone or something. These surprises feel small and irrational; you can brush them aside; yet
they also convey a sense of importance, which can make you
say afterward: "Fate."

TELOS AND TELEOLOGY

Fatalism bestows a feeling that what happens in my life is intended toward a distant misty goal. Something is "meant" for
me. I am meant to be a singer or a bullfighter. I am meant to
have success, or be cursed and wronged and luckless, or to die
in a certain way on a certain day. The image I am born with
not only pushes from the beginning; it also pulls toward an
end. "Teleology" is the term for this belief that events are
pulled by a purpose toward a definite end.

Telos means aim, end, or fulfillment. A telos is opposite to
cause as we generally think of causes today. Causality asks,
"Who started it?" It imagines events pushed from behind by
the past. Teleology asks, "What's the point? What's the purpose?" It conceives events aimed toward a goal.

Finalism, another term for teleology, maintains that each
of us, like the cosmos itself, is moving toward a final goal.
The goal may be defined in a variety of ways—reunion with
God and redemption of all sins; slow entropy running down
to stasis; ever-evolving consciousness and the dissolution of
matter into spirit; a better life or worse; apocalyptic catastrophe or divine salvation.

Tele*ology* gives a logic to life. It provides a rational account
of life's long-range purpose. And teleology reads whatever
happens in life as confirming this long-range vision—for instance, God's will, his divine plan.

If we drop the "-ology" and just stick with "telos," we can
get back to its first and original meaning (formulated by Aristotle): "that for the sake of which."[6] I go to the store to buy
bread and milk. Not because I was pulled by a vision of the

betterment of mankind; not because of a defined philosophy that governs all actions, including why I married and had children and lease a car so I can get to the store for their needs—all of which can answer any question "Why?" with one final teleological answer. Telos gives a limited, specific reason for the sake of which I perform the action. It imagines every action to be purposeful, but it does not state an overriding purpose to action in general; that would be tele*ology* or final*ism*.

For telos it's enough to say I went to the store for the sake of the family breakfast. We are spared the philosophies of breakfast: the theology of caring, the symbolism of the morning meal, the morality of duty, the pseudo-politics of "family values," the psychology of needs and wants, the economics of nutritional costs, the physiology of morning metabolism. There are many philosophies of breakfast that can satisfy your teleological vision of life. Many gods come to the breakfast table. But the telos, the purpose, of the bread and milk and run to the store is simply the breakfast itself. Eat first, talk later.

The acorn seems to follow just this sort of limited pattern. It does not indulge in long-term philosophies. It disturbs the heart, it bursts out in a temper, as it did in Menuhin. It excites, calls, demands—but rarely does it offer a grand purpose.

The pull of purpose comes with force; you may feel full of purpose. But just what it is and how to get there remains undetermined. The telos may even be double or triple and confused about whether to sing or dance, write or paint. Purpose does not usually appear as a clearly framed goal, but more likely as a troubling, unclear urge coupled with a sense of indubitable importance.

Two stories from the childhood of the Swedish filmmaker and theater director Ingmar Bergman will bring out the indeterminate determinism of the acorn. As a small boy, Bergman says, he was prone to lying and often unable to distinguish between fantasy and reality—or, as he puts it, "between magic and oatmeal porridge." At the age of seven he was taken to

the circus, an event that "drove me into a state of feverish excitement." The crucial moment came when he saw

> a young woman dressed in white, riding around on a
> huge black stallion.
>
> I was overcome with love for this young woman. She
> was included in my fantasy games and I called her Esmer-
> alda. . . . Under an oath of secrecy, I confided in the boy
> called Nisse who sat next to me at school. I told him that
> my parents had sold me to Schumann's Circus and I was
> soon to be taken away from home and school to be
> trained as an acrobat, together with Esmeralda, who was
> considered the most beautiful woman in the world. The
> next day my fantasy was revealed and desecrated.
>
> My class teacher considered the matter so serious that
> she wrote an agitated letter to my mother. There was a
> dreadful court scene. I was put up against the wall, hu-
> miliated and disgraced, at home as well as at school.
>
> Fifty years later, I asked Mother if she remembered my
> sale to the circus. . . . Did no one question the deeper
> reasons why a seven-year-old wished to leave home and
> be sold to a circus? Mother replied that they had already
> been troubled on several occasions by my lies and fan-
> tasies. In her anguish, she had consulted the paediatrician.
> He had emphasized how important it was for a child to
> learn at an early stage to differentiate between fantasy and
> reality. As they were now faced with an insolent and fla-
> grant lie, it had to be punished accordingly.
>
> I had my revenge on my former friend by taking my
> brother's sheath-knife and chasing him around the school
> playground. When a teacher threw herself between us, I
> tried to kill her.
>
> I was removed from school and severely beaten. Then
> my false friend caught polio and died, which pleased
> me. . . .
>
> But I still fantasized about Esmeralda, our adventures
> becoming more and more dangerous and our love more
> and more passionate.[7]

So much is packed into this one incident: the desperate importance of finding an actual place (the circus) where the two realms, magic and reality, combine; the first encounter with "anima," the white woman on the black horse, and the manic madness of falling in love (the romantic vision is outside of time, so Ingmar's age is irrelevant to the eternality of the archetypal emotion); the life-and-death risk, that one might kill or die for one's vision; the disciplinary countermeasures of the "real" world of teachers, doctors, parents; the value of the "secret" and the cosmic catastrophe of betrayal, which splits apart fantasy and reality, heaven and earth, Esmeralda and porridge.

Although the entire event blazes with importance and bears traces of Bergman's character and calling, there is no glimpse of future career, no message. There is no teleology, no determinism, no finalism.

The second tale, more evidently connected to Bergman's calling, is about moving pictures.

> More than anything else, I longed for a cinematograph. The year before, I had been to the cinema for the first time and seen a film about a horse. I think it was called *Black Beauty*. . . . To me, it was the beginning. I was overcome with a fever that has never left me. The silent shadows turned their pale faces towards me and spoke in inaudible voices to my most secret feelings. Sixty years have gone by and nothing has changed; the fever is the same.

Come the following Christmas:

> All the food was laid out and the distribution of Christmas gifts took place at the dining-room table. The baskets were carried in, Father officiated with a cigar and glass of sweet liqueur, the presents were handed out. . . .
>
> That was when the cinematograph affair occurred. My brother was the one who got it.
>
> At once I began to howl. I was ticked off and disappeared under the table, where I raged on and was told to

be quiet immediately. I rushed off to the nursery, swearing and cursing, considered running away, then finally fell asleep exhausted by grief.

Later in the evening I woke up. . . . Among my brother's other Christmas presents on the white gate-legged table was the cinematograph, with its crooked chimney, its beautifully shaped brass lens and its rack for the film loops.

I made a swift decision. I woke my brother and proposed a deal. I offered him my hundred tin soldiers in exchange for the cinematograph. As Dag possessed a huge army and was always involved in war games with his friends, an agreement was made to the satisfaction of both parties.

The cinematograph was mine.

The apparatus also included a square purple box which contained some glass slides and a sepia-coloured film strip (35mm). . . . Information on the lid stated that the film was called Mrs Holle. Who this Mrs Holle was no one knew, but later it turned out that she was a popular equivalent of the Goddess of Love in Mediterranean countries.

The next morning I retreated into the spacious wardrobe in the nursery, placed the cinematograph on a sugar crate, lit the paraffin lamp and directed the beam of light on to the white-washed wall. . . .

A picture of a meadow appeared on the wall. Asleep in the meadow was a young woman apparently wearing national costume. *Then I turned the handle!* It is impossible to describe this. I can't find words to express my excitement. But at any time I can recall the smell of the hot metal, the scent of mothballs and dust in the wardrobe, the feel of the crank against my hand. I can see the trembling rectangle on the wall.

I turned the handle and the girl woke up, sat up, slowly got up, stretched her arms out, swung round and disappeared to the right. If I went on turning, she would again lie there, then make exactly the same movements all over again.

She was moving.[8]

Bergman's story of the movie machine makes clearer the difference between causality (being pushed from behind by the past) and teleology (being pulled toward a goal). To the question of why that little boy so desperately wanted the cinematograph, why he was willing to yield a whole army for it, causality replies: He had seen one previously and it piqued his curiosity. When his brother received it, sibling rivalry, going back to earlier years and birth order, provoked envy. Earlier still is the black horse of the circus incident, repeating his first remembered film, *Black Beauty,* which offers liberation ("being sold" as a passive form of "running away to the circus") from the morally oppressive house of his father the pastor. Or he may have desired power over his mother, over Woman, whom he could make move merely by cranking the handle.

Causality, or what classical philosophy (Aristotle) named "efficient causality," tries to answer the question "What initiated a motion?" by working back through a series of hypothetical connections, a chain of supposedly linked events, each presumed to have been initiated by the one preceding. Even if all these links were actually connected, one pushing the next like a fantastical Rube Goldberg machine, the very first link is fastened to a bare surmise: Why that particular image of a black horse, why ravishing Esmeralda, why the circus? To what is that first, spontaneous, and long-remembered passion linked? Our answer: Ask fate.

Fate gives this reply: Ingmar Bergman, filmmaker in acorn, at age seven if not earlier, had his vision. He did not know it, could not foretell it, but something daimonic selected the events that made Esmeralda so compelling and the later cinematograph so necessary. Fate had no teleological plan, no final goal of *Through a Glass, Darkly* or *The Magic*

Flute in mind. Yet the daimon's fateful vision infuses particular events with emotional importance—thrill, feverish excitement, cursing. Bergman's fate was not sealed, but signified.

Once more, let me try to distinguish the narrower idea of telos from the broad category of teleology, mainly because the first is most useful while the second is usually not. The idea of telos gives value to what happens by regarding each occurrence as having purpose. What happens is for the sake of something. It has intention. Little boy Ingmar did not just concoct lies; his stories intended toward a lifestyle and career in which the "lying" stories not only made sense but were necessary to the illusions of his kind of work. He was already making theater of his life before he had a stage or a script. To look at the events of his childhood through the lens of purpose changes them from mere lies and temper tantrums and obsessive desires to expressions of the necessities of his soul. Telos gives events value.

But adding an "ology" to "telos" declares what that value is. It says what is intended by the tantrum and the obsession. It dares to pronounce the purpose. Such predictions are presumptuous because Bergman's lying could also belong to the pattern of a forger, of a huckster. The black horse could have carried him off in many directions; Esmeralda, Mrs. Holle, and the moving cinematograph image on the grass might have indicated painting or pimping, fashion design or crossdressing. To state the purpose as if a definite teleological end was pulling him toward it—"You are intended to be in the theater, women will be crucial, fantasy is your metier, and you must have control"—this is presumptuous. It is also laming. For if you already know what the purpose of a symptom is, you've robbed the symptom of its own peculiar intentions. You have lost respect for its own purpose and thus lessened its value.

Freud's theoretical system could state full well what was going on in a childhood obsession, but Freud said practice required withholding, abstention, reserve. He did not allow the practice of psychoanalysis to become teleological, even though he regarded all the phenomena going on in the analysis to have a telos.

The acorn acts less as a personal guide with a sure long-term direction than as a moving style, an inner dynamic that gives the feeling of purpose to occasions. You get the feeling of importance: This supposedly trivial moment is significant, while this supposedly major event doesn't matter that much.

Let's say the acorn is more concerned with the soul aspect of events, more alive to what's good for it than to what you believe is good for you. This helps explain why Socrates' daimon told him not to escape imprisonment and execution. His death belonged to the integrity of his image, to his innate form. A death—whether in the bullring, on the toilet, or in a car crash—may make more sense to the image and its trajectory than to you and your plan.

ACCIDENTS

The easy part is following the trajectory with dedication. We often feel what we must do. The image in the heart can lay down strong demands and it asks us to keep faith. The hard job is making sense of accidents, those trivial gusts that take you off course and seem to be delaying your projected arrival in the teleological harbor. Are the hindering gusts distractions? Or has each one its particular purpose? Do they together combine to advance the boat—maybe to a different port? You will not be able to find any point in an untoward incident if your compass is pointed too fixedly on the far horizon and your teleological vision knows where you should be going, what you should be doing to get there, and where you are right now.

Even more: What matters is not so much whether an interference has or does not have purpose; rather, it is important to look with a purposive eye, seeking value in the unexpected. The purposive eye starts from the assumption that events can indeed be accidents. The world is run as much by folly as by wisdom, as much by order as by chaos, but—and this "but" is huge—these accidents may still intend something interesting. It is as fatalistic and teleological to claim cosmic design as to claim cosmic randomness. The eye of purpose merely looks into each "accident," as these events are called, for what it says about itself. The soul seeks to fit it into its form.

Bette Davis, seven or eight years old and away at school, was playing Santa Claus. Real candles lit the tree, and under the tree were all the presents. As little Bette tried to get close to the presents, she touched a candle with her sleeve. It spread through her costume to her cotton beard.

> Suddenly I was on fire. I started screaming in terror. I heard voices, felt myself being wrapped in a rug. . . . When the rug was taken off, I decided to keep my eyes closed. Ever the actress! I would make believe I was blind. "Her eyes!" A shudder of delight went through me. I was in complete command of the moment.[9]

The acorn had not staged the fire, but Bette Davis could indeed turn it into theater. A person's innate form incorporates the accidents. Character is fate.

Consider the early years of two great connoisseurs of food. Pierre Franey, in a Burgundy village, caught fish by slipping a hand over a resting trout and plucking it straight from the stream, then ate the fish poached lukewarm with herb mayonnaise; he raised rabbits and killed chickens; he searched the early-morning fields for little molehills which covered and whitened dandelion stems, improving their sweetness. In short, he grew up "on intimate terms with the food we ate."[10] Such raw incidents happened to any boy in that village, but Franey's image turns them into the cooked sophistication of the professional chef. James Beard, cook, adviser to cooks, writer on cooking, gourmet extraordinaire, weighed fourteen pounds at birth; he was an oversized accident for a mother in her forties. Beard's natal body seems to have been chosen by his soul to incorporate fully the tastes and smells that were to be his kind of life. His first "accident" was also "the scene of my first gastronomical adventure. I was on all fours. I crawled into the vegetable bin, settled on a giant onion and ate it, skin and all. It must have marked me for life."[11] Franey and Beard: instances of the daimon making use of haphazard occasions.

At eighteen, Churchill cracked his skull and ruptured a kidney in an accident while playing heroic battle games. "During his convalescence . . . he found himself intellectually."[12] The form not only integrates the fall, but is fed by it.

While away at school, the elder brother of James Barrie cracked his skull on the skating pond and died. Barrie's mother went into years of seclusion and invalidism, mourning the loss of her favorite boy. Jamie (then only six or seven) kept his mother company in the sickroom, trying to make her laugh; they told each other stories, hers biographical, his more invented.[13] The acorn shaped the accident, the sorrow and the confinement according to the image of J. M. Barrie, writer of fantasy.

The accident that blinded James Thurber in one eye and eventually the other (his brother shot him with an arrow) while he was still a small boy neither set his life course nor blew him off it. The form bends to accommodate and finds purpose, like his early writing skills, like the "amateurish quality"[14] of Thurber's outsized cartoons, drawn with odd scale and perspective.

President Richard M. Nixon was especially fond of *Tom Sawyer*. It is hardly unusual to come upon that book in accounts of American boyhood reading, and Nixon was an avid reader and writer very early. "Nixon liked the episode where Tom tricks Ben Rogers into whitewashing his fence, so much so that he learned it all by heart. Nearly fifty years later [in the White House] . . . Nixon recited the episode without a mistake."[15] Incidental trivia (?) from childhood given significance by the soul.

The great fashion designer Coco Chanel, who in 1924 invented the basic "little black dress," passed all of her teen years in a rigid monastic orphanage. It was an imprisonment, and every trace of it, and her time there, has been erased from the records as well as from her memoirs. "Don't tell me what I'm feeling. . . . You can die more than once in your life, you know," she once said.[16] But the classic austerity of her suits, their symmetrical perfection, her constant use of black and white and gray, replicate the accidents of her suppression, despite her effacement of the memories. What the soul needs, it uses. It is amazing how practically wise it can be about misfortune and accidents.

Wisdom in Greek was *sophia*, as in our word "philosophy," love of wisdom. *Sophia* had a most practical meaning, referring originally to the crafts of handling things, especially to the helmsman who steers the boat. The wise one steers well; the wisdom of the helmsman shows in the art of making minor adjustments in accord with accidents of water, wind, and weight. The daimon teaches this wisdom by constant appraisals of events that seem to pull you off course. This is also philosophy: the love of making little corrections, little integrations of what seems not to fit in. Sometimes this attention to the singular event is called by philosophers "saving the phenomenon" from the metaphysical trajectories of theories.

These accidental movements neither hinder nor advance the main project. Rather they reshape its form, as if the course and the boat itself were being restructured by the soul's responses to the events of life. There is a craft of growing down; it's the wisdom of watching things with an eye to their effects.

This idea of continual, moving adjustments is nothing new or strange. As far back as Aristotle the soul was conceived to be both the form and the motion of a body. The form is given with beginnings as the image of your lot, and it shifts as we move. This form, for which we are using many interchangeable terms—image, daimon, calling, angel, heart, acorn, soul, pattern, character—stays true to form.

Some accidents swamp the boat, bust the form. For example, "shell shock," as post-traumatic stress disorder was called during the First World War; rape at knifepoint; crashes at high speed; repetitive, abusive cruelty. Some souls nonetheless seem to "work with it"; others remain fixated in the tar, struggling to "work it out," as we see in the recurring nightmares of Vietnam veterans. Has the acorn been so damaged by these accidents that its form remains incurably injured, a gestalt that cannot close, a rudder broken no matter how the helmsman steers?

Fatalism answers: Everything is in the hands of the gods. Teleological finalism says: It all has a hidden purpose and belongs to your growth. Heroism says: Integrate those shadows or slay them; put disaster behind you and get on with your life. In each of these replies, the accidental as category dissolves into the larger philosophy of fatalism, finalism, and heroism.

I would rather keep accident as an authentic category of existence, forcing speculations about existence. A serious accident demands answers. What does it mean, why did it happen, what does it want? Continuing reappraisals are part of the aftershock. The accident may never be integrated, but it may strengthen the integrity of the soul's form by adding to it perplexity, sensitivity, vulnerability, and scar tissue.

Developmental theory regards the accidents of Churchill and Chanel, of Thurber and Barrie as representing typical youthful trauma, which may be sublimated, transformed, and integrated through time. Time heals all wounds.

The acorn theory says that Churchill's fall, Thurber's lost eye, Barrie's mother's mourning, and Chanel's monastic adolescence belong appropriately to their acorns. These accidents in youth were not foretold by the acorn as if laid down in a divine plan, nor were these untoward events determinants of later career, forcing it forward along a defined path.

Rather, they were "necessary accidents," necessary and accidental both. They were means for the soul's calling to come forth, ways the acorn expresses its form and formed their lives. In Churchill's case it took a sudden shock and slow convalescence; in Barrie's and Chanel's, a long imprisonment. Inside the orphanage, Chanel was learning the discipline, as Barrie was learning by telling stories to his sick mother, as Richard Nixon's inner form picked up precisely the tale he needed from Tom Sawyer's capacity to con.

NECESSITY

There remains one last biggie, the one Plato put right in the middle of his myth: Necessity, she who turns the spindle on which are wound the threads of our lives.

Remember the tale: The goddess Ananke, or Necessity, sits on her throne amid the Fates, her daughters, companions, and aides. But it is she, Ananke, who establishes what the soul has selected for its lot to be *necessary*—not an accident, not good or bad, not foreknown or guaranteed, simply necessary. What we live is necessary to be lived. Necessary to whom? To what? To her, Goddess Necessity. Necessary because necessary? Hardly an answer. We have to speculate.

Who and what is Ananke? First, she is extremely potent among the powers of the cosmos. Plato cites only two great cosmic forces: Reason (*nous* or mind) and Necessity (*ananke*).[17] Reason accounts for what we can understand, for what follows reason's laws and patterns. Necessity operates as a "variable"— sometimes translated as "erratic," "errant," or "wandering"— cause.

When something doesn't fit, seems odd or strange, breaks the usual pattern, then more likely Necessity has a hand in it. Though she determines the lot you live, her ways of influencing are irrational. That is why it is so difficult to understand life, even one's own life. Your soul's lot comes from the irrational principle. The law it follows is Necessity, which wanders erratically. Little wonder that we readers are drawn to biographies and autobiographies, for they offer glimpses of how irrational Necessity works in a human life. Although Necessity's rule is absolute and irreversible, this determinism is indeterminate. Unpredictable.

We have already encountered this idea of irrational causes in several previous chapters: the genetic explanations that rely on chaos theory (chapter 6), the kids who wander off the beaten track to read the strange and weird fantasies of pulp fiction and penny dreadfuls (chapter 7); the "something else" breaking into intentions, as when Ella Fitzgerald suddenly sang though her reason for going onstage was to dance, and Barbara McClintock forgot her own name. And we have seen the erratic cause at work in the many school refusals and expulsions, and in mentors' sudden perceptions of the beauty and potentialities of their pupils (chapter 5). In fact, we have been following the wandering trail of Necessity all through these pages, watching how she operates and feeling her inexplicable and undeniable power.

Ancient images make visible this undeniable power, and ancient roots of the word *ananke* demonstrate it further. *Ananke* derives from a root that spreads through Old Egyptian, Akkadian, Chaldean, and Hebrew terms for "narrow," "throat," "strangle," "constrict," and the yokes and rings laid on the necks of captives.[18] *Ananke* takes you by the throat, holds you prisoner, and drives you like a slave.

Mythological images and pathological problems refer to each other. Jung's famous dictum makes this explicit: "The Gods have become diseases." Nowhere does the god in the disease show more strongly and tersely than in the tightening heart pain of angina and the anxiety states that hold you back from free action. Both "angina" and "anxiety" derive from *ananke.*

The point is that there is no escape from necessity. It will not yield, cannot submit: *ne* + *cedere.* Kant defined necessity's

German equivalent, *Notwendigkeit,* to mean that which "could not be otherwise." This makes the understanding of our lives remarkably easy: whatever we are we could not have been otherwise. There is no regret, no wrong path, no true mistake. The eye of necessity reveals what we do to be only what could have been. "What might have been is an abstraction / Remaining a perpetual possibility / Only in a world of speculation. / What might have been and what has been / Point to one end, which is always present"(T. S. Eliot)[19]

As we perform an act, make a choice, we believe there are options. Options, Personal Agency, Choices, Decisions— these are the catchwords Ego thrives on. But if we look up from the engagement for a moment and speculate, Necessity's implacable smile says that whatever choice you make is exactly the one required by Necessity. It could not be otherwise. At the moment the decision falls, it is necessary. Before it is decided, all lies open. For this strange reason, Necessity guarantees only risk. All is at risk in each decision, even though what is finally decided upon at once becomes necessary.

By claiming that Necessity has laid its hand on each of the decisive moments of my life, I can justify whatever I do. It appears as if I can slip the harness of responsibility—it's all in the cards, or the stars. Yet this unyielding dominatrix of a goddess makes me quaver over each decision, for there is no predictability in her errant irrationality. Only in hindsight can I find certitude, saying it was all necessary. How curious that life can be foreordained yet not foretold.

Then where are the errors? How can one go wrong, and why feel guilty? If all that happens is necessary, what about remorse?

Since necessity incorporates whatever decision I make as necessary, then necessity must be imagined as an inclusive principle that adjusts the image of each life to include all its actions one by one, whatever they may be. We are still collared, but the collar is adjustable. Necessity's yoke produces that feeling that we are always somewhere caught, somehow a victim of circumstances, longing for liberation. I may know that what had to be, had to be, yet nonetheless I feel remorse. Necessity says the remorse, too, is necessary as a feeling and belongs to your yoke, but it does not refer to what you actually might or should have done otherwise.

To understand necessity in this way makes mistakes tragic, rather than sins to be repented or accidents to be remedied. Things cannot be, could not have been otherwise. Inexorably everything belongs, fatal flaws and all, and the course of necessity plays out until the bull's horn finds your gut.

It takes a large heart to accept the tight collar. Most times we reject the odd irrational events that come down on us. Most times we try to ignore disturbances—until the heart calls our attention to them as possibly important, possibly necessary. The mind is the last faculty to submit, and there is usually a tug-of-war between the heart's calling and the mind's plan, a conflict within each human replicating Plato's two principles of *nous* and *ananke,* reason and unreasonable necessity.

Sure, the mind can postpone the call, suppress, and sell out. You will not therefore necessarily be punished and damned. The daimon is not necessarily a pursuing demon, a Christian hound of heaven. Revenge is not one of Necessity's daughters. Necessity, in fact, refers only to that which could not be otherwise, or that which you could not escape. Escape is not a sin, because Necessity is not a moralist. Escape can belong just as well to your soul's lot and its pattern as can facing the music and taking the arrows in the chest.

Harry Houdini built a career of escape. It was his calling. "He never ceased to invent" his own life, thereby escaping from imprisonment in "pedantic truth."[20] He managed to get out of every trap set for him, including the factual ones—such as where he was actually born (Wisconsin or Hungary?), the date of his birth (March 24 or April 6?), his given name (Ehrich or Erik?); finally he escaped from his family name (Weiss) by taking on the invention "Houdini" after reading, at seventeen, the life of Robert-Houdin, a great nineteenth-century French magician.

Houdini overcame necessity everywhere, using every mercurial turn to do so. Poverty, Unemployment, Prejudice, Failure—none of the mean gods could hold him. He escaped from every straitjacket, prison cell, and bank vault, and especially thrilled his audiences by sealing himself, tied and chained, inside a metal coffin immersed in icy waters—then getting out and coming up breathing.

He escaped the outer coffins, only to succumb inescapably to the slow death building in his tough, muscular body from a long-inflamed, finally ruptured appendix.

Isn't Houdini's story like Manolete's, and like any of ours? The acorn's eye reads the story backward. As the bull was waiting for Manolete, so the appendix was waiting for Houdini, an inescapable necessity, shadowing the extraordinary efforts and amazing accomplishments of his heroic fight that was given with his acorn—until the very last day when, on his deathbed, he said to his wife: "I'm getting tired and I can't fight anymore."

Even the escape artist meets necessity. Ananke's chains are both visible and invisible. When the "couldn't be otherwise" occurs, then the most plausible account of how life works and why things happen as they do is the acorn theory.

The truer you are to your daimon, the closer you are to the death that belongs to your destiny. We expect the daimon to have prescience about death, calling on it before an airline flight or during a sudden attack of sickness. Is this my fate, and now? And when the demands of our calling seem undeniably necessary, again death appears: "If I do what I really must, it will kill me; and yet if I don't, I'll die." To be the calling or not to be, that still and again seems to be the question.

Perhaps this intimacy between calling and fate is why we avoid the daimon and the theory that upholds its importance. We mostly invent, and prefer, theories that tie us tightly to parental powers, encumber us with sociological conditionings and genetic determinants; thereby we escape the fact that these deep influences on our fates don't hold a candle to the power of death. Death is the only complete necessity, that archetypal Necessity who rules the pattern of the life line she spins with her daughters, the Fates. The length of that line and its irreversible one-way direction is part of one and the same pattern, and it could not be otherwise.

— 🦂 —

CHAPTER 10

THE BAD SEED

CALLED TO KILL?

Crooks and criminals, sadistic guards and serial rapists—all the creatures large and small of the underworld—did their souls descend from the lap of Necessity? Again, Plotinus asked the question centuries ago: "How could a wicked character be given by the Gods?"[1] Can one be called to murder? Can the acorn harbor a bad seed? Or, perhaps the criminal psychopath has no soul at all?

In reply to this question of the bad seed, a question which asks about nothing less than the nature of evil, we shall inquire into that figure who was the ultimate criminal psychopathic murderer of modern times, if not of all times: Adolf Hitler (1889–1945).

An inquiry into Hitler offers benefits beyond a comparative study of many puzzling cases of sadistic killers and torturers. First, it furthers the method we have applied all along: Examine the extreme in order to grasp the more usual. Second, we turn to a single exemplary case to reveal how the daimon shows in traits of character and habitual actions. Third, by confronting the enormity of Hitler we are face to face with the enormities he bequeathed to our era. The phenomenon of Hitler has implications bearing on our present lives as citizens. Unlike the crimes of Charles Manson, Jeffrey Dahmer, John Wayne Gacy, and the like, "the damages wrought by individual violence . . . are insignificant compared to the holocausts resulting from self-transcending devotion to collectively shared belief systems."[2]

To be a conscious citizen in the Western post-Hitler age, not only must one recall the images and the lessons of the first half of this century, Hitler's time in Western history, but also one is obliged to reflect about Hitler as a demonic potential in this same Western world. To reflect upon Hitler is to do more than present a case study in psychopathy or political tyranny, and more than a literary departure such as performed by Mailer, Capote, and Sartre on their psychopathic subjects. It is a ritual act of psychological discovery, an act as necessary to the claim of being a conscious human as remembering the Holocaust and reviewing the Second World War. A study of Hitler is an act of contrition by all who share the Western psyche for that psyche's unconscious participation in Hitler's actions; and it is an act of propitiation of the particular demon who selected Hitler for its host. Having once appeared in such virulent form, may that demon not need to blind us again. Our inquiry also intends to lay out specific ways in which a daimon shows itself to be demonic, and a genius, evil.

One major drawback to this concentration upon the worst is that lesser crooks and smoother murderers slip by. By looking closely at Hitler, we may miss the demon closer to home. Faceless corporate boards and political administrators make decisions that wreck communities, ruin families, and despoil nature. The successful psychopath pleases the crowd and wins elections. The thick glass of the TV tube and its chameleon-like versatility in displaying whatever is wanted favors distance, coldness, and the front of charm, as do many of the sleek accoutrements of high station in the political, legal, religious, and corporate structures. Anyone who rises in a world that worships success should be suspect, for this is an age of psychopathy. The psychopath today no longer slinks like a dirty rat through the dark alleys of black-and-white 1930s crime films, but parades through the boulevards in a bullet-proof limo on state visits, runs entire nations, and sends delegates to the U.N. Hitler is therefore old-style and can divert us from seeing through the mask worn by the demonic today, and tomorrow. The demonic that is timeless nonetheless enters the world disguised in contemporary fashion, dressed to kill.

The habits of Hitler, reported by reliable informants and assessed by reliable historians and biographers, give evidence of an identification with or possession by his daimon. The principal difference between Hitler's possession and that of others in this book lies in the nature of his personality and the nature of the daimon—a bad seed in a personality that offered no doubts and no resistance.

As I want to demonstrate, the acorn theory offers as good a mode as any of imagining the Hitler phenomenon, and I will summarize the other theories later in this chapter. The idea of a demon or evil genius helps account for his appeal to the substrate of shadow in the German *Volk* and to the formation of that group ethos which, blinded by his demonic visions, complied with and executed them. By seeing how, from a single seed, the fascinating power in Hitler charmed millions into a collective demonization, we can more easily understand how individual psychopathic murderers like Jeffrey Dahmer, Andrei Chikatilo, Dennis Nilsen, Peter Sutcliffe, and Juan Corona could enchant long series of compliant victims. Perhaps innocence is a greater mystery than evil.

HITLER

We shall go about this exposure of Hitler's character, which became our civilization's fate, in two steps. First, by enumerating particular characteristics that symbolize traditional descriptions of evil, death, and destruction, and then, by analyzing a smaller set of characteristics, which reveal more nakedly the actual presence of the invisible in Hitler's biography.

1. *The Cold Heart*

Near the end, in Hitler's last speech to his district commanders, he said: "Come what may, my heart remains ice-cold." At a staff conference, he admiringly praised Göring, who, he said, "has proved himself to be ice-cold. . . . He was with me through all the difficult days, he was always ice-cold. Whenever it became really bad, he turned ice-cold."[3]

The very bottom of hell, according to Dante, is a realm of ice, inhabited by the archcriminals Cain, Judas, and Lucifer. Legends, superstitions, and the dogma of the Inquisition of the late Middle Ages through the Renaissance claim that the Devil's penis is icy and his semen cold.[4]

The psychological trait that goes with the iced heart is rigidity, an incapacity to yield, to flow, to let go. Waite reports testimony from four different periods of Hitler's life, all agreeing that "There was in his nature something firm, inflexible, immovable, obstinately rigid. . . . Adolf could simply not change his mind or nature."[5] At the very end, in Berlin, 1945, "when an aide suggested that possibly some things might have been done differently, Adolf Hitler cried out in baffled anguish, 'But don't you see, I cannot change.' " All his habits—the clothes he wore till they disintegrated, his toothbrushing routines, the music and movies he selected, his time schedules—were repetitive. When he took his dog for a walk, which he did every day at the same time, he threw the same piece of wood from exactly the same spot in the same direction.[6]

2. *Hellfire*

A more common image of Hell is fire. The daimon has long been associated with fire. For instance, a person's genius was spoken of as a fiery nimbus around the head, like a halo.

Hitler's daimon used fire for his demonic work—the Reichs-
tag fire, which set the stage for his accession to power; the
night marches with flaming torches; the fiery images in his
speeches; the burning cities of Europe; the ovens and chim-
neys of the death camps; and his body in the Berlin bunker,
doused with gasoline and set ablaze. Years before the war
(1932) in conversations with Hermann Rauschning, who was
then a major Nazi leader but later defected and published his
notes *before* the war, Hitler already knew his end and the end
of Germany. He said: "We may be destroyed, but if we are we
shall drag a world with us—a world in flames."[7] He then
began humming a theme from Wagner's *Götterdämmerung—*
Twilight of the Gods.

Fire has many symbolic values: transformational, baptismal
and initiatory, warming and culturing, and bringing light to
darkness. For Hitler, fire's potential was limited to the destructive, and the firebombing of Dresden was the apogee of
the death demon visited on the people and the culture that
had been inflamed by that demon's call.

3. *Wolf*

Hitler in his early days called himself Herr Wolf, and had
his sister change her name to Frau Wolf. During the last days
in the bunker he fed and stroked a pup, named Wolf, which he
allowed no one else to touch. This wolf spirit appeared in his
boyhood when he derived his name, "Adolf," from "Athal-
wolf," "Noble Wolf." He named three of his military head-
quarters Wolfsschanze, Wolfsschlucht, and Werwolf. His
favorite dogs were *wolfshunde,* Alsatians. "He called his SS, 'my
pack of wolves.' . . . Often and absentmindedly he whistled,
'Who's afraid of the big bad wolf?' "[8]

The archetypal power of this wolf identification affects each
of our lives still. It lies at the root of the cold war and the modern division of Europe between East and West. For American
intelligence came to believe that an entire army of Hitlerian
"werewolves," with poison gas supplies and secret weapons

and using ancient runic signs of the wolf to mark houses for vengeance, would hold out in a mountain redoubt of Bavaria with Hitler and his associates carrying on terror tactics. Not only did General Omar Bradley shift the American armies toward southern Germany to deal with this delusion of wolf power, but, to Stalin's astonishment, Allied commanders let his troops take Berlin.[9]

Without condemning the actual wolf, or forgetting its symbolic virtue as nourishing mother, protector of lost children, we may cite a long tradition that places the wolf among the nefarious death demons in many widely separated cultures, not only or mainly Germanic.[10]

4. Anality

Hitler gave himself enemas; he was immensely disturbed by his flatulence; he had obsessive ideas about touching and being touched, about diet, digestion, and personal cleanliness. There is also convincing evidence that his particular sexual pleasure involved being soiled by his women partners.[11]

Again there is a demonic association here. The devil supposedly chose the anus as his special location in the body— hence sodomy as sin, cleanliness as next to godliness, sulfuric smells as the odor of hell, and the devil's face depicted on his rear end in medieval woodcuts. Violent medical purges had a theological component: cleaning out the bad stuff. And that Antichrist of sexual practices and counterpart to Christian love, the Marquis de Sade, focused mainly on anal eroticism. Punishments aimed at the buttocks, from spanking to whipping and branding, including the cruelest Christian-ordered tortures of evildoers, could be justified as attacks on the demonic in its bodily lair.

Thus the imagination of anality goes far and deep; anality is more than merely a developmental stage in Hitler's character, accounting for his rigidity and sadism. If the anus is the erogenous zone that harbors bad spirits, then obsession with it not merely expresses toilet-training fixations, but keeps the demonic continually present, giving its symbolic locus the ritual attention it demands.

5. Suicides of Women

Six of the women—and there were not that many others—with whom Hitler is reliably reported to have had liaisons or intimate relations or to have been "in love" with killed themselves or attempted to.[12] These include a teenage girl, Mimi Reiter, for whom Hitler fell when he was thirty-seven and who tried to hang herself after he suddenly broke off, and his niece Geli Raubal, who was "the love of his life." Eva Braun shot herself over the heart in 1932, surviving only to die with him in their suicide pact in the bunker.

Psychologically we can theorize that Hitler was attracted to psychically offbeat women, and that that accounts for their destructive impulses. And we might also theorize that his sexual dysfunction and possible coprophilia produced in these women such self-loathing revulsion that they chose "death before dishonor." Or we may imagine more demonically, asking whether intimacy with the wolf, hellfire, and the ice-cold heart makes it impossible to continue living. Did these women intuit that they had loved a devil?

6. Freaks

The circuslike atmosphere of costumes, parades, ceremonies, and peculiar gestures (goose-stepping and stiff-armed salutes) also included freaks. Hitler's longtime personal chauffeur was so tiny that blocks were put under his seat so that he might see over the steering wheel. The Brownshirt leader who replaced the murdered Ernst Röhm was one-eyed; Joseph Goebbels had a clubfoot; the official photographer was an alcoholic and had a deformed back. Hitler's press manager, Max Amann, and his first treasurer were one-armed; Amann was also dwarflike. The assistant press chief was stone deaf. Martin Bormann was alcoholic, Rudolf Hess paranoid, Hermann Göring a morphine addict; Robert Ley, master of the labor camps, had a speech defect.[13]

The disfigured, the halt, and the blind populated the marketplaces and begged on streetcorners all through Europe during the twenties and thirties as a result of the Great War; Expressionist art, cabaret humor, and the night-world bordellos placed the freak in public view. Hitler's entourage, however, was most unusual for its collection of freaks in high places, even as others physically like them were systematically expunged in the death camps.

Perhaps this is not so unusual, for the history of demonology shows that the half-human figure represents the inhuman, menacing the normal world as does the hook-handed, one-eyed pirate, the limping pursuer, the hunchback in fantasies and films. Hitler's two favorite movies, which he repeatedly viewed, were freak shows: *King Kong* and *Snow White and the Seven Dwarfs.*

It is a praiseworthy accomplishment of the American democratic spirit to have legally integrated the disabled into the society and pursued this incorporation with such vigor. Not only does the integration of the "freakish" enrich society and extend a gesture of compassion. It also attempts to remove a symbolic curse from the impaired and disabled, who in many cultures still carry the imagination of a sinister and demonic underworld.

7. *Humorless Hitler*

Freaks, costumes, theater, pageant—but no comedy. "Hitler had no humor," said Albert Speer, his architect and armaments minister. A secretary who worked daily with him said, "I must say I never heard him laugh heartily," and a companion of his youth said that "he was totally lacking in a spirit of self-irony. . . . He could not . . . pass over something with a smile." Among soldiers on the front, "he never laughed or joked." He had a horror of being laughed at; he told no suggestive jokes and forbade them in his presence.[14]

The devil may act like a trickster, show wit, play the clown, dance a jig, and be a jokester, but the humus and humility of humor—never! Humor as the word also implies,

moistens and softens, giving life a common touch; it is anath-
ema to grandiosity, fostering self-reflection and distancing us
from self-importance. By taking us down a peg, humor is essential to growing down (see chapter 2). The laughing recognition of one's own absurdity in the human comedy bans the
devil as effectively as garlic and the cross. Chaplin's *The Great
Dictator* did more than mock Hitler; it revealed the absurdity,
the triviality, and the tragedy of demonic inflation.

GENERAL CHARACTERISTICS OF THE DEMONIC

I want now to introduce more evidence of the demonic in
Hitler to give greater understanding of how the Bad Seed
works and how it might be recognized.

August Kubizek, a school friend of Hitler, said his mother
was afraid of Hitler's eyes—light blue, startlingly intense, and
lashless. Hitler's high school teacher described his eyes as
"shining." Kubizek also wrote: "If I am asked where one
could perceive, in his youth, this man's exceptional qualities,
I can only answer, 'In the eyes.' " Hitler considered his eyes
to be like those of his mother, which "in turn reminded him
of the Medusa" as depicted by his favorite painter (Franz von
Stuck). Hitler practiced "piercing glances in front of a mirror," and played the game of "staring down" other people.
The old English fascist (and Wagner's son-in-law) Houston
Chamberlain wrote him: "It is as if your eyes were equipped
with hands, for they grip a man and hold him fast. . . . At one
stroke you have transformed the state of my soul."

Around 1909 Hitler met one of his intellectual mentors,
Georg Lanz, an anti-Semitic fantast of prodigious output who
had written weirdo tracts with such titles as *Theo-zoology,
or Tales of the Sodom-Ape Men . . . ,* and "The Dangers of
Women's Rights and the Necessity for a Masculine Morality
of Masters." Lanz also wrote these words: "The most impor-

tant and decisive erotic force for the people of the higher race is the *eye*. . . . Heroic eroticism is a love with the eyes."[15] One who, of the many captivated by Hitler's "heroic eroticism" reported: "I looked into his eyes, he looked into mine, and I was left with only one wish—to be at home and alone with the great, overwhelming experience."[16]

"The veteran German dramatist" Gerhart Hauptmann finally had the occasion to meet Hitler. "The Führer shook hands with him and looked into his eyes. It was the famous gaze that makes everyone tremble. . . . Later Hauptmann said to his friends: 'It was the greatest moment of my life!' "[17]

If the eyes are the mirror of the soul as tradition declares, then was the compelling power of Hitler's eyes the stare of the demon? Did his eyes reveal the hollowness within, a glimpse into the ice-cold abyss, the utter absence of soul? Although no one can answer, at least we cannot attribute the strangeness of these eyes to environmental conditioning, and even if their color is genetically determined, is their Medusa-like, benumbing power reducible to chromosomes?

As we noted in so many of the biographies, the urgent certainty given by the acorn seems to put life in the hands of a stronger power. "I go the way that Providence dictates for me with all the assurance of a sleepwalker," Hitler said in a speech in 1936. He was spared, he was meant, he was different. In the trenches through the whole of the 1914–1918 war (where he suffered a flesh wound, only once, and was once lightly gassed, with effects mainly on his eyes) other soldiers regarded Hitler as a "white crow," unapproachable and apart. His comrades felt he lived a charmed life. "His regiment fought in 36 major battles. . . . Death surrounded Hitler for more than a thousand days, and the ways in which he avoided it were uncanny."[18] "Time after time he seemed to court death, but when the bullets claimed a comrade, he escaped unscathed. After one notable attack that left the regiment decimated, someone turned to Hitler and said, "*Mensch, für dich gibt es keinen Kugel.* (Man, there's no bullet with your name on it.)"[19] During the failed "Beer Hall Putsch" to seize power (1923), Hitler's bodyguard "leapt in front of Hitler to take the half-dozen bullets meant for him."[20] The carefully planned and courageous assassination attempt of July 1944 failed; Hitler was saved as if by the chance intervention of a faulty firing pin and a thick table leg.

Once, when he was seventeen, fortune did fail him. He had taken a lottery ticket and had grandiose plans for what he would do with the winnings. He did not win and he went into a blind fury. He had been let down by this same "Providence," Moira, Fortuna, or Lady Luck in whom he had absolute faith. Moira, you will recall, was another name for the personal daimon.

He spoke of the goddesses of fate, destiny, and history. *Mein Kampf,* setting forth his vision, opens with his version of the Platonic myth. He states that Brunau, Austria, had been selected by fate for his entry into the world.

Hitler's call gave him the self-appointed right to be a sleep-walker outside the human world. Outside also means transcendent, where the gods themselves live. Hitler's certitude also confirmed his sense of always being right, and this utter conviction utterly convinced his nation, carrying it forward in its wrongs. Absolute certainty, utter conviction—these, then, are signs of the demonic.

Already at age seven, "Hitler was imperious and quick to anger and would not listen to anyone," said his half brother Alois, just as later he would not listen to his generals.[21] No woman had his ear, either; it heard only his daimon, his sole true companion. We begin to see how power corrupts as the guiding whisper becomes a demonic voice obliterating all others. The seed comes with sure and uncanny knowledge. But while a god is omniscient, a human becomes a know-it-all, and so Hitler had no use for exchange with others. There was nothing they could teach him.

To show this omniscience he memorized masses of facts—locations of regiments and reserves, displacement and armature of ships, kinds of vehicles—all of which he used to over-power his questioners and embarrass his commanders. This information "proved" his transcendence and disguised his lack of thought and reflection and his inability to hold a con-versation. The demonic does not engage; rather, it smothers with details and jargon any possibility of depth.

Our republic should learn this lesson from Hitler, for we might one day vote into power a hero who wins a giant TV trivia contest and educate our children to believe the Infor-mation Superhighway is the road to knowledge. If one clue to psychopathy is a trivial mind expressing itself in high-sounding phrases, then an education emphasizing facts rather than thinking, and patriotic, politically or religiously correct "values" rather than critical judgment may produce a nation of achieving high school graduates who are also psychopaths.

The daimon's transcendence places it outside time, which it enters only by growing down. In order to grasp the biogra-phy of the daimon from the chronology of a life, we must "read life backward," by means of intuition (see chapter 4). Intuition sees everything at once, given as a whole. Time strings things out into a chain of successive events leading toward a finishing line. But Hitler's programs and powers did not develop through time; they were there in youth, as was his death among the Wagnerian ruins.

Hitler felt himself trapped by time. Often he said: "I have no time." "Time always . . . works against us." He never wore a wristwatch, and on the occasions when he carried a pocket-watch he let it run down. He ignored the day's division into light and darkness, drawing shades in daytime and burning lights all night. The kingdom he was erecting on earth would last a thousand years, he said, and the figures with whom he identified were of another era: Frederick the Great, Bismarck, Christ. Insomnia was one of his major symptoms.

To the pattern in the seed all is present at once, and it pushes toward simultaneous articulation. You want it all and you want it all at once, because you feel and see it all at once.

This is a transcendent kind of perception, appropriate to an omnipresent God. As the old preacher explained: God created time so that everything wouldn't happen at once. Time slows; events unfold one by one, and we, committed to time-bound consciousness, believe that each one causes the next. But for the daimon, time can't cause anything that is not already present in the whole image. Time only slows and holds back realization, thereby furthering "growing down."

This timelessness of the acorn and its push to make everything happen at once indicates possession by the daimon, daimon becoming demonic. The appreciation of everything having its season, of giving time and having time and taking time, does not apply to the Bad Seed, which promulgates manic inflation that brooks no interruptions (Hitler's invention of blitzkrieg and his fury at anything blocking his way), and that demands impulsiveness and hurry. The alchemists said, "In your patience is your soul" and "All haste comes from the devil."

Finally, this evidence of direct demonic intrusion, perhaps the devil himself:

A man in the closest daily association with him gave me this account: Hitler wakes at night with convulsive shrieks. . . . He shakes with fear, making the whole bed vibrate. . . . Hitler stood swaying in his room, looking wildly about him. "It was he! It was he! He's been here!" he gasped. His lips were blue. Sweat streamed down his face. Suddenly he began to reel off figures, and odd words and broken phrases, entirely devoid of sense. It sounded horrible. He used strangely constructed and entirely un-German word formations. Then he stood quite still, only his lips moving. He was massaged and offered something to drink. Then he suddenly burst out—

"There, there! In the corner! Who's that?"

He stamped and shrieked in the familiar way. He was shown that there was nothing out of the ordinary in the room, and then he gradually grew calm.[22]

EIGHT EXPLANATIONS

Alice Miller, who retells this story, imagines that Hitler is imagining his ordeals with a punishing father. Her conventional angle of insight reduces the demon that Hitler sees to a conjured father. She believes the war games he directed with his playmates, fighting as underdog Indians and Boers, also to have been battles against this oppressive father. Moreover, for Miller, not only was Hitler opposing his oppressive father, he was also unconsciously identified with him as an oppressor himself; for Alice Miller, the motivating force and haunting demon in the horror of Hitler was not a daimon at all but an introjected father image.[23] Thus does the parental fallacy exorcise the evil.

Accounts of Charles Manson, a figure of terror who has floated through the Western imagination of the last three decades as did Jack the Ripper in the last century, also put the prime blame on bad parenting. These accounts locate the seed of his evil in the mother who supposedly "sold him to a bar waitress for a pitcher of beer." Manson told this story to his biographer to explain why "he always felt he was an outsider."[24] Our pop psychology has no other explanation than parentalism and developmental psychology for the original loneliness and the isolating effects of the daimonic call, whether in Hitler or any of the other natural-born killers.

Woody Harrelson, playing the psychopath in Oliver Stone's film, states outright that he is a "natural born killer," giving an explanation for his acts and a title to the film. Yet Quentin Tarantino, who wrote the script, and Stone, who directed, seem unable to accept the implications of their own film. They pay tribute to outworn psychological "reasons" by flashbacks to scenes of sexual abuse. These irrelevant inserts not only establish the psychopath as a victim himself, but they confuse the film's own important insight. Its main themes give the true reasons for the "senseless behavior" in a three-way combination of irresistible motives: the isolating, antisocial inflation of American being-in-love; the delusional transcendence of media acclaim; and the inborn Bad Seed that calls to kill.

This inborn Bad Seed shows nowhere more clearly, perhaps, than in the case of Mary Bell of Newcastle, England. With her bare hands, this ten-year-old girl strangled Martin (age four) and Brian (age three) two months apart, in 1968. Gitta Sereny studied Mary Bell's early life with an immensely destructive and schizoid mother who never wanted the baby—indeed, tried to get rid of it many times—so that, in Sereny's version, the two murdered boys become victims of Mary Bell's own soul murder at her mother's hands. Inhumanity is due to inhuman parenting. Sereny's book is written to improve social conditions and disprove the acorn theory, the theory of the Bad Seed. "Are we still not beyond the point where we call sick children monsters and believe in evil birth?"[25]

There are, however, incidents in Mary Bell's earliest years that can be read to indicate an uncanny fate. She was disliked and kept at a distance by other children: "Nobody wants to play with me." Her primary school teachers thought her cunning, cheeky, crafty; she told stories all the time, and it was hard to distinguish between her truth and her lies. In the witness stand, "she provoked an unwilling and perplexed sense of distaste, not only in those who attended her but in many of those who watched." Something about her repelled human closeness.

This was already true in infancy. Her father's sister, who cared for her for a while, said: "She was only a baby then, but she wouldn't have anything done for her. She wouldn't let anybody hug or kiss her. It was always like this. She'd turn her face away." Sereny notes that just as for Mary's mother, "there was a wealth of love available for Mary. But both seemed unable to accept it."[26]

Then, the attraction to death: On four different occasions before she was four Mary came close to dying. She found poisons and pills and nearly fell to her death from a window. Did the acorn already know it should not enter the world? Visiting her grandmother, a "very responsible woman," Mary—but a year old!—was able to get hold of the older woman's pills. "To achieve this, the baby had to find the knitting needle [that opened the hiding place], get up to where the gramophone stood [this was the hiding place], open it, dig out the carefully hidden bottle, unscrew it, and take out and eat enough of the unpleasant little pills almost to kill her."

As to the stranglings, " 'Death,' 'murder,' 'killing,' had a different connotation for Mary. . . . For her all of it had been a game."[27]

Mary Bell takes us directly into the puzzle of causes. Gitta Sereny clearly believes that had Mary's mother received proper psychiatric attention, had there been better school counseling and less-deplorable socioeconomic conditions, Brian and Martin would not have been murdered.

Alice Miller would agree with Sereny, for she states clearly that "All absurd behavior has its roots in early childhood" and that "Hitler actually succeeded in transferring the trauma of his family life onto the entire German nation."[28] Helm Stierlin's "psychohistory," *Adolf Hitler: A Family Perspective*, concurs. It sounds as if the whole course of world history could have been altered by early therapeutic intervention in that obscure Austrian household. Twenty million Russian casualties and six million Jews, not to mention the victims from all the other places, and the dead Germans, too, caused by young Adolf's beatings and the behavior of his mother, etc.

Even if Sereny and Miller are holding on to some piece of truth, we are still left asking: Were there perhaps genetic factors in these cases and other cases of criminal psychopathy, that "run in the family"? Are certain people by nature demonic and beyond human reach? Shakespeare's Prospero, sounding like a frustrated therapist, says of the monster Caliban: "A devil, a born devil on whose nature / Nurture can never stick; on whom my pains, / Humanely taken, all, all lost, quite lost!" (*The Tempest,* IV, i, 189). Then, too, when we read of the odd coldness in Mary and in Hitler, of that impulse toward death, there seems to be something else apart from both upbringing and possible heredity, some lack in their souls, or a lack of soul altogether.

So we shall set forth the major models for explaining the Bad Seed. While I list them one by one so that they stand one against another in sharp delineation, that all eight play into one another should go without saying. Any one of the eight may contribute hypotheses to any other one. No single model would claim to be the only truth.

That this chapter shows more rigid lines in its presentation than any other in the book may be the result of its main material, Hitler. The image is so toxic, so explosive, that it asks for special handling. Every bit of evidence and accusation must be numbered and separately labeled. Perhaps, too, we can understand the labored, obsessive methods used from the Inquisition through the trials of Adolf Eichmann in Israel, Klaus Barbie in France, and in the Nuremburg trials themselves. This controlling carefulness of step-by-step rationalism defends against the demonic force under discussion. Let us imagine the Bad Seed itself on trial, with each of the eight models sketched below as a primary explanation of the behavior of the accused.

1. *Early Traumatic Conditioning*

You have become as you are owing to abusive, brutalizing, and uncaring surroundings during infancy and early years.[29] Perhaps you have suffered perinatal complications, malnourishment, early head injuries. As soon as you were born you were unwanted and had to survive in a cruel and violent atmosphere. Messages transmitted to you were double-binding; they denied actual reality; and you were subject to unpredictable moods and arbitrary whims. Every moment of your life was spent in extremis; powerless before tyranny, robbed of dignity, you learned a pattern that established itself early and became continuous and progressive. You went from bad to worse.

2. *Hereditary Taint*

You are the bearer of a dysfunctional physiological structure: too much testosterone; not enough serotonin; hormonal imbalance; electrical misfirings; autonomic insensitivity; genetic anomalies. The idea of a physical taint determining behavior carried great weight in the psychiatry of the last century. The theory derived from longitudinal histories of families through several generations to show degeneration marks in ears and hand lines. Psychiatry books presented a rogues' gallery of grotesque "degenerates" whose "substance" had declined in vitality and viability because their grandparents drank heavily or were sexually odd. A criminal psychopath was the consequence of biophysical forces and endowed with a particular physiology shared also by geniuses and artists and strongly influenced by sexual libido.[30] The condition is fundamentally unalterable except by physical means, a fact that justifies such "treatments" as lifelong incarceration in institutions for the "criminally insane," castration, electroshock, lobotomy, and under the Nazi regime, vivisection and extermination. Today's physiological model more subtly recommends a pharmaceutical armament for subduing your behavior: popping pretty little pills.

3. *Group Mores*

Though biological nature and social conditioning may lay a groundwork, the crucial release factor is your societal milieu, especially from the onset of puberty through prolonged adolescence. The habits of the streets, the gang's code, the unwritten laws of the prison, the military indoctrination of special forces, militia ideology, the compound of the concentration camp, the *omertà* of the Mafia family: These conventions of the group with which you are identified determine the value system that styles your behavior. These styles become inculcated and become your fall-back reactions when under threat, as at My Lai or when "dissed" in your neighborhood. Criminality and violence belong to a group ethos—like that of the early street gangs of Hitler's storm troopers—and burning, looting, and raping belong to victorious armies after battle. All this is relatively independent of physiological and early environmental factors. When in Rome you do as the Roman Legions do.

A biographer of Al Capone, the ruthless Chicago crime lord, provides the usual explanation of the criminal calling by referring to his early Brooklyn environment and group mores:

> What boy would want to linger an instant longer than necessary where eight, ten, twelve people ate and slept, washed and dressed in two or three dank, dingy rooms, where the fetor of excrement from rotten drains filled the hallways and vermin feasted on the garbage dumped out of windows, where you either froze or sweltered, where the grown-ups, in their distress and bewilderment, constantly screamed at one another and at you and whipped you for the least offense?
>
> The street gang was escape. . . . They formed their own street society, independent of the adult world and antagonistic to it. Led by some older, forceful boy, they pursued the thrills of shared adventure, of horseplay, exploration, gambling, pilfering, vandalism, sneaking a smoke or snuff or alcohol, secret ritual, smut sessions, fighting rival gangs.[31]

4. *The Choice Mechanism*

Your behavior is your choice, and conditioned by your choices all along. That your choices are themselves conditioned by your physiology, your early upbringing, your group mores in adolescence, still does not determine the cost-benefit analysis you are making with each of your murderous moves. Clearly, there must be a profit in it for you. The scale is simple: a pain/pleasure ratio as proposed by Jeremy Bentham's utilitarian calculus of human action and which appears again in James Q. Wilson and Richard Herrnstein's punishment/reward concept.[32] If for your kind of personality the rewards from impulsive acts and premeditated killing outweigh the anticipated punishments, then you will automatically, mechanistically, go for it. Moreover, if each choice is met with accumulating success, as was the case with Hitler for an entire decade, then those successes will reinforce your belief that fate has you on the right track.

5. Karma and Zeitgeist

Some portion of your past life is being enacted in this. The hereditary taint may lie in your chromosomes, but what put it there is karma. The Bad Seed reflects something you must endure personally and also something belonging to the history of the world, its zeitgeist. Whether you fall in with Fagin's gang of thieving kids or are initiated into the Thugs of India, or whether your body is set up so as to produce unusual physiological reactions—all this is karma resulting from previous incarnations. There is a metaphysical mystery at work, which the limits of human reason cannot grasp: Even the worst of the Bad Seeds takes part in a cosmic pattern of the zeitgeist. Hitler's personal karma belongs to a world plan.

6. The Shadow

Apart from biological and environmental factors, the psychological propensity to destroy exists within all human beings. Violence, crime, murder, and cruelty belong to the human soul as its shadow. The Bible gives this shadow due respect by issuing outright, as five of the Ten Commandments, prohibitions against theft, murder, adultery, lying, and envy. These universal tendencies, latent in everyone, are the basis for protective societal forms, political organizations, and moral constraints. If the human soul had no shadow, who'd need lawyers, criminologists, or confessors? At any moment the autonomy of the shadow may emerge like Mr. Hyde from Dr. Jekyll, or come slowly to the fore under extreme conditions, as in the novel *Lord of the Flies*. The natural-born killer is all too human. Since humans have shadows whose depths reach to the collective level of murder, human behavior is prompted by this archetypal force. Hitler knew the shadow all too well, indulged it, was obsessed by it, and strove to purge it; but he could not admit it in *himself,* seeing only its projected form as Jew, Slav, intellectual, foreign, weak, and sick.

7. *Lacuna*

Something fundamentally human is missing. Your character, your personality inventory has a hole in it. Your crimes are not due so much to the *presence* of the shadow (since everyone is subject to that universal archetype), but rather to a specific absence, the lack of human feeling. Adolf Guggenbuhl-Craig's theory calls this missing essential eros.[33] Catholic theology called the absence *privatio boni,* deprivation of goodness, as we say colloquially, "That boy is no good."

Other traits may fill in the absence: impulsiveness (the short fuse), shortsightedness (immediate gratification outweighs long-term consequences), repetitive rigidities, emotional poverty, stunted intellect, imperviousness to guilt and remorse (the Teflon shrug), projection and denial—all these are noted, but principal and more basic is that erotic lacuna, that cold absence, that inability to feel for and into another living creature.

When British serial killer Dennis Nilsen keeps dead boys in his room to sleep with and fondle and make love to, and when Jeffrey Dahmer eats his pickups' flesh, they are like the demon figures in the underworld pictured by Christian, Tibetan, and Japanese art. They may be attempting to find some way out of exile in emptiness, some way back into common humanity. The sexual component in the crime is not the cause but a symptom trying to ignite a dead fire, arouse a life force, to touch, to connect, to have intercourse with human flesh.

8. *The Demonic Call*

There is a specific calling that belongs inescapably to you. How it fits into past lives, present body, or the developing zeitgeist in the history of the world is beyond your knowledge and our theoretical concerns. The call offers *transcendence,* becoming as necessary to a person's life on earth as performance to Garland, battle to Patton, painting to Picasso. As the potential for art and thought were given with the acorn, so is the potential for demonic crime.

> . . . people don't understand. . . . People in the life ain't looking for no home and grass in the yard and shit like that. We the show people. The glamour people. Come on the set with the finest car, the finest woman, the finest vines. Hear people talking about you. Hear the bar get quiet when you walk in the door. You make something out of nothing.[34]

Transgression as transcendence; lifted out of your circumstances, filled with the power or the "glamour," and in touch with the transcendent origin of the calling urge.

In the last scene of the tragedy *Othello,* when Iago is revealed to be the malicious cause of murders and the destruction of Othello's noble and gullible character, Othello asks him: "Why he hath thus ensnar'd my soul and body?" Shakespeare has Iago reply: "Demand me nothing: what you know, you know." These are Iago's final words, and they leave interpreters guessing about his motives. But this statement by one of Shakespeare's archvillains is not enigmatic at all. Iago says, in essence, "You already know, Othello. In the lines just preceding you have already twice named me a devil." Iago made tragedy out of nothing—as if a sport, a game.

The Bad Seed takes pleasure in malice, enjoying destruction. Mary Bell told the woman psychiatrist interviewing her about Brian's murder: "I was full of laughter that day." The only witness, a girl of thirteen, stated, "She said she had enjoyed it."[35] There is satisfaction in just doing the demonic deed, a gratification that may be accompanied by sexual pleasure in postpuberty males, but is hardly a factor, for instance, in the case of Mary Bell.

Materialism cannot explain the urge. Hitler did not institute his murder-based nation for economic gains. In fact, the diversion of infrastructure and effort, as his war was being lost, into the killing camps cost him immeasurably more than the property confiscated and gold gained. Nor can material poverty account for the Bad Seed—or what Jack Katz, sociologist, calls the "drive toward deviance"—even if oppressive conditions may well be a major contributing factor.

Katz's account relies on philosophical concepts (some from the French thinker Paul Ricoeur's *Symbolism of Evil*) by which "senseless" acts take on meaning rather than merely being insane. They close the gap between the mundane and the divine. Breaking all commandments frees you from human bondage, opening a door to a suprahuman condition where devil and divinity are indistinguishable.

Radical mysticisms, such as the celebrations of the Black Mass, Jewish Frankism, Christian Antinomianism and satanic cults, and Tantric practices ritually break taboos that keep the sacred in a moral precinct. Elevation of the profane by the most profane acts imaginable raises its power until it is indistinguishable from the sacred.

Psychopathic killings are called senseless not only because they are a-rational and arbitrary, their motivation so obscure. They are senseless because of the "dizziness of deviance," a radical plunge or ascent by means of crime that is a transformation, an "apotheosis."[36] Katz indicates that the senselessness makes sense from its otherworldly side, not from who you were or are, but who you might thereby become.

This derangement of the senses is present during the acts. Brian Masters's conclusions about the psychopathic killer (his focus was on Dennis Nilsen, murderer of fifteen young men) say "at the time of the murder the killer's reason is dulled."[37]

A German torturer and killer of little boys, Jürgen Bartsch, stated: "From a certain age (around thirteen or fourteen) I always had the feeling of no longer having any control over what I was doing. . . . I prayed, and I hoped at least that it would do some good, but it didn't."[38] He turned to divine intervention because he sensed the cause was out of the human sphere. Jeffrey Dahmer, who beat and sliced young men to death and ate their flesh, had no explanation for what came over him. He chose to go to trial rather than plead guilty because he "wanted to find out just what it was that caused me to be so bad and evil."[39]

During the trial, in 1992, his father, Lionel Dahmer, was struck by recollections of incidents and conditions of his own youth that paralleled his son's: the "taste" for control and wish for power; experiments with destructive materials; distancing and coldness of feeling; an attempted seduction of a little girl—and having dreams between the ages of eight and twenty of committing horrible murders. On awakening, the crimes seemed real: "I would literally hang between fantasy and reality, I would be terrified at what I might have done. I would feel lost, as if I had gone out of control, and in that instant, done something horrible."

Lionel Dahmer does hold himself responsible for having been an inadequate father, "evasive and uninsightful." However, he goes beyond the parental fallacy espoused by Alice Miller and others who blame the parents for the criminal child. He brings in an uncanny component. This father assumes a kind of *participation mystique,* a demonic potential shared with his son. He, too, knew the overpowering reality of demonic intervention. This Bad Seed already showed its fury in Jeffrey when he was four.

The family was carving pumpkins for Halloween (the night devoted to making visible the invisible presence of demons, devils, witches, and the dead in our midst). They were about to carve a smile on the pumpkin's face. Jeffrey screamed suddenly: "I want a mean face." As they tried to coax him toward the smile, "he began to pound the table, his voice high and vehement, 'No, I want a mean face!'"

Supposedly the numerically worst of all serial killers, Andrei Chikatilo, who was tracked down in southern Ukraine after some fifty murders of adolescents, mainly girls, said when interrogated: "It was as if something directed me, something outside me, something supernatural. I was absolutely not in control of myself when I committed these murders, when I stabbed people, when I was cruel." In his confession he repeated such phrases as: "I was in an animal fever and I remember some of my actions only vaguely.... At the moment of the crime I wanted to tear everything.... I don't know what happened to me . . . seized by an uncontrollable urge . . . overwhelmingly drawn . . . I started to shake.... I was shaking violently.... I literally started to shake...."[40]

The acorn appears not only as a guiding angel who warns, protects, counsels, urges, and calls. It also uses deadly force, as when it terrified Hitler and made him shake in the night, a terror not reported in other circumstances—in the trenches, after the July 1944 assassination attempt, during the last days in the bunker. The only comparable seizures were those he had when possessed on the podium, writhing in fury and charming the crowd, or the tantrums he had when opposed.

PREVENTION?

The inevitable practical question arises at the end: If Hitler monstrously exemplifies the Bad Seed, could future Hitlers be prevented?

That the seed was there in childhood seems clear enough. The uncertain ancestry and apocryphal tales of his beginnings emphasize the daimonic inheritance. The fervent pro-Germanism he exhibited at age twelve, though he was an Austrian, predicts what was to come. Even at ten he led his school chums in mock Boer battles against the English. At eleven, Hitler was "top boy," running younger ones, and was observed to be reserved and yet fanatic. His romanticism in adolescence fastened on the staginess of myth, opera, and Wagner.

Even earlier (at seven) he draped an apron over his shoulders, "climbed on a kitchen chair and delivered long and fervent sermons." By fourteen or fifteen he could make extraordinary ranting displays of rhetoric as if speaking to the wind, transcending his personality and visible shape, "looking almost sinister," as if possessed by the voice of another being. "He just *had* to talk," said a friend from boyhood.[41]

The book, *Mein Kampf*, that he wrote in prison in his early thirties, lays out the visionary project he intended to fulfill. The entire disaster is there in a nutshell for anyone to read. Yet the Jews, the Western statesmen, the intellectuals and democrats, the church, could not see the demonic. The dark eye that can see evil had been blinded by bright hopes in human progress and faith in goodwill and peace.

Without a profound sense of psychopathy and a strong conviction that the demonic is always among us—and not only in its extreme criminal forms—we hide in denial and wide-eyed innocence, that openness which also opens wide the gate to the worst. Again: Note how political tyranny lives on a gullible populace, and how a gullible populace falls for tyranny. Innocence seems to ask for evil.

Hitler's biographies give us some diagnostic signs of what to look for both from his childhood and from early adult years: the cold eyes and icy heart; the humorlessness; the certitude, arrogance, inflexibility, purity; the fanatical projection of shadow; the being out of step with time; the mystical sense of luck; rage at being blocked, crossed, or dissed; the paranoid demand for trust and loyalty; the attraction to myths and symbols of "evil" (wolf, fire, apocalypse); raptures, seizures, and moments of estrangement and/or call to transcendence; the fear of powerlessness as ordinariness, ignorance, impotence.

About this last—the fear of powerlessness. We need to keep quite clear a distinction between inadequacy and impotence. The attribution of Hitler's psychopathy to his supposed monorchidism—like the attribution of Chikatilo, Gilmore, and Nilsen's crimes to sexual dysfunction—puts the cart before the horse. The driving animal is the terrible fear of being inadequate to the demanding vision of the daimon. This fear afflicts all ordinary humans when in touch with the extraordinary claims of the daimon. Demonism arises, not because of supposed or actual sexual dysfunction, but because of the dysfunctional relation with the daimon. We strive to fulfill its vision fully, refusing to be restrained by our human limitations—in other words, we develop megalomania.

That inequality between what a personality has available and what the daimon demands sets up feelings of inadequacy. These feelings of inferiority narrow down to sexual inadequacy, in keeping with the basic concretism of psychopathology in general. (Psychopathology can be generally defined by one catchword: *concretism,* taking psychological events such as delusions, hallucinations, fantasies, projections, feelings, and wishes as actually, literally, concretely real. For instance, the wishful fantasies of strengthening the nation by overcoming weakness after defeat in World War I, Hitler took literally, eliminating "weakness" by concrete measures of rearmament and death camps. The same concretistic thinking convinces child molesters and repetitive rapists that castration is the cure, since they assume that what appears as sexual is literally only sexual.)

Only in our Western psychological theories does the tail wag the dog. For our theories tend to share the same concretistic imagination as the pathologies they want to explain. Our theories, too, are as obsessed by the sexual fantasies that permeated our culture even before Freud, perhaps as far back as St. Paul. Since our theories of psychopathologies are themselves pornographic (hence the voyeurism and prurience of our case histories), they must be just as degrading to the soul and its daimons as the commercial pornography which puritans delight in blaming.

To reduce the Bad Seed to an inadequately filled seed bag of monorchidism—itself a questionable fact, since Hitler did not allow his doctors to examine him below the waist—misses the deepest feelings of inadequacy, the feeling of failing the daimon, that I am not up to its call, its boundless vision and manic impulsion. The "cure" is not recovery of sexual potency—that is, "more balls"—but recovery from concretism, which trivially reduces the potency of the acorn to the "little sac and its contents," as Freud called the scrotum.

It is as difficult to resist the call as it was for Judy Garland to resist singing even when her voice could not reach the notes or her mind hold the lyrics, as difficult as it was for Manolete not to enter the ring even on a day when he had forebodings. As Garland's and Manolete's potential was given with the acorn, so is the psychopathic potential for demonic crime. The crimes are not choices as much as necessities, though they may be diverted, inhibited, thwarted, sublimated, as psychiatry and criminology hopefully sometimes believe. For the psychopath the call is to exercise power with your eyes, your voice, your charm, your lies and cunning resilience, your physical body, which disguises the fundamental weakness of your person. Since the power is in the seed rather than in the person, the person, like Hitler, is often a vagabond, a misfit, half-educated and given to trivial pursuits, even if slightly gifted with artistic talent and heightened imagination (as Capote, Mailer, and Sartre emphasize in their discussion of their criminal psychopath subjects).

The discrepancy between human personality and daimonic seed is so great that it is as if the human world were drained to feed the seed. The human being, more and more narrowed and "inhuman," seeks blood as the figures in the Greek underworld begged those who descended (Ulysses) for blood. The Bad Seed—perhaps, to a lesser degree, any acorn—acts as a parasite on the life of the person it has selected to inhabit, often leaving the person disorganized, symptomized, boring, emptied of eros, and unable to connect. We call such people loners.

But the loner is not alone. He or she is in communion with the daimon, drawn apart from the human by the invisibly inhuman, and attempting to create a world modeled upon the grandeur and the glamour of a world unseen but envisioned. The loner commingles with a solitary, transcendent God, monomania and monotheism indistinguishable, performing a parody of this last and famous passage in Plotinus' *Enneads:* "This is the life of gods and of godlike and blessed men . . . a life which takes no delight in the things of this world, the passing of solitary to solitary."[42]

Hitler's own greatest passion was neither the German Reich, nor war, nor victory, nor even his own person. It was architectural construction. Megalomaniac emperors, from Nebuchadnezzar and the Egyptian pharaohs through the Roman rulers to Napoleon and Hitler, construct in concrete what the daimon envisions. For this reason, megalomania haunts the actual architect—as the Bible warns with the story of the Tower of Babel, which is not only about the origin of language but also about the megalomania inherent in all attempts to make concrete the grandeurs of fantasy, especially in architecture. Tribal peoples are usually careful to keep their sacred altars movable, their architecture vernacular, but their visions otherworldly.

PREVENTION AND RITUAL

Prevention therefore would focus on redressing the balance between the psyche's weakness and the daimon's potential, between the transcendent call and the personality to which it is calling. Building the personality is a psychological task beyond "strengthening the ego." The psyche's construction is also beyond *Bildung,* the German idea of cultural and moral education. Josef Mengele, the worst of the concentration-camp doctors who cruelly experimented on inmates, was well educated, loved music, and studied Dante.[43] Chikatilo was a teacher; Hitler painted and was making architectural designs right to the last days; Manson writes pop music and lyrics in jail; Mary Bell wrote poems; Gary Gilmore painted well, and his brother

Gaylen, who has a long sociopathic history of crime and jails, has read the great authors and written poetry.[44] As we've already learned, the psychological task is "growing down."

Growing down shifts the focus of the personality from the single-minded egocentricity of the daimon into common humanity, twisting the call to transcend toward extension into the world and its claims, as we read in the life of Josephine Baker, and also in those of Canetti and Einstein, Menuhin and Bernstein.

But growing down cannot be forced upon youth. Hitler was incensed by suggestions he enter the conventional professions and become a civil servant. The French mathematician Évariste Galois could not comply with the routines of school. His arrogance and his brilliance increased, together with his estrangement, in proportion as he was forced into harness, until he was dead at twenty.

Before growing down can even be considered, let alone managed, full recognition of the genius is unconditionally required. This means admitting that the acorn, even as Bad Seed, is the most deeply driving motivation in life, especially in a young life. Often this recognition comes from a solitary friend (like Hitler's Kubizek, who patiently listened to tirades for years, or Izambard, who accompanied and admired Rimbaud), from a perceptive teacher (like Kazin's Miss Shank), or from a coach (like Manolete's Camará). Recognition comes from those who see the daimon and pay it homage. Then it may enter the traces more willingly.

What these mentors perceived, theory too must recognize. So thwarting the Bad Seed begins with a theory that gives it full recognition. That's what this chapter, this book, is all about. So long as our theories deny the daimon as instigator of human personality, and instead insist upon brain construction, societal conditions, behavioral mechanisms, genetic endowment, the daimon will not go gently into obscurity. It drives toward the light; it will be seen; it asks for its place in the sun. "Hear people talking about you. . . . We the show people."

Dick Hickcock, who killed the Clutter family in cold blood, said: "I thought a person could get a lot of glory out of killing. The word glory seemed to keep going through my mind. . . . When you bump somebody off you are really in the big time."[45] Television offers the daimon that light, that celebration. If TV can be blamed for serious criminality, it is less because of what it shows than simply because it shows, affording instant worldwide recognition, full exposure. Yet the seed that desires to enter the world remains encapsulated in a delusion above the world, as a superstar. TV provides merely a quick simulacrum of growing down.

Above the world is also where M. Scott Peck places some of his patients who have in common a condition that Peck calls "evil." He uses the term as a diagnosis: evil basically consists in arrogant, selfish narcissism or supreme willfulness.

This notion of evil is hardly a startling discovery—supreme willfulness was known to the Greeks as *hubris* and appears in the Christian tradition as *superbia* or overweening pride. The idea that evil people choose their path with their own will carries Herrnstein's explanation (No. 4 above) of criminal behavior into moral territory. And Peck, although a psychiatrist, is decidedly a moralist.

The criminal's attempt at transcendence and the invocation of invisible powers like Fame and Fortune ("We the show people. The glamour people.") is altogether lost on Peck, who finds that evil makes people ugly, cheap, tawdry, impotent, and small, all the while deluding them with romantic superiority. Thus, his "own latest vision of hell" is a Dante-esque Las Vegas, "jammed with dull-eyed people . . . yanking machines for all eternity."[46]

The rigid frame enclosing his vision does not allow Peck to see the daimon in the demonic. A deep-seated Manichaeism divides his world into saints and sinners, saved and damned, healthy and sick. "Evil is the ultimate disease . . . the evil are the most insane of all." By means of a psychiatric diagnosis the moralist can place a patient among the damned.

A logic that so radically divides good and bad can offer only the same old standardized recommendation we've heard for centuries in the Christianized West: Fight the good fight. Peck calls it "combat." "Our most basic data about the nature of evil will be won from hand-to-hand combat with evil itself." Therapists will be in the front lines of this fight because of their capacity for and training in love. "I think we can safely study and treat evil only through the methods of love."

"Love" is surely the most omnipotent word in current usage, since the Christian God himself is defined as love. It can do all things. I would insist, however, that it can do very little with "evil" unless this "love" first recognizes the soul's call within the bad seed. Love, as I am trying to argue in this chapter, may be less an exercise of the will in an act of combat and more an exercise of intellectual comprehension of that daimonic necessity that calls above and beyond the world to the sinner as to the saint. Strangely enough, as martyrdom for some saints may be their way down into the world, so may atavistic acts be the way down for the one called by a bad seed—although, let us be clear, the call does not justify the crime or relieve the criminal acts of their reprehensibility. I am claiming that the acorn theory allows a wider comprehension of the Bad Seed than the diagnosis of evil does.

Prevention, as I understand it, may neither restrict nor admonish. It has to address the same seed, the same call, and invoke the same invisibles that are claiming the price of life itself. The most immediately dangerous of all invisibles is the explosive charge in the seed, its obsessive, compelling potency, like Hitler's raging obstinacy. Before dismantling the bomb or isolating it in solitary confinement, we may need to lengthen its fuse. We need to encourage slowness, which is what "serving a sentence" and "doing time in the cooler" intend.

Therefore, effective rituals begin as downers, with mourning. Even if there is no remorse about vicious acts, there can be increased awareness about the demon that prompted them. Hitler only followed the demon, never questioned it, his mind enslaved by its imagination rather than applied to its investigation.

After the downers comes not repressions disguised as conversion and born-again reform but that turn toward community service we can witness every day when ex-cons take to the schools and grow down into the kids' worlds, explaining how the Bad Seed works, what it wants, what it costs, and how to be smart. Mentoring juveniles as a regular repetitive service of dedication is also a kind of ritual.

Finally, prevention of the demonic must be based in the invisible ground "above the world," transcending the very idea of prevention itself. Prevention requires not combat but seduction, inviting the daimon in the acorn to move out from the hard-shell confines of an only-bad seed, so as to recover a fuller image of glory. For what makes the seed demonic is its single-track obsession, its monotheistic literalism that follows one prospect only, perverting the larger imagination of the seed toward serial reenactments of the same act. (Performing the same act over and over again is one description of ritual, too.)

My notions of ritual suggest ways of respecting the power of the call. They suggest disciplines imbued with more-than-human values, whose rituals will be touched by beauty, transcendence, adventure, and death. Like cures like—again that old adage. We must go toward where the seed originates and attempt to follow its deepest intentions.

Society must have rituals of exorcism for protecting itself from the Bad Seed. Yet it must also have rituals of recognition that give the demonic a place—other than prisons—as Athena found an honored place for the destructive, blood-angered Furies in the midst of civilized Athens.

These rituals of societal protection take the demons in. They see the daimon in the demon. And these rituals sharply contrast with current ideas of prevention, which, following Hitler's own preferred methods for purifying society, would eradicate the Bad Seed. Public programs are being proposed to test schoolchildren for their "genetic predispositions," to uncover potentials for crime and violence in terms of character traits and personality, "weeding out" those who show such factors as "early irritability and uncooperativeness."[47]

These traits, as we have seen in the examples in this book, indicate not mainly crime, but that genial exceptionality on which a whole society depends for leadership, invention, and culture. Besides, once sorted out, on what compost heap would the weeds be thrown? Or would they merely be "improved" and rendered compliant by drugs to which you may not say no, or kept in privately owned, for-profit penitentiaries exempt from labor laws and minimum-wage scales?

For adequate rituals we substitute rigidities and formulaic fixes like "three strikes and you're out." Without exorcisms that attempt to separate the Devil and the daimon, we have only eradications that get rid of both. Rituals not only protect society from the demonic; they also protect it from its own paranoia, from falling prey to its own obsessive and vicious measures of purification, that ever-present American myth: the return to innocence in a Puritan paradise.

Innocence is America's mystical cloud of unknowing. We are forgiven simply by virtue of not knowing what we do. To wrap ourselves round in the Good—that is the American dream, leaving place for the evil nightmare only in the "other," where it can be diagnosed, treated, prevented, and sermonized about. A history of this habit of the heart has been exposed by Elaine Pagels (in her important study *The Origin of Satan*[48]) as a disastrous, perhaps "evil" essential, an inherent bad seed, in Western religious denominations, making obligatory as countermeasure their relentless insistence on "love."

A society that willfully insists upon innocence as the noblest of virtues and worships innocence at its altars in Orlando and Anaheim and on Sesame Street, will be unable to see any seed of any kind unless it be sugar-coated. Like Forrest Gump eating chocolates and offering sweets to strangers before he ever looks into their eyes, stupid is indeed as stupid does. The idea of the Bad Seed, the idea that there is a demonic call, should startle our native intelligence, awakening it from the innocence of our American theories so that as a nation we can see that evil is attracted to, belongs with, innocence. Then we might finally recognize that in America, Natural Born Killers are the secret companions of, are even prompted by, Forrest Gumps.

— ❧ —

CHAPTER 11

MEDIOCRITY

Can there be a mediocre angel? A call to mediocrity? After all, most of us pass our time sheltered under the middle bulge in the bell curve. Huddled there in the mean, we look with envy and fear at the exceptional few pushing out the edges. The middling majority, whether in talent, in opportunity, in background, in luck, in brightness and beauty, are neither born great nor have greatness thrust upon them. So it surely seems.

Let's first acknowledge that snobbish prejudices are packed into the term "mediocre." To apply this word to anything implies our own distance from it. I stand apart, am different from, don't belong among, and therefore can pass judgment upon whatever I am naming mediocre.

"Mediocre" tends to mean "undistinguished," while snobs enjoy their distinguishing hallmarks of style—how they wear clothes, use words, where they go and gather and gossip. The literature of Western civilization since the eighteenth century mainly turns on snobbish appraisals of mediocrity, and this tradition can catch up anyone attempting to deal with the theme. Whatever the circumstances the genius has put you into, the fact of individuality defends the soul against all class-action claims. No soul is mediocre, whatever your personal taste for conventionality, whatever your personal record of middling achievements.

Common expressions make this quite clear. A soul is said to be old, or wise, or sweet. We speak of someone having a beautiful soul, a wounded soul, a deep soul, a large soul, or one that is simple, childlike, naive. We might say, "She's a good soul"—but terms like "middle-class," "average," "usual," "regular," "mediocre" do not adhere to "soul." There are no standard benchmarks for a daimon; no usual angels, no regular genius.

Let's try to imagine a mediocre soul. What would it look like? Wishy-washy, nondescript, chameleonlike, would it pass completely by fitting with any and every external cliché? Even that conformist Eichmann was not ordinary. We may not identify mediocrity of soul with the ordinary jobs of repairman, receptionist, road worker, since their jobs may be mediocre but not their performance. Millions may eat cornflakes for breakfast and popcorn at the movies, but this does not attest to their average souls. Everyone is a "one" because of his or her style. The only possible mediocre soul would have to be one without marks of any kind, utterly innocent, imageless and therefore unimaginable, and also damned to an existence without a daimon.

Soulless individuals do appear in the literature of Western civilization, but even these have images. They are imagined as the Golem, the Zombie, the Robot, the existential Stranger. To be at all is to be defined by a form, a style. You never lose the image in which your soul is shaped, that pattern of your lot. Everyone is marked; each of us is singular. For the soul the idea of mediocrity is meaningless.

Let us not confuse a particular gift—like Menuhin's for the violin, or Teller's for physics, or Ford's for mechanics—

with the call. The talent is only a piece of the image; many are born with musical, mathematical, and mechanical talent, but only when the talent serves the fuller image and is carried by its character do we recognize exceptionality. Many are called, few are chosen; many have talent, few have the character that can realize the talent. Character is the mystery, and it is individual.

Some may come with little special talent. Omar Bradley's talent was sports, especially baseball. His daimon was his character. Bradley—trudging the back roads of farm-country Missouri in winter to the one-room schoolhouse with his schoolteacher father, seventeen miles to the hour, shooting game for table food (he had his own BB gun at six)—showed diligence, study, obedience, physical coordination. Bradley's fate was there in his character. His future did not have to entail West Point and Army Chief of Staff, though the military was the career that allowed his character to fulfill its image. (And was he not already enduring the Battle of the Bulge in the frozen Ardennes on those side-by-side marches in the Missouri winter?)

What determines eminence is less a call to greatness than the call of character, that inability to be other than what you are in acorn, following it faithfully or being desperately driven by its dream. Many heroes and heroines of this century, like Bradley, appeared in mediocre circumstances with hardly a hint of their rising star. Nixon, Reagan, Carter, Truman, Eisenhower—many whom we vote for, listen to, watch on TV—might have lived lives like our own, unblessed by the sun, their feet stuck to the shady side of the street. And yet they were singled out.

The acorn theory states that each of us is singled out. The very fact of eachness presumes a unique acorn that characterizes each person. Sun or shade, each has a character. In rare instances, the acorn shouts loud and clear at an early age. Musicians often hear the call first: At six Pablo Casals already knew piano and organ music; Marian Anderson gave her first paid performance (she earned fifty cents) at eight; Mozart, of course, and Mendelssohn too; "even before Mahler could stand, he would hum tunes he had heard"; Verdi's father, to stop his son's pleading, acquired a spinet for Giuseppe, age seven; Tchaikovsky was pleading already at age four.[1]

These are the examples that show, and show business shows this best. But most times, the angel does not shout, and instead governs the slow and quiet revelation of character. Not simply the pronounced calling to show business that led them to the heights (Judy Garland, Ingrid Bergman, Leonard Bernstein), but the character with which each performed the calling.

So let's clear away a typical mistake: identifying vocation only with a specific kind of job, rather than also with the performance in the job. This mistake unfortunately is given with the Platonic myth itself, which puts souls into jobs—Ajax the warrior; tired traveler and homecoming husband Ulysses. In the myth, the soul selects its lot in terms of a job. The activity of butchering, say, and the soul of the butcher are not sharply separated in the myth. You are what you do, and therefore if you have a mediocre job like cutting meat in a supermarket you are not called.

Again the mistake; for character is not what you do, it's the way you do it. Each butcher is different, because each has an individual daimon. Ernest Borgnine's Marty, in the film of that name, was a "good butcher," bearing all the traits of mediocrity within the norms of the bell curve, but Marty's character made him memorable and unique.

Uniqueness in the midst of societal mediocrity is the subject of Studs Terkel's interviews. Who does not remember a local "character" from childhood—a mailman, a teacher, the lady who ran the candy store, the liquor store, the pet shop. Trying to salvage unique individuality from desultory, humdrum case histories is the deeper impetus in social workers and therapists. Therapists write *up* the cases; they don't merely write *down* the facts. They want to arrive at an insight, a vision, that holds the facts in pattern. Inside the normative diagnostics and statistics of Mary Doe and Joe Average lies an idiopathic, idiosyncratic image in the heart of each single case. Inside each case is a person; inside each person, a character, which is, according to Heraclitus, a fate.

We will get very soon to Heraclitus' famous dictum, "Character is fate." First, we have to answer the opening question of this chapter: Is there a mediocre angel? Is there a call to mediocrity? Here are four answers.

1. No; only stars have acorns. The rest of us mosey along, picking through the help wanted ads.
2. Yes; we in the middling majority are called too, but we miss the call for many reasons: parents block it, doctors diagnose it, poverty ruins it, no one recognizes it; faith falters, accidents happen. We settle in and make do. The mediocrity of an old shoe.
3. Yes, but the old shoe never really fits; the acorn develops into a corn. While traveling the middle path, I feel all along that something else was meant. I could have, I should have . . . I wish and wait for something to move my feet to the sunny side of the street where my true self really belongs. As Shakespeare wrote: "We, the poorer born / Whose baser stars do shut us up in wishes" (*All's Well That Ends Well*, I, i, 198) begin to believe the mediocrity of our lot is an error of the gods. Bitterly, I believe I am shut into an unauthentic self.
4. Yes, but. For many the call is to keep the light under a bushel, to be in service to the middle way, to join the rank-and-file. It is the call to human harmony. It refuses to identify individuality with eccentricity. The calling stays through life and guides it in subtle ways and into less dramatic forms than we witness in exemplary figures such as those presented in this book. All are called; never mind the chosen few.

The first answer—only stars have acorns—is mainly to be found in studies of creativity, theories of genius, and biographies of standouts. The first answer also divides humanity into haves and have-nots—which is not the intention of this book. Besides, that Augustinian-Calvinist division between the saved and the damned dissolves, since everyone has been individually elected by his or her daimon elector.

The second answer—most people miss their call and settle for something else—appears in sociological accounts. The third provides the stuff of therapeutic idealism, which seeks to uncover the true self or the inner child and put the patient on the creative track by freeing genius from hindering developmental abuses.

The fourth is the one that interests me in this chapter and that drives our inquiry further. For it is the one that both makes a calling of mediocrity and redefines it altogether, away from social and statistical norms.

This position finds its main advocates in contemporary feminist views of biography (and of life itself), which set out to show that greatness of character matters as much as recognition by acclaim. New writings about history and historical figures look carefully at ordinary lives, rather than at political and gifted heroes. Roger North's (1653–1734) "General Preface" to his *Lives* (written c. 1720) espoused this "new" antiheroic and antihierarchical view of biography quite a while ago.[2] These writings look at styles of relating, at social customs, at the tiny daily accomplishments of courage that shift the values of a culture, at the moral trials, at the ideals expressed, to show the subtleties of individuality apart from what went on around the emperor's throne.[3] For character we look as much to the soldier's letter on the eve of battle and the families at home away from the action as to the plans laid out in the general's tent.

These revisions of biographical and historical writing aim to display individual souls amidst the mess of events. Their underlying theory is the same one I would like to claim here:

Character forms a life regardless of how obscurely that life is lived and how little light falls on it from the stars.

Calling becomes a calling to life, rather than imagined in conflict with life. Calling to honesty rather than to success, to caring and mating, to service and struggle for the sake of living. This view offers a revision of vocation not only in the lives of women or as viewed by women; it offers another idea of calling altogether, in which life is the work.

Therefore old questions fall away, questions that ask "Why are some great and others less so?" "Why the minor leaguer who never makes it to the majors, the middle manager who never gets the corner office with the wide window, the salesman who receives no plaque, stays unadvanced, neither fired nor retired, continuing the mediocre performance of an undistinguished person with a modicum of talent?"

No, they have not been doomed by a mediocre daimon, nor is their genius merely average. In fact we are unable to estimate them at all. As long as we regard people in terms of earning power or specific expertise, we do not see their character. Our lens has been ground to one average prescription that is best suited for spotting freaks.

Why do we believe angels prefer angelic persons? Why assume that the genius wants only to be with geniuses? Maybe the invisibles are interested in our lives for the sake of *their* realization and as such are inherently democratic: Anyone will do. Maybe they do not recognize the concept "mediocre." The daimon gives importance to each, not only to the Important. Moreover, they and we are linked in the same myth. We are divine and mortal twins, and so they are in service to the same social realities as we. Because of this linkage, the angel has no way of descent into the streets of the public common except via our lives. In the film *Wings of Desire,* angels fall in love with life, the street-life of ordinary human predicaments.

Our sociology, psychology, and economics—that is, our civilization itself—seem unable to estimate the worth of people who do not stand out. Such people are relegated to the mediocrity of average intelligence in middle America. That's why "success" takes on such exaggerated importance: It offers the only way out of the limbo of the middle. The media pull you out only when you are weeping after tragedy, raging on-stage, or posing for an opinion; then they drop you back into the melting pot of undifferentiated mediocrity. The media can adulate, celebrate, exaggerate, but they cannot imagine and therefore cannot see.

To say it quick and plain: There is no mediocrity of soul. The two terms do not converge. They come from different territories: "Soul" is singular and specific; "mediocrity" sizes you up according to social statistics—norms, curves, data, comparisons. You may be found mediocre in every sociological category, even in your personal aspirations and achievements, but the manner in which this social mediocrity appears will throw a unique spike into any bell curve. No size fits all.

ETHOS ANTHROPOI DAIMON

In the beginning, even before Socrates and Plato, was Heraclitus. His three little words "Ethos anthropoi daimon," frequently rendered as "Character is fate," have been quoted again and again for twenty-five hundred years. No one can know what he meant, though few fail to offer interpretations, as this list of English translations demonstrates:

> "Man's character is his Genius."
> "Man's character is his daimon."
> "A man's character is his guardian divinity."
> "A man's character is the immortal and
>   potentially divine portion of him."
> "Man's own character is his daimon."
> "Man's character is his fate."

"Character is fate."
"Character for man is destiny."
"Habit for man, God."[4]

The *daimon* part is easy enough, for we have already accepted the translation of *daimon* as *genius* (Latin) and then transposed it into more modern terms such as "angel," "soul," "paradigm," "image," "fate," "inner twin," "acorn," "life companion," "guardian," "heart's calling." This multiplicity and ambiguity inhere in the daimon itself as a personified imaginal spirit who in Greek psychology was also your personal fate. You carried your fate with you; it was your particular accompanying genius. That's why translators of *daimon* sometimes say "fate" and sometimes "genius." But never "self."

Among native peoples on the North American continent, we find a parade of terms for the acorn as an independent spirit-soul: *yega* (Coyukon); an owl (Kwakiutl); "agate man" (Navaho); *nagual* (Central America/southern Mexico); *tsayotyeni* (Santa Ana Pueblo); *sicom* (Dakota) . . . these beings accompany, guide, protect, warn. They may even attach to a person, but they do not merge with your personal self. In fact, this "native" acorn belongs as much to the ancestors, the society, the ambient animals as it does to "you" and its power may be invoked for crops and hunting, for community inspiration and health—the actual world. The acorn stands apart from the inflated self of modern subjectivity, so separate, personal and alone. Though *your* acorn, it is neither you nor yours.

The "self" that permeates our daily language has expanded to titanic proportions. *The New Oxford English Dictionary*—the "shorter" edition!—gives ten columns in its small print to compounds of "self": "self-satisfaction," "self-control," "self-defeating," "self-approval," "self-contempt," "self-satisfied" . . . and maybe five hundred more. The majority of these compounds, which attach so many psychological phenomena to this "self" entered English usage along with the rise of rationalism and the Enlightenment, which blinded the modern eye to the invisibles, and consequently to the independence from the self of the genius and the daimon.

A daimon in the ancient world was a figure from somewhere else, neither human nor divine, something in between the two belonging to a "middle region" (*metaxu*) to which the soul also belonged. The daimon was more an intimate psychic reality than a god; it was a figure who might visit in a dream or send signals as an omen, a hunch, or an erotic urge. Eros, too, belonged in this middle region that was not truly divine and yet always partly inhuman. So for the Greeks it was clear why erotic events are always hard to locate, heavenly and cruelly inhuman both. The translation of Heraclitus' fragment into "Character is fate" keeps your life's way tightly tied to the way you perform. The most simple reading would be: If you do a mediocre job, then you have a mediocre fate.

Of course there are other readings of the phrase. Some want Heraclitus to be countering popular superstitions, which grant to the daimons all sorts of destiny-determining powers. They read Heraclitus as a moralist attacking the fatalism that justifies personal irresponsibility, as if Heraclitus were arguing against Shakespeare: "It is the stars, / The stars above us, govern our conditions" (*King Lear,* IV, iii, 35). No, says Heraclitus, it's not the stars; it's your character. But then wily Shakespeare says that too: "The fault, dear Brutus, is not in our stars, / But in ourselves" (*Julius Caesar,* I, ii, 139).

Others derive from the fragment a transcendental ego, an ancestral mentor spirit who looks after individual persons and guards their behavior, as Socrates was guarded from wrong moves by his daimon. So, this reading says, following the daimon makes for character or right behavioral habits. The daimon would be the ingrained character traits that inhibit excesses, prevent inflated pride, and get you to stick to the patterns of your image (genius). These patterns show up in how you behave. Therefore, you find your genius by looking in the mirror of your life. Your visible image shows your inner truth, so when you're estimating others, what you see is what you get. It therefore becomes critically important to see generously, or you will get only what you see; to see sharply, so that you discern the mix of traits rather than a generalized lump; and to see deeply into dark shadows, or else you will be deceived.

CHARACTER

What about *ethos,* the first term of Heraclitus' fragment? To our ears it sounds like "ethics." This loads *ethos,* a Greek word unencumbered by piousness, with all the moralism of Hebrew, Roman, and Christian religiosity. If we try to strip away the ethics from *ethos,* we find it carries more the meaning of "habit." Heraclitus might be saying that *ethos* is habitual behavior. As you conduct your life, so you are and so you shall be. It's quite illusory to hang on to a private, hidden, truer self apart from how you actually are, even if therapy promotes this grand illusion and profits from it. Instead, the realism of Heraclitus: You are how you are. "How" is the crucial term, which links life as it is habitually "behaved" with the call of your image.

Is Heraclitus, then, the first behaviorist? Is he saying, "Alter your habits and you alter your character and thus your fate"? "Never mind the underlying reasons; change your habits and your fate changes"?

I feel Heraclitus is implying much more. This behaviorism sounds too willful, too Protestant, too American, and altogether too humanistic. Though Heraclitus connects character (*ethos*) and human ethics directly with the daimon, it is *its* fate that becomes our concern. The egocentric focus of humanism makes us believe that the daimon, having chosen us to inhabit, concerns itself with our fate. But what about *its* fate?

Maybe the human task is to bring our behavior into line with its intentions, to do right by it, for its sake. What you do in your life affects your heart, alters your soul, and concerns the daimon. We make soul with our behavior, for soul doesn't come already made in heaven. It is only imaged there, an unfulfilled project trying to grow down.

The daimon then becomes the source of human ethics, and the happy life—what the Greeks called *eudaimonia*—is the life that is good for the daimon. Not only does it bless us with its calling, we bless it with our style of following.

Since "back" of the daimon are the invisibles, the ethics that please the daimon cannot be made clear and standardized. Good habits to make good character and therefore a good life cannot conform with Boy Scout principles. Instead the ethics will be daimonic and inscrutable, and will include the character of Elias Canetti going for his sister with an ax for the sake of words and of Ingmar Bergman wanting to knife his traitorous school friend for the sake of a secret fascination. It will even include the character of the Bad Seeds. The claims of the daimon do not always accord with reason, but follow their own irrational necessity. Tragic flaws and character disorders have an inhuman quality, as if following invisible orders.

The invisible source of personal consistency, for which I am using the word "habit," psychology today calls character.[5] Character refers to deep structures of personality that are particularly resistant to change. When they are socially harmful they are named character neuroses (Freud) and character disorders. These hard-to-change lines of fate are like the fingerprints of the daimon, each whorl different from every other. The very word "character" originally meant a marking instrument that cuts indelible lines and leaves traces. And "style" comes from *stilus* (Latin), a sharp instrument for incising characters (for instance, letters). No wonder style reveals character and is so hard to change; no wonder character disorders lie at the core of diagnosed psychopaths and sociopaths. Something is deeply, structurally, characterologically amiss, or missing, if they can smile and torture, kill with no remorse, betray, deceive, deny, and never wince. Serial murderers, impostors and embezzlers, obsessive pedophiles betray a consistency of style. Their habits tend to repeat; generally, they fall back rather than reform, programmed by the character of their wiring.

It is not, however, to diagnose psychopaths and their daimons that we now turn for examples of character to three eminent witnesses to the American dream. Each of these three men shows an undeviating firmness of habits and has been acclaimed for never stepping out of character. The three are also men of the middle range of circumstances and whose years bridge the history of the twentieth century: America from 1902, when Thomas E. Dewey was born in Owosso, Michigan, through 1995, when Billy Graham still functioned as a national religious monument and Oliver North was the standout folk hero of the mean.

The task in the following excursion is to single out a central configuration, the daimon in the ethos of each, and curiously similar in all three, through which we can understand what it is in their habits that has found chords of response in the American public. Through them we may glimpse a daimon that is essential to the American ethos.

AMERICAN CHARACTER

At first look these three seem very different: Governor Dewey, clipped mustache, five foot six, tight-packed in his dark suits, fastidiously careful ("when he tours a state prison, he will not touch a door handle himself, but wait for someone else to open it. If no one picks up his message, he will remove a handkerchief from his coat pocket, discreetly cover his palm, and lightly brush the metal the prisoners hold daily"). Graham fresh out of high school, age eighteen, "in a peacock-hued tie and a gabardine suit of bottle-green with thin yellow piping"; North "arriv[ing] in Vietnam in camouflage fatigues, ready to do battle. He wore a flak jacket and black greasepaint under his eyes to cut the glare, and in the field he always kept his helmet buckled. He was squared away. In addition to the .45-caliber revolver issued each officer, Ollie opted to carry a 12-gauge shotgun for extra firepower. And if that wasn't enough protection, he also wore a crucifix."[6]

One could recite a litany of their differences—generational differences; differences in educations, careers, professions; differences in youthful temperament (Graham was naive and flamboyant; North, dogged and decent; Dewey, bright and arrogant). Our eye, however, has chosen to focus on sameness.

The first piece of this sameness was their gift of undiluted energy. Dewey: dedicated, head-on, and hard-to-please executive, the first "gangbuster," as he was called; never absent a day and never missed a football practice in his entire school life. North: well-liked and "always willing to do whatever was asked of him," including the missions in Vietnam for which he was awarded "a Bronze Star with Combat 'V,' a Silver Star, two Purple Hearts and a Navy Commendation Medal"; leading charges and ignoring pain. Graham: "so lavishly energied that, in his early teens, his parents took him to be examined by a doctor. . . . One of his relatives asserts that as soon as he learned how to work a tricycle . . . he would *zoom* back and forth, his feet working so fast you couldn't see them." What brought the energies under control was a similar firmness of belief.

The second similarity among them is self-discipline. North's choice of the Marines epitomizes a life of discipline. As a young boy, he was already obedient to orders. North "didn't hang around much. . . . His mother used to blow a whistle for him when it was time to come home. . . . He was more apt to dress neater than we did." Graham "grew up in a regimen of diligent pieties in his household; by the time he was ten he had memorized all 107 articles of the Shorter Catechism." As for Dewey, his lot dropped him straight into a severely disciplined life: "When Tommy was three, he was given a bicycle with the strict admonition that it would be reclaimed if he were to fall off while riding. The child promptly mounted . . . and promptly lost it to his mother's unrelenting grip for a full year."

In college, Dewey "seems to have abstained from sowing wild oats." Graham was often smitten, was girl crazy, went to "the communal spooning ground," "kissing girls until my mouth was chapped." But "somehow I never engaged in sexual amorality. For some reason God kept me clean. . . . I never even touched a girl's breast." In high school, North "dated infrequently." When he was ten, he and a pal were mistakenly dropped off at a Brigitte Bardot movie. "Ollie's eyes fairly bugged out as she steamed across the screen. 'There's no way we ought to be seeing this,' Ollie reportedly told his pal. . . . So they got up and went to an ice-cream parlor instead."

I believe that the crucial common denominator shared by these three is their *belief,* the pure persuasive power of belief.

> When Tommy [Dewey] was seven, he dragged a cart to a neighbor's house and asked if he might collect her old newspapers to sell. . . . At the age of nine, he began selling magazines and newspapers. . . . His dedication was sometimes carried to curious extremes. . . . "Tom seemed possessed when he came around selling the *Saturday Evening Post.*" [A purchaser remembers,] "I told him I didn't want the magazine, but he just looked at me defiantly with those dark piercing eyes and left it on my desk. He gave me a dozen reasons why I should buy it. I couldn't outargue him; it was easier to become his steady customer."

During the drought and depression of the southern summer of 1936, Billy Graham, out of high school, sold Fuller Brushes door to door in both Carolinas.

> The area sales manager was absolutely overwhelmed at the Fuller Brushes that Billy sold those few weeks. . . . He didn't quite see how just one single human being could possibly sell that many brushes in that space of time. Billy himself professes, "I believed in the product. Selling those little brushes became a cause to me. I felt every family ought to have a Fuller Brush as a matter of principle." . . . "Sincerity is the biggest part of selling anything, I found out—including salvation."

He brought Fuller Brushes to his girl as gifts and brushed his own teeth with them so often and so sincerely, "his gums started receding."

North's product was America itself, rather than its symbolic representations in Fuller Brushes and the *Saturday Evening Post,* and he was equally convinced of its virtue and equally persuasive in his passion. Long before he sold it openly to the United States Senate and on TV, "America" was his belief. A high school classmate remembers: "One of the guys in school said something about how stupid the Army was. Then he said that we, meaning the U.S., shouldn't get involved in any wars overseas. Well, Larry [Ollie] got pretty mad. He told the guy, 'If you don't like living in America, you can just get the hell out.' "

Though the product may represent collective mediocrity—the brush, the magazine, the love-it-or-leave-it patriotism—there is nothing mediocre in selling performance. Habit is character, and becomes fate. This high school incident already reveals the acorn's belief in all the future foreign operations that North subsequently executed.

Ambition, high ideals, clean living, long hours: the signs of alpha animals harnessed by the work ethic, pulling big loads of reform uphill. Their values and practices, their tastes and associates may not have risen above the middlebrow range, but they nonetheless went to the peaks. By his early thirties Graham had already seized the popular evangelical imagination, drawing huge crowds of the lost and seeking—and the wealthy, too—into his tent. At age thirty-five Dewey was sworn in as district attorney of Manhattan, becoming the youngest man ever to hold this title. At thirty-eight he was close to winning the Republican nomination to run against Roosevelt, which he did four years later at age forty-two. He had already busted bosses and bootleggers, racketeers and hit men. One after another they were trapped by his relentless, meticulous prosecutions—Waxey Gordon, Dutch Schultz, Joseph Castalado (the Artichoke King), the Gorilla Boys, the Black Hand, Lucky Luciano, Jimmy Hines, and Louis Lepke of Murder, Inc.

Before he was forty, North was moving easily among the Washington power elite. Congressman Michael Barnes reports:

> He hung out with Henry [Kissinger]. . . . Ollie has a rather remarkable facility for ingratiating himself with important people. . . . Here he was hobnobbing with Supreme Court justices . . . generals and senators, and very relaxed about the whole thing. . . . Ollie was more a peer. He arrived with the imprimatur of the White House, and more often than not he was at Henry's elbow.

A few years later North was in charge of major portions of United States foreign affairs in the Caribbean (Grenada), Central America, and the Middle East (Iran, Libya, and Israel).

Graham's operations were also worldwide. As prayer man for Eisenhower, Johnson, Nixon, Ford, and Reagan, he, too, belonged to the cadre of power. Dewey may have reached fewer people, but in the modern Republican party it was he who masterminded the nominations of both Eisenhower and

Nixon, two men who dominated America in the middle years of this century. Hardly a life on this planet has not been affirmed or afflicted by the eager actions of these three men of the virtuous middle.

They stayed the course, stood for principle, kept tight the purse strings. At thirty-two, Dewey still "continued his methodical notation of every fifteen-cent shoeshine and eighty-five-cent dinner in a tiny pad." When he left the governorship of New York, state taxes were 10 percent lower than when he had first taken office. Graham, whose cause received giant donations and who golfed with the rich, "spends hours, *hours,* trying to figure out how not to make money," said his wife, Ruth. Each man married the right girl, raised his children, and stood for honesty and, above all, self-control, the idealized habits of middle America's Great White Way.

Perhaps the one god that provides the common denominator here is just this habit of self-control. But not self-control as such; rather, its shadow: control in service of belief, in particular, of a belief that required control over the shadow.

This is abundantly clear in North's statements of belief before Congress. There was an enemy to be faced: international Communism and the compromising that weakens the patriotic fiber of America. Things must be put in order. Dewey's target was crime, the gangsters in the dark tenements of Manhattan, the Irish Tammany Hall, the Jewish racketeers and the Italian mobsters and extortionists. Dewey was cleaning up America, remaking it on the model of his own fastidiousness. Graham's charge was the cleansing of the spirit throughout the world; his enterprise was called a crusade.

Control over the weakness and evil in self, and control over evil in others go together: for Dewey, by convicting criminals to the penitentiaries; for North, by bombing the bad guys in El Salvador, Grenada, and Libya; for Graham, by beating sin and Satan through converting sinners to Christ. In all, belief justifies the control and the *furor agendi* with which the shadow is opposed, whether the shadow be

Tammany Hall, or the mullahs of Tehran, or the Evil One himself.

Is it belief in the cause, or belief in belief itself? When accused of "intellectual suicide," Graham answered: "I know I just believe. I just know what belief, without question, without reserve, has let God do in my life. . . . I have decided to believe." North lodged his defense of lying to Congress upon the rock of belief in America and its commander in chief. The faith that moves mountains becomes its own shadow. The nobility of the ideals hollows out as the belief intensifies. What did Santayana say about fanaticism? It loses the purpose and redoubles the effort.

After his unexpected loss to Truman in the 1948 election, Dewey put it behind him. "That's that, I am going to go ahead," he said, and indeed he did, denying by machinations of power the depth of his rejection by the electorate. North's redoubled effort on behalf of his belief included his plan while at Annapolis to alter (or steal, from a closed office after hours) the record of his leg injuries, which might have kept him out of the Marines.

In his devotion to his beliefs each tried to eliminate what might have held him back. This is called denial. Of Graham, his wife said: "Of course he had doubts but not for long—because he never really *entertains* them." His ultimate denial followed Nixon's fall from power—and from Graham's grace. So firm was his belief, so unentertaining was he of his doubts, that Graham never picked up on Nixon's shadow. When it growled forth from the Watergate tapes, Graham entered the deepest depression of his life and suffered a crisis of faith. He paced, bit his fingernails, was nauseated, could not sleep. He was temporarily cornered in the contradiction posed by belief—that it requires some sort of suicide; intellectual, moral, perceptual. "I really believed [in Nixon] as the greatest possibility ever for leading this country on into its greatest and finest days. He had the character for it. I'd never heard him tell a lie." "Those tapes revealed a man I never knew; I never saw that side of him."

From blindness to denial. In time Graham recovered from this trial; faith refound, restored to innocence, he kept on going.

The common denominator in all three is the invincibility of belief. Though each can be found morally reprehensible—Graham for his denial, North for his lies, Dewey for his manipulations—belief allowed them to go forward uncorrupted in the midst of dirty doings, untouched by their own shadows, innocent. And I submit that it is precisely this American habit of belief that appeals to our Main Street mediocrity. Therefore, this same component—whether it be named innocence by literary critics, denial by psychologists, or belief by believers—must be the essence of the American character, which accounts for why Dewey, Graham, and North are such eminent representatives of its style.

We must also admit, despite our previous judgment against mediocrity as a psychologically valid term, that we have uncovered the psychological condition that generates American mediocrity. The capacity to deny, to remain innocent, to use belief as a protection against sophistications of every sort—intellectual, aesthetic, moral, psychological—keeps the American character from awakening. The American character remains blind to the fact that the virtues of mediocrity—those pieties of disciplined energy, order, self-control, probity, and faith—are themselves messengers of the devil they would overcome.

We need to emphasize the exceptional in a society that now, owing to a reverse snobbism, is enthralled with the ordinary, with the newly knighted hardworking, taxpaying, moral, and deserving middle class. If the society suffers a loss of soul, a loss of daimonic inspiration, of angel and genius, then before starting off in search of them, why not ask what might be driving them away? Maybe inviting mediocrity in—just doing a passable job as a team player, not upsetting the boat, holding on to "family values," joining the Wal-Mart community, staying cool, fearing extremists and ungrounded underground ideas—is precisely what drives the invisibles away.

Why is the exceptional suspect? Do we resist it because we fear inspiration, conceiving it to be an elitist condition of the private mind, privileging communication with spirits over community with peers? And what about a culture that imagines inspiration to be asocial—will it not cling ever more tenaciously to uninspired mediocrity?

Let us not forget that societies are elevated and rewarded by those who are inspired: the emergency nurse; the teacher of the year; the basketball guard who arcs a perfect three-pointer. The inspired moment does not invalidate the team, but belongs to the context of the team and to its wider hometown public. To sink the shot in the final second and thereby save a crucial game is not merely an isolated heroic act. It reconstitutes the hero itself within an archetypal context: The hero is the one who performs inspired deeds for the glory of the city and its gods. Our civilization's egocentric, competitive notions of inspired actions make us miss their societal service. "Inspiration" means simply "inbreathing of spirit," not "exaltation of the spirited."

Some societies require their members to seek inspiration for the sake of the society. For instance, Native American vision quests, sweat lodges, peyote sessions, and dances; Quaker meetings, which attend the appearance of the indwelling spirit. The social philosophy here is that you can best serve others when you are in service to the Others.

I have not been adulating fame for its own sake, but rather to display the daimon in an enlarging mirror. To use the exceptional person as an example of an idea is not to literalize exceptionality as embodied only in exceptional people. The persons in this book are *personifications* of the effect of the invisible daimon. They are heightened visibilities of the daimonic phenomenon. These outstanding figures make human the general idea that *all* lives have an exceptional component that has not been accounted for by the usual psychological and biographical theories.

Manolete and Ingmar Bergman, for instance, are availabilities. They are not available for imitation or cloning, but as exhibitions of the daimon. The blessing shown in their lives to such an exceptional degree is a universal phenomenon. It is yours, too. They are enlarged witnesses to the availability of blessing.

This old method of magnification aims to inspire the weak and weary to feel again the grandeur latent in the acorn of Everyman and Everywoman no matter their statistical mediocrity. But only after we have invalidated mediocrity as a psychological concept may we legitimately enthuse over exceptionality. Otherwise such enthusiasm, our name-dropping and our introducing the reader to so many stars, would appear to be snobbish fawning over the famous. So we have kicked the notions of "mean," "average," "middle," and "mediocre" out of psychology altogether and back to where they better serve (economics, epidemiology, sociology, marketing), that readers may imagine themselves more in terms of the extraordinary for which the models in this chapter and book serve.

North and Graham and Dewey are each exceptional; whatever clings to them as mediocre comes from snobbish sniggerings at Graham's gabardine suits or Dewey's "little-man-on-the-wedding-cake" look or North's good-boyism. Thereby we miss the fact that each is faithful to his acorn and exemplifies his particular character including its vices in every consistent motion of his conduct.

In a society and at a time when oddballs are shelved in shelters, medicated into serotonin serenity, and recovered by groups from compelling individual intensities, when anything too different becomes marginalized, it becomes especially important for the consciousness of the nation to actively affirm the extraordinary. If eminence depends on fate and fate on character, then the three terms may also be reversed: to improve character, moral instruction is not enough. We can ignore the exhortations of William Bennett and Allan Bloom, and rather look at fate and particularly at the fate of the eminent. Their images—their courage, their ambition, and their risk—are our instructors. These three extreme representatives of the middle, who fired the faith and political engagements of millions of Americans, do not have middling characters themselves.

Images of eminence from the middle show that the middle is also a path. This allows us to grasp the innate value of the middle rather than sneering at it for its collective petit-bourgeois limitations or retreating into it for fear of the edge. Despite whatever snobbism the chapter may still betray, it is a chapter written with idealism, for I have tried to change "mediocrity" from a term of contempt into a concept of value where the daimon may also appear. The word remains a social put-down until we uncover within each example of mediocrity the specific character it carries, that eachness of the acorn.

A DEMOCRAT'S PLATONISM

The underlying tension in this chapter is one I have wrestled with for a long time. Twenty-five years ago, maybe more, Gilles Quispel, the Dutch scholar of early Christian Gnosis and the sects of the time, and I were sitting beside Lake Maggiore, he puffing his pipe and twinkling with a certain malicious glee like an old Dutch sea captain from a Conrad novel, when he asked me, "How can you, Hillman, be both a Platonist and a democrat?"

Quispel had glimpsed the daimon of my destiny, and so the question has taken some years to answer. Of course, assumed by the question is a certain common view of Plato and Platonism—that is, that they are totalitarian, elitist, patriarchal, and have laid an authoritative groundwork for the authoritarian state. Quispel's question assumes, as well, a certain notion of democracy as popularist, secular, and unanchored in transcendence. Democracy may have Founding Fathers, but not angels. Hence Quispel's question: How can one embrace elitism *and* populism, eternal principles *and* vagaries of persuasion—or, in the classical language of philosophy, with which Quispel was far more familiar than I, how can one embrace the realms of Truth *and* Opinion. This conundrum has bothered Western thinkers as far back as Parmenides.

In our nation the distinction between truth and opinion has solidified into the wall between church and state, between revealed truth and polls of popular opinion. Yet the Declaration of Independence asserts that the American democratic state is founded upon a transcendent "Truth": "All Men are created equal."

What is the basis of this claim? Inequalities are there before the first breath. Any nurse in the birthing section of a hospital can confirm that inequality exists from the beginning. Infants differ from one another. Genetic studies show innate differences of skills, temperaments, intensities. As for the circumstances into which we descend, what could be more unequal than our environments? Some are disadvantaged, others privileged by nurture and nature both—and from the beginning.

Since neither nurture nor nature gives equality, where do we even get the idea? It cannot be induced from the facts of life; nor can equality be reduced to a factor common to all human beings, such as erect posture, symbolic language, or manipulation of fire, because individual differences elaborate the common factor in billions of ways. Equality can only be deduced from uniqueness, from what the Scholastic philosophers called the "principle of individuality." I am imagining this uniqueness as the *haeccitas* (Medieval Latin for "thisness") in the genius as the formative factor given with each person's birth so that he or she is *this* one and not some other one, anyone, no one.

So equality must be axiomatic, a given; as the Declaration of Independence says, that we are equal is a truth self-evident. We are equal by the logic of eachness. Each by definition is distinct from every other each and therefore equal as such. We are equal because each brings a specific calling into the world, and we are unequal in every other respect—unfairly, unjustly, utterly unequal, except in the fact of each's unique genius. Democracy rests, therefore, upon the foundations of an acorn.

The acorn pushes beyond the edge; its principal passion is realization. The calling demands untrammeled freedom of pursuit, a freedom "live on arrival," and this freedom cannot be guaranteed by society. (If the opportunities for freedom are decreed by society, then society has the superior power, and freedom becomes subject to society's authority.) As democratic equality can find no other logical ground but the uniqueness of each individual's calling, so freedom is founded upon the full independence of calling. When the writers of the Declaration of Independence stated that all are born equal, they saw that the proposition necessarily entailed a companion: All are born free. It is the fact of calling that makes us equal, and the act of calling that demands we be free. The principle guarantor of both is the invisible individual genius.

Let us forgo both reading Plato as a nasty fascist with unreal ideals and imagining democracy as a directionless collection of opinionated victims. Then we may see that Platonism and democracy do not need to repel each other like the ends of opposing magnets, but are both built upon the same charge: the importance of the soul of the individual. Plato's state exists for the sake of that soul, not for the sake of the state or for any particular group within it. In fact, the main analogy running through his *Republic* is the parallel between the layers of the soul and the strata of the state. What we do in the state we do to the soul, and what we do in the soul, we do for the state—if Platonism is carried to term and not aborted before its implications are fully formed.

Furthermore, as we have seen in this chapter, the only theoretical guarantor of the individuality required by democracy and for the sake of whom the American democracy was brought into being is that same soul, here called angel, acorn, genius, by any name as sweet. Platonism and democracy share a vision of the principal importance of the individual soul.

This soul or daimon or genius, by the way, also seems to be not only a Platonist in its origins in Plato's own myth, but also a democrat, because it enters the world of interactions; it shows itself in geography, as if to say it so enters the world that it takes on the garments of place, as if it wants to abide in the world and live in its body. Only theologians and shamans dare speak about the invisibles apart from the visible world. Death and another realm are surely not the aim of the acorn's push, but rather the visible world, where it acts as guide. Loss of the daimon collapses democratic society into a crowd of shoppers wandering a mall of mazes in search of the exit. But there is no exit without the guide of an individual direction.

So, Professor Quispel, should we meet again under the thick trees, I'd say Platonism and democracy can get along with each other very nicely. Both are based on soul. Both are similarly concerned with how the soul can be in the world and in the best manner fulfilled. To focus on the best and on fulfillment does not force elitism. Nor does it abandon democracy.

CODA: A NOTE
ON METHODOLOGY

Is it a mistake to choose an organic metaphor for this theory? Doesn't the very term "acorn" put us immediately into an organic model of natural growth and attach our theory both to genetic determinism and to evolution through time, two ideas our theory intends to circumvent, even undermine? Is the theory not being subverted willy-nilly by its own name?

The naming of species, of heavenly bodies, of diseases always entraps the thing named in a root metaphor, claiming it for a worldview, as for instance the naming of mountains and islands during the period of colonial explorations. The names of European potentates and heroic scientists colonized all sorts of natural phenomena: planets, plants, processes. Liberation movements cast off the oppression of words that represented the old order. Should we not let go of the residue of evolutionary organicism represented by the word "acorn" and rename this theory the essence theory, the image theory, or the genius theory, or even call it, boldly, the theory of angelic psychology?

I hold to "acorn" because it demonstrates how to read organic images without falling prey to organicism. If we are able to use a natural image in an unnatural way, then we will have shown, by means of the term "acorn," the very kernel of our archetypal point of view, which aims to turn the organic, time-bound developmental view of human life backward on itself, to read life against the stream of time. If we want to revise the developmental model of human nature, we may as well take on one of its seed images to begin with.

We keep the term, but we shall dislodge it from our usual patterns of thought. It is not the acorn that needs to be discarded, but the habit of thinking of acorns only naturalistically and temporally.

However, once the acorn is imagined archetypally, imagined as an archetypal idea, it is not confined by either the laws of nature or the processes of time. A narrow, naturalistic definition of "acorn" as the seed or fruit of the oak tree establishes only one level of its meaning, giving it only a literal, botanical place in the mind. This first level can block others from showing; the acorn also has *mythological, morphological,* and *etymological* meanings.

The acorn is also a *mythical symbol;* it is a *shape;* and it is a *word* with ancestries, tangents and implications, and suggestive power. By amplifying "acorn" in these different directions, as we are now about to do, we will be carried beyond the naturalistic strictures of its standard meaning. And by turning the sense of "acorn" and expanding its potential we shall be demonstrating how to turn the biology of the human beyond its organic setting.

Let's take the mythological symbolism of oak and acorn, for a start. In the ancient Mediterranean and in northern Germanic and Celtic Europe, the oak was a magical ancestor tree. Whatever was closely associated with the oak partook of its power—birds nesting there, gall wasps in its boles, bees and their honey, the entwining mistletoe, and, of course, the oak's acorns. Oaks were father trees that drew down fire bolts from the sky and belonged to such major gods as Zeus and Donar and Jupiter and Wotan. And they were mother trees (*proterai materes*—first mothers, in Greek), giving birth to humans in the various myths that tell tales of how humans first came to be in the world. We are born from acorns, as acorns are born from oaks. And as the words "tree" and "truth" are cognates, so the tree in its acorn form bears truth, too, *in nuce.* Such would be a rhapsodic reading of the little cupped pellets lying around the forest floor.[1]

Mythological language composes in images what conceptual language states in sentences. The reason acorns are images of primordial personality is that oaks are inhabited by oracular soul figures. Oaks in particular are soul trees, because they are the haunts of bees and harbor honey, which was considered in Mediterranean antiquity, and in many other parts of the world, to be a divine nectar for the gods, an otherworldly primordial "soul food." But more significantly, oaks are soul trees because nymphs, diviners, and priestesses lived in or by them and could express the oaks' foreknowledge and understanding of events in hints and sayings. All tall trees are wise, according to the West African teacher Malidoma Somé, because their movement is imperceptible, the connection between above and below so firm, their physical presence so generously useful. The oak, with such size and age and beauty and solidity, would therefore be especially wise, and its acorns will carry all the tree's knowledge compressed into a tiny core, as endless angels of vast awareness can dance on the head of a pin. Invisibles require minimal space. But to some they can speak loud and clear, and they do so from oaks.

Whether this speaking was heard in the rustling of wind in the leaves, the creaking of limbs, the rubbing of branches, or without any external verifiable sensations, it could be interpreted by specially gifted priestesses, as for instance at Dodona in northwestern Greece, already mentioned in Homer. People came to ask the oracular tree about their fate. Embodied in the oak was knowledge of fate, and so an inquirer could ask: "Gerioton asks Zeus concerning a wife whether it is better for him to take one." "Callicrates asks the god whether I will have offspring from Nike the wife whom I have by remaining with her and praying to which of the gods." "Cleotas asks Zeus and Dione if it is better and profitable for him to keep sheep." Or, to uncover the more simple yet also stressful mysteries of life: "Did Dorkilos steal the cloth?"[2]

Assumed in these oracular oaken practices at Dodona and elsewhere are two facts relevant to our thesis. First, the oak knows what is concealed from ordinary eyes; second, this knowledge can be revealed to persons, in most cases women, who can "hear" and let it speak through them. Robert Graves claims the Dodona priestesses, and Gallic Druids too, literally chewed acorns to induce prophetic trance.[3] Parke, who collected the evidence, does not report the interpreters' answers. *What* they heard through the tree may have been enormously important to the inquirers, but for our inquiry what matters is *that* they heard.

The acorn, botanically, is like an angiosperm, a fully endowed embryonic plant. The essence of the oak is all there at once. Theologically, the acorn is like one of Augustine's *rationes seminales* or seminal reasons. As far back as the Stoics, Gnostics, and Platonists such as Philo, some ancient thought held that the world was filled with *spermatikoi logoi*—word seeds or germinal ideas. These are present in the world from its beginning as the primordial *a priori* that gives form to each thing. And these spermatic words make it possible for each thing to tell of its own nature—to ears that can hear. The idea that nature speaks, especially through the voice of a talking oak, remained a vivid fantasy through the ages and was still a subject of paintings a hundred years ago.[4]

Awakening to the original seed of one's soul and hearing it speak may not be easy. How do we recognize its voice; what signals does it give? Before we can address these questions, we need to notice our own deafness, the obstructions that make us hard of hearing: the reductionism, the literalism, the scientism of our so-called common sense. For it is hard to get it through our hard heads that there can be messages from elsewhere more important to the conduct of our lives than what comes through Centel and Internet, meanings that don't slide in fast, free, and easy, but are encoded particularly in the painful pathologized events that perhaps are the only ways the gods can wake us up.

A Scandinavian tale in Jacob Grimm's *Teutonic Mythology* expresses this idea in the language of myth.

> The big old giant Skrymir went to sleep under a big old oak. Thor came and hit him on the head with his hammer. Skrymir woke up wondering if a leaf had fallen on him. He went back to sleep and snored outlandishly. Thor hit him again, harder; the giant again woke up and asked whether an acorn had fallen on his head. He went back to sleep. Thor

hit him even a greater blow to his head with that divine hammer, but the giant, rousing himself from sleep, said, "Must be birds up in the tree; they must have dropped on my head."[5]

The acorn theory is bird shit to the giant. Giants are notoriously slow-witted, cursed with physical thinking, short-sighted, and always hungry (because they are so empty?). Skrymir is our literalist, our reductionist, who never can quite get it. And so the giant is counterpoised in fairy tales with the cunning animal, the elf or gnome, the savvy maiden or the little tailor. These would never equate an acorn with a leaf blown by or a drop of dung. They can pick up a metaphor when they see one, while the giant can only think in *onlys*, reducing everything to its least common denominator so that he never has to leave the cave or awaken from his stentorian snoring stupor. Little wonder that when we were very small we all feared giants and thrilled to stories about those who could kill them, like David or Jack, or outwit them, like Ulysses. The giant, with its grown-up stupidity, threatens a child's imagination, a child's ecological connections with a wondrous world. Stupidity is the giant that misses the small things. After all, it's a bean that saves Jack, and a pebble that saves David from Goliath. The giant in the psyche is another name for Plato's cave of ignorance, and so it's in a cave that Ulysses meets Cyclops, the one-eyed giant, who takes literally Ulysses' witty way with words and is thereby fooled.

Although the talking oak spoke oracularly through women, and though all trees have been categorized as symbolically female because of their sheltering, nourishing, cyclical behavior, and because they provide the basic *hyle*, or matter, for so many human actions, the oak and the acorn were imagined as particularly male. Not only was the oak a Great-Father-God-tree (Jupiter in Roman Europe and Donar in the North), but also— and now we move from the mythic to the morphological—because the acorn was called the *juglans*, or glans penis of Jupiter.

The English language hides from us what many other languages reveal: the smooth head of the penis and its rolled-back and cupping foreskin display the shape of an acorn. In German, *Eichel* means both acorn and glans. In French the word for both is *gland;* in Latin, *glans;* in Greek, *balanos;* in Spanish, *bellota.* Medical writers like Celsus and naturalists like Pliny and Aristotle made this equation of penis-head and acorn, and fertility rites conjoined the mythological understanding of the oak with the morphological appearance of its fruit.

Etymologically, at our third level of elaboration, the word "acorn" is related to "acre," "act," and "agent." "Acorn" derives most closely from Old High German *akern* (fruit, produce), not merely as a seed but as an already fulfilled fruition. *Actus* (action, activity, agency) is associated with "acorn" so that the acorn must be understood as an accomplished result and not merely as a beginning (in a developmental sense) of a new tree. The entire order of thinking is reversed.

More distantly, "acorn" comes from the Sanskrit via the Greek *ago, agein* and their various forms and derivatives, which mean basically to push, to direct toward, to lead or guide. (A chief in Homer is an *agos.*) The imperative *age, agete* means: move, get going, go. From this same ancient stem derive your "agenda" and your "agony," the ordinary experience of the pushy "acorn" in any of our lives.[6]

Isn't it surprising to find this cornucopia of verbal riches packed into the acorn? And we're not done yet, because the Greek word for glans penis and for acorn (*balanos*) derives from *ballos* and *bal,* meaning that which is cast or falls, like the nut from the tree, or is thrown, like the throw of the dice. And it also means to fling. There is a parallel here between this root, *ballos,* for the fall or throw that may decide your case, and the source of the word "case" itself, which comes from the Latin *caere,* to fall. Your case is simply the fate that befalls you, and your case history tells the story of how your lot has been cast. A fatal element lies condensed into the very word "acorn," and your life is its project.

Cognate with *balanos,* acorn, is *ballizon,* to throw the leg about, and *balletus,* a throwing, from which our words "ballistic" and, via the Romance languages, our "ballet" and "ball" as a large dancing event. A primordial loveliness resides in the ety-mological acorn; it dances with life and is full of projections; and it is as sensitive as the tip of the penis. Moreover, it is ballistic with action. All this we have harvested from its myths, its shape, and its words. It seems precisely the right image for the theory we are examining.

———

The acorn theory of biography seems to have sprung from and to speak the language of the *puer eternus,* the archetype of the eternal youth who embodies a timeless, everlasting, yet fragile connection with the invisible otherworld.[7] In human lives he accounts for the precocious child and the undeniable call of fate, such as we saw in Menuhin and Garland. He appears espe-cially as the dominant archetype in those visionary figures who make their mark early, disturb the commonplace, and vanish into legend, like James Dean and Clyde Barrow and Kurt Cobain, like Mozart and Keats and Shelley, like Chatterton and Rimbaud and Schubert, like Alexander the Great (dead at thirty) and Jesus (dead at thirty-three), like that brilliant boy Alexander Hamilton, at eighteen already a Founding Father of a revolution and an idealized new nation. Charlie Parker was gone at thirty-five, Bunny Berigan at thirty-three, Jimmy Blan-ton at twenty-three, Buddy Holly at twenty-two; and think of the dead young painters like Jean-Michel Basquiat and Keith Haring. Any of us could make a list—and not only of the cele-brated and notorious, but of those elemental young men and women who touched our lives with their promise and then were gone.

And of course the *puer eternus,* as archetype, is beyond gen-der: Jean Harlow, dead at twenty-six, Carole Lombard at thirty-three, Patsy Cline at thirty. Janis Joplin, Eva Hesse, Moira Dwyer, Amelia Earhart . . .

These figures of fame find backing in figures of myth: Icarus and Horus, who flew higher than their fathers; fleet Atalanta; young Lancelot and Gawain; marvelous Theseus; St. Sebastian, pierced through the breast; boy David, sweet singer of psalms;

Ganymede, cup-bearer of ambrosia on Olympus; and all the luminous lovers, Adonis, Paris, and Narcissus.

Colloquial speech calls bright young stars "geniuses." Especially relevant to this connection of genius with *puer,* of glans with acorn, is the Roman primary identity of the *genius* with procreative phallic power so that the spontaneity of the penis represents, *pars pro toto,* the *genius* itself.[8] For this reason a man may speak of his member as having its own intuitive eye, its own will, and feel that it plays a major role in his fate. Men may fetishize the organ, conferring upon it the mysterious motions of an invisible divinity. This delusional, narcissistic, obsessive, overvalued idea of the penis (in the terms of conventional therapy) can best be accounted for by placing this style of *puer* phallicism against a background in myth.

The *puer* figure—Baldur, Tammuz, Jesus, Krishna—brings myth into reality. The message is mythical, stating that he, the myth, so easily wounded, so easily slain, yet always reborn, is the seminal substructure of all imaginative enterprise. These figures, like myths themselves, seem not "real." They feel insubstantial; tales of them say they are quick to bleed, fall, wither, vanish. But their devotion to the other world—they are missionaries of transcendence—is never forsaken. Somewhere over the rainbow. *"La lune, c'est mon pays,"* says the white-faced clown in the film *Les Enfants du Paradis.* Looney and lonely, lovely and pale— this is the *puer,* touching earth tentatively, and of course promiscuously, by the glans of the penis, wanting to be received by the ground.

The devotion to an altered state of mind propels *puer* fantasy toward altering the mind of the state by setting fires of rebellion. The calling from the eternal world demands that this world here be turned upside down, to restore its nearness to the moon; lunacy, love, poetics. Flower power, Woodstock, Berkeley, the cry of the students of Paris '68: *"Imagination au pouvoir."* No gradualism, no compromise because eternity doesn't make deals with time. Inspiration and vision are results in themselves. But then what happens? Immortal ideals fall to mortality: Kent State; then baby boomers and business. "Golden girls and lads all must, / As chimney-sweepers, come to dust." Manolete, bleeding in the sand.

Not only a biography can be touched by an archetypal figure. There are archetypal styles of theories as well. Any theory that is affected by the *puer* will show dashing execution, an appeal to the extraordinary, and a show-off aestheticism. It will claim timelessness and universal validity, but forgo the labors of proof. It will have that *puer* dance in it, will imagine ambitiously and rebel against convention. A *puer*-inspired theory will also limp among the facts, even collapse when met with the questioning inquiries of so-called reality, which is the position taken by the *puer*'s classical opponent, the gray-faced king or Saturn figure, old hardnose, hardass, hardhat. He wants statistics, examples, studies, not images, visions, stories. Knowing about these constellations and how they affect what we read and how we react to what we read helps readers find where they are on the archetypal map—at one moment entranced by the revolution in ideas, at another thoroughly skeptical of the bullshit.

This kind of self-reflection belongs to psychological method. Unlike the methods used by other disciplines when positing their ideas, an archetypal psychology is obliged to show its own mythical premises, how it is begging its first question, in this case the myth of the acorn. Because theories are not merely cooked up in the head or induced from cold data, they represent the dramas of myth in conceptual terms, and the drama is played out in arguments over paradigm shifts.

———

Having uncovered the *puer* in our method, let us go on with the acorn. Galen, the learned and prolific medical writer (A.D. 129 to 199), confirms the ancient belief that acorns are a primordial food, which is a mythical way of saying that you feed off your inner kernel. Your calling is your psyche's first nourishment. Galen said that the Arcadians were still eating acorns even after the Greeks had learned to cultivate cereals. This is another way of saying that the support of the acorn precedes the practical civilizing effects of your natural mother, the mother world of

Demeter-Ceres, the nourishing civilizing goddess after whom cereal is named. The acorn is a gift of nature before nurture, but a nature that is mythical and virgin (that is, never known, never grasped); so acorns, according to Sir James George Frazer's compilations, belonged to the realm of Artemis, who presided at childbirth.

Then, and up into modern times in French and English poetry and painting, this Arcadia of the ur-acorn was the imaginal landscape of primitive nature, similar to Eden or Paradise, where the untrammeled natural soul lived in accord with nature. Therapy has transplanted Arcadia to childhood; the natural being, feeding on acorns, therapy has christened the inner child. Replacing the Garden of Eden, filled with animals and serpents and sin and knowledge, as well as replacing the Arcadia of rough acorn-eaters with an abused and idealized inner child is an abuse itself. For the pagan mind you did not go "back to childhood," nor did you idolize innocence to recover the idylls of free being; you went to Arcadia, an imaginal terrain where we are cared for by our genius.

In the acorn lies not only the completion of life before it is lived but the dissatisfied frustration of unlived life. The acorn sees, it knows, it urges—but what can it do? This discrepancy between seed and tree, between the spindle in the lap of the gods in heaven and the traffic in the lap of the family on earth, packs the acorn with the fury of incapacity, of reach without grasp; the acorn is like a tiny child empurpled with rage because it cannot do what it imagines.

Although the inner taste of the acorn may be nourishing, and communion with the angel sweet, the acorn is also bitter. It is astringent and tannic. It shrinks back; says no, as Socrates' daimon only cautioned negations. Maybe that's why actual acorns must be soaked and leached, boiled and blanched again and again, undergoing long softening before their meat can be ground into palatable flour. As the recipes say: "You'll know they're done when they no longer taste bitter." Inside the beautiful *puer* is a terrifying, even toxic, bitterness. See it in the gestures of Basquiat, the sounds of Cobain, Hendrix, Joplin, the suicidal desperation that can't wait into the time of the oak. Theories, too, are afflicted with shadow. The acorn theory and the extraordinary lift to life that it offers—vision, beauty, destiny—is also a tough nut to swallow.

This coda proved to be a necessary and final excursus on method. It tied the acorn theory with its founding image and tied the founding image yet further out to a mythical configuration called *puer eternus.* By means of this excursus I was able to show how one can transplant an organic metaphor from its usual pot in a philosophy of organicism, which would have confined our acorn theory in a developmental model of human life.

Life is not only a natural process; it is as well, and even more, a mystery. To account for life's occluded revelations by analogies with nature commits a "naturalistic fallacy," that is, assuming psychic life obeys only natural laws as described, for instance, by evolution and genetics. Humans ever and again try to crack the soul's code, to unlock the secrets of its nature. But what if its nature is not natural and not human? Suppose what we seek is not only something else, but somewhere else, in fact, having no "where" at all despite the call that beckons us to search. There is, therefore, nowhere to look beyond the fact of the call. It seems wiser to attend to the call than to avoid it by searching for its source.

The invisibility at the heart of things was traditionally named the *deus absconditus,* the "concealed god," that could be spoken of only in images, metaphors, and paradoxical conundrums, gems of immense worth buried within giant mountains, sparks that contain the flammable force of wildfire. The most important, said this tradition, is always the least apparent. The acorn is one such metaphor, and the acorn theory draws upon this tradition that goes back to Blake and Wordsworth, to the German Romantics, and to Marsilio Ficino and Nicholas of Cusa in the Renaissance.

As the acorn is one such metaphor of smallness, so, too, are the daimon and the soul metaphors. They are even smaller than small because they belong among the invisibles. For the soul is not a measurable entity, not a substance, not a force—even if we are called by the force of its claims. Nothing corporeal at all, says Ficino, and therefore the daimon's nature and the soul's code cannot be encompassed by physical means—only curious thought, devotional feeling, suggestive intuition, and daring imagination, each a mode of puer knowing.

In keeping with the specific archetypal figure of the puer, this theory is meant to inspire and revolutionize, and also to excite a fresh erotic attachment to its subject: your subjective and personal autobiography, the way you imagine your life, because how you imagine life strongly impinges upon the raising of children, the attitudes toward the symptoms and disturbances of adolescents, your individuality in a democracy, the strangeness of old age and the duties of dying—in fact, upon the professions of education, psychotherapy, the writing of biography, and the life of the citizen.

NOTES

CHAPTER 1: IN A NUTSHELL

1. E. R. Dodds, *Proclus: The Elements of Theology,* 2d ed. (Oxford: Oxford Univ. Press, 1963), 313–321.
2. Edward B. Tylor, *Primitive Culture,* vol. 1 (London, 1871), 387.
3. Åke Hultkrantz, *Conceptions of the Soul Among North American Indians* (Stockholm: Statens Etnografiska Museum, 1953), 387.
4. Jane Chance Nitzsche, *The Genius Figure in Antiquity and the Middle Ages* (New York: Columbia Univ. Press, 1975), 18, 19.
5. Sid Colin, *Ella: The Life and Times of Ella Fitzgerald* (London: Elm Tree Books, 1986), 2.
6. R. G. Collingwood, *An Autobiography* (Oxford: Oxford Univ. Press, 1939), 3–4.
7. Barnaby Conrad, *The Death of Manolete* (Boston: Houghton Mifflin, 1958), 3–4.
8. Evelyn Fox Keller and W. H. Freeman, *A Feeling for the Organism: The Life and Work of Barbara McClintock* (New York: W. H. Freeman, 1983), 22.
9. Yehudi Menuhin, *Unfinished Journey* (New York: Alfred A. Knopf, 1976), 22–23.
10. Ibid.
11. Colette, *Earthly Paradise: An Autobiography,* trans. Herma Briffault, Derek Coltman, and others, Robert Phelps, ed. (New York: Farrar, Straus and Giroux, 1966), 48, 76, 77.

12. Golda Meir, *My Life* (New York: Putnam, 1975), 38–39.

13. Eleanor Roosevelt, *You Learn by Living* (New York: Harper and Bros., 1960), 30.

14. Blanche Wiesen Cook, *Eleanor Roosevelt,* vol. 1, *1884–1933* (New York: Viking Penguin, 1992), 70–72.

15. Roosevelt, *You Learn by Living,* 18.

16. Brian Crozier, *Franco: A Biographical History* (London: Eyre and Spottiswoode, 1967), 34–35.

17. Desmond Young, *Rommel: The Desert Fox* (New York: Harper and Bros., 1950), 12.

18. References to Peary, Stefansson, and Gandhi drawn from Victor Goertzel and Mildred G. Goertzel, *Cradles of Eminence* (Boston: Little, Brown, 1962).

19. James Hillman, "What Does the Soul Want—Adler's Imagination of Inferiority," in *Healing Fiction* (Dallas: Spring Publications, 1994).

20. Steven Naifeh and Gregory W. Smith, *Jackson Pollock: An American Saga* (New York: Clarkson Potter, 1989), 62, 50–51.

21. David Irving, *The Trail of the Fox* (New York: E. P. Dutton, 1977), 453.

22. Albert Rothenberg, *Creativity and Madness: New Findings and Old Stereotypes* (Baltimore: Johns Hopkins Univ. Press, 1990), 8.

23. Elias Canetti, *The Tongue Set Free: Remembrance of a European Childhood* (London: André Deutsch, 1988), 28–29.

24. Peter R. Breggin and Ginger R. Breggin, *The War Against Children: The Government's Intrusion into Schools, Families and Communities in Search of a Medical "Cure" for Violence* (New York: St. Martin's Press, 1994).

25. Mary Sykes Wylie, "Diagnosing for Dollars?" *The Family Therapy Networker* 19(3) (1995): 23–69.

26. Patricia Cox, *Biography in Late Antiquity: A Quest for the Holy Man* (Berkeley: Univ. of California Press, 1983).

27. Edgar Wind, *Pagan Mysteries in the Renaissance* (Harmondsworth, England: Penguin, 1967), 238.

28. Wallace Stevens, "Notes Toward a Supreme Fiction," in *The Collected Poems of Wallace Stevens* (New York: Alfred A. Knopf, 1978), 383.

CHAPTER 2: GROWING DOWN

1. Gershom Scholem, ed., *Zohar—The Book of Splendor: Basic Readings from the Kabbalah* (New York: Schocken Books, 1963), 91.
2. Charles Ponce, *Kabbalah* (San Francisco: Straight Arrow Books, 1973), 137.
3. Plato, *Republic*, trans. Paul Shorey, in *Plato: The Collected Dialogues*, Edith Hamilton and Huntington Cairns, eds., Bollingen Series 71 (New York: Pantheon, 1963), 614ff.
4. Gerhard Kittel, ed., *Theological Dictionary of the New Testament*, 3d ed., vol. 3 (Grand Rapids, Mich.: Eerdmans, 1968).
5. Plato, *Republic*, 617d.
6. Plotinus, *Enneads*, vol. 2, trans. A. H. Armstrong, Loeb ed. (Cambridge, Mass.: Harvard Univ. Press, 1967), 3.15.
7. Joel Covitz, "A Jewish Myth of a Priori Knowledge," *Spring 1971: An Annual of Archetypal Psychology* (Zurich: Spring Publications, 1971), 55.
8. Aristotle, *Nicomachean Ethics*, trans. Martin Ostwald (Indianapolis: Bobbs-Merrill, 1962), 1106b.
9. Quotes re Judy Garland drawn from David Shipman, *Judy Garland: The Secret Life of an American Legend* (New York: Hyperion, 1993).
10. Additional quotes re Judy Garland from Mickey Deans and Ann Pinchot, *Weep No More, My Lady* (New York: Hawthorne, 1972).
11. All quotes re Josephine Baker from Jean-Claude Baker and Chris Chase, *Josephine: The Hungry Heart* (New York: Random House, 1993).

CHAPTER 3: THE PARENTAL FALLACY

1. All quotes re Thomas Wolfe drawn from Andrew Turnbull, *Thomas Wolfe* (New York: Scribners, 1967).
2. Peter B. Neubauer and Alexander Neubauer, *Nature's Thumbprint: The Role of Genetics in Human Development* (Reading, Mass.: Addison-Wesley, 1990), 20–21, as quoted

in David C. Rowe, *The Limits of Family Influence: Genes, Experience and Behavior* (New York: Guilford, 1993), 132.

3. Stephen Citron, *Noel and Cole: The Sophisticates* (Oxford: Oxford Univ. Press, 1993), 8.

4. Victor Goertzel and Mildred G. Goertzel, *Cradles of Eminence* (Boston: Little, Brown, 1962), 13.

5. Stanley A. Blumberg and Gwinn Owens, *Energy and Conflict: The Life and Times of Edward Teller* (New York: Putnam, 1976), 6.

6. Pupul Jayakar, *Krishnamurti: A Biography* (New York: Harper and Row, 1988), 20.

7. All quotes re Van Cliburn drawn from Howard Reich, *Van Cliburn: A Biography* (Nashville: Thomas Nelson, 1993).

8. Lee Congdon, *The Young Lukács* (Chapel Hill: Univ. of North Carolina Press, 1983), 6.

9. Joan Peyser, *Leonard Bernstein* (London: Bantam, 1987), 22.

10. Patricia Bosworth, *Diane Arbus: A Biography* (New York: Alfred A. Knopf, 1984), 25.

11. Roy Cohn and Sidney Zion, *The Autobiography of Roy Cohn* (Secaucus, N.J.: Lyle Stuart, 1988), 33.

12. Elisabeth Young-Bruehl, *Hannah Arendt: For Love of the World* (New Haven: Yale Univ. Press, 1982), xii, 4.

13. Evelyn Fox Keller and W. H. Freeman, *A Feeling for the Organism: The Life and Work of Barbara McClintock* (New York: W. H. Freeman, 1983), 20.

14. Goertzel and Goertzel, *Cradles of Eminence,* 255.

15. Tina Turner and Kurt Loder, *I, Tina: My Life Story* (New York: William Morrow, 1986), 8, 10.

16. Rowe, *The Limits of Family Influence,* 193.

17. Diane E. Eyer, *Mother-Infant Bonding: A Scientific Fiction* (New Haven: Yale Univ. Press, 1992), 2, 199, 200.

18. John Bowlby, *Child Care and the Growth of Love,* 2d ed., abridged and edited by Margery Fry (Harmondsworth, England: Penguin, 1965), 53.

19. Rowe, *The Limits of Family Influence,* 163.

20. Robert Coles, *The Spiritual Life of Children* (Boston: Houghton Mifflin, 1990).

21. John Demos, "The Changing Faces of Fatherhood," in *The Child and Other Cultural Inventions,* Frank S. Kessel and Alexander W. Siegel, eds. (New York: Praeger, 1983).

22. Rainer Maria Rilke, *Selected Poems of Rainer Maria Rilke,* trans. Robert Bly (New York: Harper and Row, 1981).

23. Michael Ventura and James Hillman, *We've Had a Hundred Years of Psychotherapy—And the World's Getting Worse* (San Francisco: Harper, 1993).

24. Camille Sweeney, "Portrait of The American Child," *The New York Times Magazine* (October 8, 1995): 52–53.

25. Edith Cobb, *The Ecology of Imagination in Childhood* (Dallas: Spring Publications, 1993).

26. Paul Arthur Schilpp, *The Philosophy of Alfred North Whitehead* (New York: Tudor, 1951), 502.

CHAPTER 4: BACK TO THE INVISIBLES

1. A. Hilary Armstrong, "The Divine Enhancement of Earthly Beauties," *Eranos-Jahrbuch 1984* (Frankfurt a/M.: Insel, 1986).

2. Paul Friedländer, *Plato,* vol. 1 (New York: Bollingen Series 59, Pantheon, 1958), 189.

3. Henri Bergson, *Creative Evolution* (London: Macmillan, 1911), ix.

4. William Wordsworth, "The Prelude," in *The Poems of William Wordsworth* (London: Oxford Univ. Press, 1926).

5. William James, "On a Certain Blindness in Human Beings," *Talks to Teachers on Psychology: And to Students on Some of Life's Ideals* (London: Longman's, Green, 1911).

6. Horace B. English and Ava C. English, *A Comprehensive Dictionary of Psychological and Psychoanalytical Terms* (New York: David McKay, 1958).

7. Howard C. Warren, ed., *Dictionary of Psychology* (Boston: Houghton Mifflin, 1934).

8. English and English, *A Comprehensive Dictionary of Psychological and Psychoanalytical Terms.* See further, K. W. Wild, *Intu-*

ition (Cambridge, England: Cambridge Univ. Press, 1938); Malcolm R. Westcott, *Toward a Contemporary Psychology of Intuition: A Historical, Theoretical and Empirical Inquiry* (New York: Holt, Rinehart and Winston, 1968); Josef Koenig, *Der Begriff der Intuition* (Halle, Germany: Max Niemeyer, 1926); Sebastian J. Day, *Intuitive Cognition: A Key to the Significance of the Later Scholastics* (St. Bonaventure, N.Y.: Franciscan Institute, 1947).

9. C. G. Jung, *Psychological Types* (London: Routledge and Kegan Paul, 1923).

10. Quote re poetic inspiration and mathematics from Rosamond E. M. Harding, *An Anatomy of Inspiration,* 2d ed. (Cambridge, Mass.: Heffer and Sons, 1942); re mathematical invention from Jacques Hadamard, *The Psychology of Invention in the Mathematical Field* (Princeton: Princeton Univ. Press, 1945).

11. Ralph Waldo Emerson, "Self-Reliance," in *Essays: First Series,* vol. 1 (New York: Harper and Bros., n.d.), 43.

12. As can be gathered from the text, many famous people had great difficulties in school. The individual stories can be found in the following books. School problems in general, and Mann: Victor Goertzel and Mildred G. Goertzel, *Cradles of Eminence* (Boston: Little, Brown, 1962); Gandhi and Undset: Robert Payne, *The Life and Death of Mahatma Gandhi* (New York: Dutton, 1969); Feynman: James Gleick, *Genius: The Life and Science of Richard Feynman* (New York: Vintage Books, 1993); Branagh: Kenneth Branagh, *Beginning* (London: Chatto and Windus, 1989); Fassbinder: Robert Katz, *Love Is Colder Than Death: Life and Times of Rainer Werner Fassbinder* (London: Jonathan Cape, 1987); Pollock: Steven Naifeh and Gregory W. Smith, *Jackson Pollock: An American Saga* (New York: Clarkson Potter, 1989); Lennon: Albert Goldman, *The Lives of John Lennon: A Biography* (New York: William Morrow, 1988); Browning: Maisie Ward, *Robert Browning and His World: The Private Face (1812–1861)* (London: Cassell, 1968); Bowles: Christopher Sawyer-Laucanno, *An Invisible Spectator: A Biography of Paul*

Bowles (London: Bloomsbury, 1989); Saroyan, Grieg, Crane, O'Neill, Faulkner, Fitzgerald, Glasgow, Cather, Buck, Duncan, Anthony, Churchill: Goertzel and Goertzel, *Cradles of Eminence;* Einstein: Roger Highfield and Paul Carter, *The Private Lives of Albert Einstein* (New York: St. Martin's Press, 1993); Arbus: Patricia Bosworth, *Diane Arbus: A Biography* (New York: Alfred A. Knopf, 1984).

13. Quotes re Puccini, Chekhov, and Picasso's troubles with exams are taken from the Goertzels' *Cradles of Eminence.* Additional material on Picasso is from Roland Penrose, *Picasso: His Life and Work,* 3d ed. (Berkeley: Univ. of California Press, 1981).

14. Goertzel and Goertzel, *Cradles of Eminence.*

15. Omar N. Bradley, Jr., and Clay Blair, *A General's Life: An Autobiography* (New York: Simon and Schuster, 1983).

16. Paul D. Colford, *The Rush Limbaugh Story: Talent on Loan from God* (New York: St. Martin's Press, 1993), 12.

17. James Grant, *Bernard M. Baruch: The Adventures of a Wall Street Legend* (New York: Simon and Schuster, 1983).

18. Eric Lax, *Woody Allen* (New York: Alfred A. Knopf, 1991), 20, 32.

19. Marshall Frady, *Billy Graham: A Parable of American Righteousness* (Boston: Little, Brown, 1979), 61.

20. Robert Sardello, ed., *The Angels* (Dallas: Dallas Institute of Humanities and Culture, 1994).

21. David L. Miller, *Hells and Holy Ghosts: A Theopoetics of Christian Belief* (Nashville: Abingdon Press, 1989).

CHAPTER 5: *"ESSE IS PERCIPI"*:
TO BE IS TO BE PERCEIVED

1. Barnaby Conrad, *The Death of Manolete* (Boston: Houghton Mifflin, 1958), 9–10.

2. Robert A. Caro's essay "Lyndon Johnson and the Roots of Power" can be found in *Extraordinary Lives: The Art and Craft of American Biography* (Boston: Houghton Mifflin, 1988).

3. James Thomas Flexner, *The Young Hamilton: A Biography* (Boston: Little, Brown, 1978), 143.

4. James Hillman, *Egalitarian Typologies Versus the Perception of the Unique,* Eranos Lecture Series (Dallas: Spring Publications, 1986), 4–5.

5. Elia Kazan, *Elia Kazan: A Life* (New York: Doubleday Anchor, 1989), 26.

6. All quotes re Truman Capote from Gerald Clarke, *Capote: A Biography* (New York: Simon and Schuster, 1988).

7. Golda Meir, *My Life* (New York: Putnam, 1975), 40–42.

8. Karen Monson, *Alban Berg* (London: MacDonald General Books, 1980), 6.

9. Wiktor Woroszylski, *The Life of Mayakovsky* (London: Victor Gollancz, 1972), 11.

10. All quotes re Rimbaud from Elisabeth Hanson, *My Poor Arthur: A Biography of Arthur Rimbaud* (New York: Henry Holt, 1960).

11. David Leeming, *James Baldwin: A Biography* (New York: Alfred A. Knopf, 1994), 14–16, 19.

12. Andrés Rodríguez, *The Book of the Heart: The Poetics, Letters and Life of John Keats* (Hudson, N.Y.: Lindisfarne Press, 1993), 48.

13. James Hillman, "Oedipus Revisited," in *Oedipus Variations: Studies in Literature and Psychoanalysis* (Dallas: Spring Publications, 1991), 137–145.

14. E. H. Gombrich, *Art and Illusion: A Study in the Psychology of Pictorial Representation,* Bollingen Series 35 (Princeton: Princeton Univ. Press, 1961), 6.

15. José Ortega y Gasset, *On Love: Aspects of a Single Theme* (London: Victor Gollancz, 1959), 116.

16. Rodríguez, *Book of the Heart,* 51.

17. The sources for the anecdotes re "late" development are as follows. Teller: Stanley A. Blumberg and Gwinn Owens, *Energy and Conflict: The Life and Times of Edward Teller* (New York: Putnam, 1976); Spock: Lynn Z. Bloom, *Doctor Spock: Biography of a Conservative Radical* (Indianapolis: Bobbs-Merrill, 1972); Buber: Maurice Friedman, *Encounter on the Narrow Ridge: A Life of Martin Buber* (New York: Paragon House,

1991); Thurber: Neil A. Graver, *Remember Laughter: A Life of James Thurber* (Lincoln: Univ. of Nebraska Press, 1994); Wilson: Edwin A. Weinstein, *Woodrow Wilson: A Medical and Psychological Biography* (Princeton: Princeton Univ. Press, 1981).

CHAPTER 6: NEITHER NATURE
NOR NURTURE—SOMETHING ELSE

1. Robert Plomin, J. C. De Fries, and G. E. McClearn, *Behavioral Genetics: A Primer* (New York: W. H. Freeman, 1990), 314.
2. Judy Dunn and Robert Plomin, *Separate Lives: Why Siblings Are So Different* (New York: Basic Books, 1990), 38.
3. Plomin et al., *Behavioral Genetics*, 370.
4. Dunn and Plomin, *Separate Lives*, 16.
5. Ibid., 159.
6. Ibid., 49, 50.
7. Plomin et al., *Behavioral Genetics*, 371.
8. Robert Plomin, "Environment and Genes," *American Psychologist* 44(2), (1989): 105–111.
9. Jerome Kagan, *Galen's Prophecy: Temperament in Human Nature* (New York: Basic Books, 1994).
10. Paul Radin, *Monotheism Among Primitive Peoples* (Basel: Ethnographic Museum, Bollingen Foundation, Special Publ. 4, 1954). On the psychological characteristics of monotheism, see James Hillman, "Archetypal Psychology: Monotheistic or Polytheistic?" in *Spring 1971: An Annual of Archetypal Psychology and Jungian Thought* (Zurich: Spring Publications, 1971), 193–230.
11. Cesare Lombroso, *The Man of Genius* (London: Walter Scott, 1891).
12. Plomin et al., *Behavioral Genetics*, 334.
13. Richard J. Herrnstein and Charles Murray, *The Bell Curve: Intelligence and Class Structure in American Life* (New York: Free Press, 1994), 108.
14. Plomin et al., *Behavioral Genetics*, 366.
15. Ibid., 334.

16. Ibid., 365.
17. Herrnstein and Murray, 105.
18. Plomin et al., *Behavioral Genetics*, 35.
19. Bard Lindeman, *The Twins Who Found Each Other* (New York: William Morrow, 1969).
20. D. T. Lykken, M. McGue, A. Tellegen, and T. J. Bouchard, "Emergenesis: Genetic Traits That May Not Run In Families," *American Psychologist* 47(12) (December 1992): 1565–1566.
21. Ibid., 1575.
22. Dunn and Plomin, *Separate Lives*, 146, 147.
23. Ibid., 148–149.
24. Niels G. Waller and Phillip R. Shaver, "The Importance of Nongenetic Influences on Romantic Love Styles: A Twin-Family Study," *Psychological Science* 5(5) (1994): 268–274.
25. Helen E. Fisher, *Anatomy of Love: The Natural History of Monogamy, Adultery, and Divorce* (New York: W. W. Norton, 1992), 45.
26. Emma Jung, *Animus and Anima* (Dallas: Spring Publications, 1979).
27. John R. Haule, *Divine Madness: Archetypes of Romantic Love* (Boston: Shambhala, 1990); Jan Bauer, *Impossible Love—Or Why the Heart Must Go Wrong* (Dallas: Spring Publications, 1993).
28. Plato, *Phaedrus*, trans. R. Hackforth, in *Plato: The Collected Dialogues*, Edith Hamilton and Huntington Cairns, eds., Bollingen Series 71 (New York: Pantheon, 1963), 511b.
29. Fisher, *Anatomy of Love*, 273.
30. Ellen Berscheid and Elaine Hatfield Walster, *Interpersonal Attraction* (Menlo Park, N.J.: Addison-Wesley, 1983), 153.
31. Lawrence Wright, "Double Mystery," *The New Yorker* (August 7, 1995): 52.
32. Nathaniel Branden, "A Vision of Romantic Love," in *The Psychology of Love*, Robert J. Sternberg and Michael L. Barnes, eds. (New Haven: Yale Univ. Press, 1988), 224.
33. Susan S. Hendrick and Clyde Hendrick, *Romantic Love* (Newbury Park, Calif.: Sage Publications, 1992), 23.

34. Wright, "Double Mystery," 58.

35. José Ortega y Gasset, *On Love: Aspects of a Single Theme* (London: Victor Gallancz, 1959).

36. Joseph Gantner, "L'Immagine del Cuor" in *Eranos-Yearbook,* 35–1966 (Zurich: Rhein Verlag, 1967), 287ff.

37. Zoltan Kovecses, "A Linguist's Quest for Love," *Journal of Social and Personal Relationships* 8(1) (1991): 77–97.

38. Ricardo C. Ainslie, *The Psychology of Twinship* (Lincoln: Univ. of Nebraska Press, 1985), 133–141.

39. Plomin, "Environment and Genes," 110.

40. David Reiss, Robert Plomin, and E. Mavis Hetherington, "Genetics and Psychiatry: An Unheralded Window on the Environment," *American Journal of Psychiatry* 148(3) (1991): 283–291.

41. Plomin, "Environment and Genes," 110.

42. T. S. Eliot, "The Dry Salvages," in *Four Quartets* (London: Faber and Faber, 1944).

CHAPTER 7: PENNY DREADFULS AND PURE FANTASY

1. E. T. Bell, *Men of Mathematics* (New York: Simon and Schuster, 1937), 341–342.

2. D. W. Forrest, *Francis Galton: The Life and Work of a Victorian Genius* (London: Paul Elek, 1974), 6.

3. Peter Kurth, *American Cassandra: The Life of Dorothy Thompson* (Boston: Little, Brown, 1990), 24.

4. Edith Cobb, *The Ecology of Imagination in Childhood* (Dallas: Spring Publications, 1993).

5. Albert Goldman, *The Lives of John Lennon: A Biography* (New York: William Morrow, 1988), 56.

6. Anecdotes re great writers and their trashy reading habits appear in the following. Porter: George Eells, *The Life That Late He Led: A Biography of Cole Porter* (London: W. H. Allen, 1967); F. L. Wright: Meryle Secrest, *Frank Lloyd Wright* (New York: Alfred A. Knopf, 1992); Barrie: Janet

Dunbar, *J. M. Barrie: The Man Behind the Image* (Newton Abbot, England: Readers Union, 1971); R. Wright: Margaret Walker, *Richard Wright: Daemonic Genius* (New York: Amistad, 1988); Ellis: Vincent Brome, *Havelock Ellis: Philosopher of Sex* (London: Routledge and Kegan Paul, 1979).

7. Sir Edmund Hillary, *Nothing Venture, Nothing Win* (New York: Coward, McCann and Geoghegan, 1975), 22.

8. Kate Meyers, "Tarantino's Shop Class," *Entertainment Weekly* (October 14, 1994): 35.

9. Eells, *The Life That Late He Led,* 17.

10. Richard Holmes, *Coleridge—Early Visions* (London: Hodder and Stoughton, 1989), 6.

11. Laurence Leamer, *As Time Goes By: The Life of Ingrid Bergman* (London: Hamish Hamilton, 1986), 7.

12. Samuel Abt, *LeMond* (New York: Random House, 1990), 18.

13. Howard Reich, *Van Cliburn: A Biography* (Nashville: Thomas Nelson, 1993), 7.

14. Daniel J. Levinson, *The Seasons of a Man's Life* (New York: Alfred A. Knopf, 1978), 97–101.

15. David McCullough, *Truman* (New York: Simon and Schuster, 1992), 837–838.

16. Mikal Gilmore, "Family Album," *Granta* 37 (Autumn 1991): 15.

17. Bob Mullan, *Mad to Be Normal: Conversations with R. D. Laing* (London: Free Associations Books, 1995), 93–95.

18. All quotes re the Loud family from Anne Roiphe in *An American Family,* Ron Goulart, ed. (New York: Warner, 1973), 22–25.

19. Mary Watkins, *Invisible Guests: The Development of Imaginal Dialogues* (Hillsdale, N.J.: Analytic Press, 1986).

CHAPTER 8: DISGUISE

1. Jean-Claude Baker and Chris Chase, *Josephine: The Hungry Heart* (New York: Random House, 1993), 12.

2. Timothy Wilson-Smith, *Delacroix—A Life* (London: Constable, 1992), 21.

3. Maurice Zolotow, *Shooting Star: A Biography of John Wayne* (New York: Simon and Schuster, 1974), 37.

4. Robert A. Caro, "Lyndon Johnson and the Roots of Power," in *Extraordinary Lives: The Art and Craft of American Biography* (Boston: Houghton Mifflin, 1988), 218.

5. Tad Szulc, *Fidel: A Critical Portrait* (New York: William Morrow, 1986), 112.

6. John Raymond, *Simenon in Court* (New York: Harcourt, Brace and World, 1968), 35.

7. Victor Seroff, *The Real Isadora* (New York: Dial Press, 1971), 14.

8. All quotes re Leonard Bernstein from Joan Peyser, *Leonard Bernstein* (London: Bantam, 1987), 12.

9. Robert Lacey, *Ford: The Men and the Machine* (Boston: Little, Brown, 1986), 10.

10. All stories re Henry Kissinger from Walter Isaacson, *Kissinger: A Biography* (New York: Simon and Schuster, 1992), 26–27.

11. Michael Holroyd, "Literary and Historical Biography," in *New Directions in Biography*, A. M. Friedson, ed. (Manoa: Univ. of Hawaii Press, 1981).

12. Leon Edel, *Writing Lives—Principia Biographica* (New York: W. W. Norton, 1984), 20–21.

13. Carolyn G. Heilbrun, *Writing a Woman's Life* (New York: W. W. Norton, 1988), 14.

14. Isaacson, *Kissinger,* 26.

15. Seroff, *The Real Isadora,* 14, 50.

16. American Psychiatric Association Staff, *Diagnostic and Statistical Manual of Mental Disorders,* 3d ed., vol. 3 (Washington, D.C.: American Psychiatric Press, 1987), 301.51.

17. Ake Hultkrantz, *Conceptions of the Soul Among North American Indians* (Stockholm: Statens Etnografiska Museum, 1953).

18. *The World Almanac and Book of Facts* (New York: Pharos Books, 1991).

19. Evelyn Fox Keller and W. H. Freeman, *A Feeling for the Organism: The Life and Work of Barbara McClintock* (New York: W. H. Freeman, 1983), 20, 36.

20. Oliver Daniel, *Stokowski: A Counterpoint of View* (New York: Dodd, Mead, 1982), xxiv, xxv, xxiii, 10.

21. Abram Chasins, *Leopold Stokowski: A Profile* (New York: Hawthorn Books, 1979), 148–149.
22. Daniel, *Stokowoski,* 923.
23. Holroyd, "Literary and Historical Biography," 18.
24. William H. Epstein, *Recognizing Biography* (Philadelphia: Univ. of Pennsylvania Press, 1987), 6.
25. Hultkrantz, *Conceptions of the Soul,* 383, 141.

CHAPTER 9: FATE

1. Plotinus, *Enneads,* vol. 3, trans. A. H. Armstrong, Loeb ed. (Cambridge, Mass.: Harvard Univ. Press, 1967), 4.5.
2. E. R. Dodds, *The Greeks and the Irrational* (Berkeley: Univ. of California Press, 1951), 6.
3. Ibid., 23.
4. B. C. Dietrich, *Death, Fate and the Gods: Development of a Religious Idea in Greek Popular Belief and in Homer* (London: Athlone Press, Univ. of London, 1965), 340; see also William Chase Greene, *Moira: Fate, Good, and Evil in Greek Thought* (New York: Harper Torchbooks, 1963).
5. H. W. Parke, *The Oracles of Zeus: Dodona, Olympia, Ammon* (Oxford: Basil Blackwell, 1967).
6. Aristotle, *Physics II,* trans. R. P. Hardie and R. K. Gaye, in *The Works of Aristotle,* W. D. Ross, ed. (Oxford: Clarendon Press, 1930), 3.194b.
7. Ingmar Bergman, *The Magic Lantern: An Autobiography,* trans. Joan Tate (London: Hamish Hamilton, 1988).
8. Ibid.
9. Bette Davis, *The Lonely Life: An Autobiography* (London: MacDonald, 1963), 23.
10. Pierre Franey, *A Chef's Tale: A Memoir of Food, France, and America* (New York: Alfred A. Knopf, 1994), 12.
11. Evan Jones, *Epicurean Delight: The Life and Times of James Beard* (New York: Alfred A. Knopf, 1990), 4.
12. Victor Goertzel and Mildred G. Goertzel, *Cradles of Eminence* (Boston: Little, Brown, 1962), 267.

13. Janet Dunbar, *J. M. Barrie: The Man Behind the Image* (Newton Abbot, England: Readers Union, 1971).

14. Thomas Kunkel, *Genius in Disguise: Harold Ross of* The New Yorker (New York: Random House, 1995), 326.

15. Stephen E. Ambrose, *Nixon: The Education of a Politician, 1913–1962* (New York: Simon and Schuster, 1987), 36–37.

16. Edmonde Charles-Roux, *Chanel: Her Life, Her World—And the Woman Behind the Legend She Herself Created,* trans. Nancy Amphoux (London: Jonathan Cape, 1976), 40.

17. Francis MacDonald Cornford, *Plato's Cosmology: The "Timaeus" of Plato Translated with a Running Commentary* (London: Routledge and Kegan Paul, 1948).

18. Heinz Schreckenberg, *Ananke* (Munich: C. H. Beck, 1964).

19. T. S. Eliot, "Burnt Norton," in *Four Quartets* (London: Faber and Faber, 1944).

20. Ruth Brandon, *The Life and Many Deaths of Harry Houdini* (New York: Random House, 1993), 11, 292.

CHAPTER 10: THE BAD SEED

1. Plotinus, *Enneads,* vol. 3, trans. A. H. Armstrong, Loeb ed. (Cambridge, Mass.: Harvard Univ. Press, 1967), 1.6.

2. Arthur Koestler, *The Ghost in the Machine* (New York: Viking Penguin, 1990), 384.

3. Robert G. Waite, *The Psychopathic God: Adolf Hitler* (New York: Basic Books, 1977), 412, 379.

4. James Hillman, *The Dream and the Underworld* (New York: Harper and Row, 1979), 168–171.

5. Waite, *The Psychopathic God,* 14.

6. Ada Petrova and Peter Watson, *The Death of Hitler: The Full Story with New Evidence from Secret Russian Archives* (New York: W. W. Norton, 1995), 16.

7. Hermann Rauschning, *The Voice of Destruction* (New York: Putnam, 1940), 5.

8. Waite, *The Psychopathic God,* 26–27.

9. Petrova and Watson, *The Death of Hitler,* 9–13.

10. Edgar Herzog, *Psyche and Death: Death-Demons in Folklore, Myths and Modern Dreams* (Dallas: Spring Publications, 1983), 46–54.

11. Waite, *The Psychopathic God*, 237ff.

12. Werner Maser, *Hitler: Legend, Myth and Reality*, trans. Peter and Betty Ross (New York: Harper and Row, 1973), 198.

13. Waite, *The Psychopathic God*, 44–45.

14. Ibid., 13, 201, 14.

15. Ibid., 7, 114, 92–95.

16. Joachim Fest, *Hitler*, trans. Clara Winston (New York: Harcourt Brace and Company, 1974), 4.

17. Rauschning, *The Voice of Destruction*, 257–258.

18. Charles Bracelen Flood, *Hitler: The Path to Power* (Boston: Houghton Mifflin, 1989), 25.

19. Waite, *The Psychopathic God*, 202.

20. John Toland, *Adolf Hitler* (New York: Doubleday, 1976), 170.

21. Waite, *The Psychopathic God*, 176, 155.

22. Rauschning, *The Voice of Destruction*, 256.

23. Alice Miller, *For Your Own Good: Hidden Cruelty in Child-rearing and the Roots of Violence* (New York: Farrar, Straus and Giroux, 1983).

24. Joel Norris, *Serial Killers: The Causes of a Growing Menace* (New York: Doubleday, 1988), 157–158.

25. Gitta Sereny, *The Case of Mary Bell* (New York: McGraw-Hill, 1973), xv.

26. Ibid., 74, 197.

27. Ibid., 195, 130.

28. Miller, *For Your Own Good*, 132, 161.

29. Lonnie H. Athens, *The Creation of Dangerous Violent Criminals* (Urbana: Univ. of Illinois Press, 1992).

30. Cesare Lombroso, *The Man of Genius* (London: Walter Scott, 1891); Richard von Krafft-Ebing, *Psychopathia Sexualis: A Medico-Forensic Study* (New York: Pioneer Publications, 1946).

31. John Kobler, *Capone: The Life and World of Al Capone* (New York: Putnam, 1971), 27–28.

32. James Q. Wilson and Richard J. Herrnstein, *Crime and Human Nature* (New York: Simon and Schuster, 1985).

33. Adolf Guggenbühl-Craig, *The Emptied Soul: The Psychopath in Everyone's Life* (Woodstock, Conn.: Spring Publications, 1996).

34. Jack Katz, *Seductions of Crime: Moral and Sensual Attractions of Doing Evil* (New York: Basic Books, 1988), 315.

35. Sereny, *The Case of Mary Bell,* 66, 41.

36. Katz, *Seductions of Crime,* 289f, 301.

37. Brian Masters, *Killing for Company: The Story of a Man Addicted to Murder* (New York: Random House, 1993), 238.

38. Miller, *For Your Own Good,* 225.

39. Lionel Dahmer, *A Father's Story* (New York: Avon, 1995), ix, 175, 204, 190.

40. Robert Cullen, *The Killer Department: The Eight-Year Hunt for the Most Savage Killer of Modern Times* (New York: Pantheon, 1993), 209, 194–203.

41. Quotes re Hitler as a child are drawn from Toland, *Adolf Hitler,* 12, 22, and Waite, *The Psychopathic God,* 147.

42. Plotinus, *Enneads,* vol. 6, 9.11.

43. Gerald Astor, *The "Last" Nazi: The Life and Times of Dr. Joseph Mengele* (New York: Donald I. Fine, 1985).

44. Mikal Gilmore, "Family Album," *Granta* 37 (Autumn 1991): 11–52.

45. Katz, *Seductions of Crime,* 301.

46. M. Scott Peck, *People of the Lie: The Hope for Healing Human Evil* (New York: Simon and Schuster, 1983), 261–265.

47. Peter R. Breggin and Ginger R. Breggin, *The War Against Children: The Government's Intrusion into Schools, Families and Communities in Search of a Medical "Cure" for Violence* (New York: St. Martin's Press, 1994), 15.

48. Elaine Pagels, *The Origin of Satan* (New York: Random House, 1995).

CHAPTER 11: MEDIOCRITY

1. George R. Marek, *Toscanini* (New York: Atheneum, 1975), 22.

2. William H. Epstein, *Recognizing Biography* (Philadelphia: Univ. of Pennsylvania Press, 1987), 71–73.

3. Theodore Zeldin, *An Intimate History of Humanity* (New York: HarperCollins, 1995).

4. The translations of Heraclitus were drawn from the following sources: M. Marcovich, *Heraclitus: Editio Maior* (Merida, Venezuela: Los Andes Univ., 1967); G. S. Kirk and J. E. Raven, *The Presocratic Philosophers: A Critical History with a Selection of Texts* (Cambridge, England: Cambridge Univ. Press, 1957); Philip Wheelwright, *Heraclitus* (New York: Atheneum, 1968); W. K. C. Guthrie, *A History of Greek Philosophy*, vol. 1 (Cambridge, England: Cambridge Univ. Press, 1962); Werner Jaeger, *Paideia: The Ideals of Greek Culture*, vol. 1, trans. Gilbert Highet (Oxford: Oxford Univ. Press, 1965); John Burnet, *Early Greek Philosophy* (London: Adam and Charles Black, 1948); *Herakleitos and Diogenes*, trans. Guy Davenport (San Francisco: Grey Fox Press, 1979); Kathleen Freeman, *Ancilla to the Pre-Socratic Philosophers: A Complete Translation of the Fragments in Diels, Fragmente der Vorsokratier* (Oxford: Blackwell, 1948); Albert Cook, "Heraclitus and the Conditions of Utterance," *Arion* 2(4) (n.d.).

5. Thomas L. Pangle, *The Laws of Plato* (New York: Basic Books, 1980), 792e.

6. Quotes re Thomas Dewey are from Richard Norton Smith, *Thomas E. Dewey and His Times* (New York: Simon and Schuster, 1982); re Billy Graham, from Marshall Frady, *Billy Graham: A Parable of American Righteousness* (Boston: Little, Brown, 1979); re Oliver North, from Ben Bradlee, Jr., *Guts and Glory: The Rise and Fall of Oliver North* (New York: Donald I. Fine, 1988).

CODA: A NOTE ON METHODOLOGY

1. Alexander Porteous, *Forest Folklore, Mythology, and Romance* (London: George Allen and Unwin, 1928); Dr. Aigremont, *Volkserotik und Pflanzenwelt* (Halle, Germany: Gebr. Tensinger, n.d.); Angelo de Gubernatis, *La Mythologie des plantes*, vol. 2 (Paris: C. Reinwald, 1878), 68–69.

2. H. W. Parke, *The Oracles of Zeus: Dodona, Olympia, Ammon* (Oxford: Basil Blackwell, 1967), 265–273.

3. Robert Graves, *The White Goddess: A Historical Grammar of Poetic Myth* (London: Faber and Faber, 1948), 386.

4. On the speaking of trees in the contemporary United States, see Michael Perlman, *The Power of Trees: The Reforesting of the Soul* (Dallas: Spring Publications, 1994); on the relation of language to landscape, see David Abram, *The Spell of the Sensuous: Perception and Language in a More-than-Human World* (New York: Pantheon, 1996).

5. Jacob Grimm, *Teutonic Mythology*, 4th ed., trans. James S. Stallybrass (London: George Bell, 1882–1888).

6. Translations of terms drawn from the following sources: Julius Pokorny, *Indogermanisches etymologisches Wörterbuch* (Bern: Francke Verlag, 1959); Pierre Chantraine, *Dictionnaire étymologique de la langue grecque* (Paris: Klincksieck, 1968); Henry George Liddell and Robert Scott, *A Greek-English Lexicon,* 7th ed. (Oxford: Clarendon Press, 1890); *Oxford Latin Dictionary,* P.G.W. Glare, ed. (Oxford: Clarendon Press, 1982); *The New Oxford English Dictionary,* corrected ed., Leslie Brown, ed. (Oxford: Clarendon Press, 1993).

7. James Hillman, ed., *Puer Papers* (Dallas: Spring Publications, 1980).

8. Jane Chance Nitzsche, *The Genius Figure in Antiquity and the Middle Ages* (New York: Columbia Univ. Press, 1975), 7–12.

BIBLIOGRAPHY

Abram, David. *The Spell of the Sensuous: Perception and Language in a More-than-Human World.* New York: Pantheon, 1996.

Abt, Samuel. *LeMond.* New York: Random House, 1990.

Aigremont, Dr. *Volkserotik und Pflanzenwelt.* Halle, Germany: Gebr. Tensinger, n.d.

Ainslie, Ricardo C. *The Psychology of Twinship.* Lincoln: Univ. of Nebraska Press, 1985.

Ambrose, Stephen E. *Nixon: The Education of a Politician, 1913–1962.* New York: Simon and Schuster, 1987.

American Psychiatric Association Staff, *Diagnostic and Statistical Manual of Mental Disorders,* 3d ed., vol. 3. Washington, D.C.: American Psychiatric Press, 1987.

Aristotle. *Nicomachean Ethics.* Trans. Martin Ostwald. Indianapolis: Bobbs-Merrill, 1962.

———. *Physics II.* Trans. R. P. Hardie and R. K. Gaye. In *The Works of Aristotle,* W. D. Ross, ed. Oxford: Clarendon Press, 1930.

Armstrong, A. Hilary. "The Divine Enhancement of Earthly Beauties." *Eranos-Jahrbuch 1984.* Frankfurt a/M.: Insel, 1986.

Astor, Gerald. *The "Last" Nazi: The Life and Times of Dr. Joseph Mengele.* New York: Donald I. Fine, 1985.

Athens, Lonnie H. *The Creation of Dangerous Violent Criminals.* Urbana: Univ. of Illinois Press, 1992.

Baker, Jean-Claude, and Chris Chase. *Josephine: The Hungry Heart.* New York: Random House, 1993.

Bauer, Jan. *Impossible Love—Or Why the Heart Must Go Wrong.* Dallas: Spring Publications, 1993.

Bell, E. T. *Men of Mathematics.* New York: Simon and Schuster, 1937.

Bergman, Ingmar. *The Magic Lantern: An Autobiography.* Trans. Joan Tate. London: Hamish Hamilton, 1988.

Bergson, Henri. *Creative Evolution.* London: Macmillan, 1911.

Berscheid, Ellen, and Elaine Hatfield Walster. *Interpersonal Attraction.* Menlo Park, N.J.: Addison-Wesley, 1983.

Bloom, Lynn Z. *Doctor Spock: Biography of a Conservative Radical.* Indianapolis: Bobbs-Merrill, 1972.

Blumberg, Stanley A., and Gwinn Owens. *Energy and Conflict: The Life and Times of Edward Teller.* New York: Putnam, 1976.

Bosworth, Patricia. *Diane Arbus: A Biography.* New York: Alfred A. Knopf, 1984.

Bowlby, John. *Child Care and the Growth of Love,* 2d ed. Abridged and edited by Margery Fry. Harmondsworth, England: Penguin, 1965.

Bradlee, Ben, Jr. *Guts and Glory: The Rise and Fall of Oliver North.* New York: Donald I. Fine, 1988.

Bradley, Omar N., Jr., and Clay Blair. *A General's Life: An Autobiography.* New York: Simon and Schuster, 1983.

Branagh, Kenneth. *Beginning.* London: Chatto and Windus, 1989.

Branden, Nathaniel. "A Vision of Romantic Love." In *The Psychology of Love,* Robert J. Sternberg and Michael L. Barnes, eds. New Haven: Yale Univ. Press, 1988.

Brandon, Ruth. *The Life and Many Deaths of Harry Houdini.* New York: Random House, 1993.

Breggin, Peter R., and Ginger R. Breggin. *The War Against Children: The Government's Intrusion into Schools, Families and Communities in Search of a Medical "Cure" for Violence.* New York: St. Martin's Press, 1994.

Brome, Vincent. *Havelock Ellis: Philosopher of Sex.* London: Routledge and Kegan Paul, 1979.

Burnet, John. *Early Greek Philosophy.* London: Adam and Charles Black, 1948.

Canetti, Elias. *The Tongue Set Free: Remembrance of a European Childhood*. London: André Deutsch, 1988.

Caro, Robert A. "Lyndon Johnson and the Roots of Power." In *Extraordinary Lives:The Art and Craft of American Biography*. Boston: Houghton Mifflin, 1988.

Chantraine, Pierre. *Dictionnaire étymologique de la langue grecque*. Paris: Klincksieck, 1968.

Charles-Roux, Edmonde. *Chanel: Her Life, Her World—And the Woman Behind the Legend She Herself Created*. Trans. Nancy Amphoux. London: Jonathan Cape, 1976.

Chasins, Abram. *Leopold Stokowski: A Profile*. New York: Hawthorn Books, 1979.

Citron, Stephen. *Noel and Cole:The Sophisticates*. Oxford: Oxford Univ. Press, 1993.

Clarke, Gerald. *Capote: A Biography*. New York: Simon and Schuster, 1988.

Cobb, Edith. *The Ecology of Imagination in Childhood*. Dallas: Spring Publications, 1993.

Cohn, Roy, and Sidney Zion. *The Autobiography of Roy Cohn*. Secaucus, N.J.: Lyle Stuart, 1988.

Coles, Robert. *The Spiritual Life of Children*. Boston: Houghton Mifflin, 1990.

Colette. *Earthly Paradise: An Autobiography*. Trans. Herma Briffault, Derek Coltman, and others. Robert Phelps, ed. New York: Farrar, Straus and Giroux, 1966.

Colford, Paul D. *The Rush Limbaugh Story: Talent on Loan from God*. New York: St. Martin's Press, 1993.

Colin, Sid. *Ella: The Life and Times of Ella Fitzgerald*. London: Elm Tree Books, 1986.

Collingwood, R. G. *An Autobiography*. Oxford: Oxford Univ. Press, 1939.

Congdon, Lee. *The Young Lukács*. Chapel Hill: Univ. of North Carolina Press, 1983.

Conrad, Barnaby. *The Death of Manolete*. Boston: Houghton Mifflin, 1958.

Cook, Albert. "Heraclitus and the Conditions of Utterance." *Arion* 2(4) (n.d.).

Cook, Blanche Wiesen. *Eleanor Roosevelt,* vol. 1, *1884–1933.* New York: Viking Penguin, 1992.

Cornford, Francis MacDonald. *Plato's Cosmology: The "Timaeus" of Plato Translated with a Running Commentary.* London: Routledge and Kegan Paul, 1948.

Covitz, Joel. "A Jewish Myth of a Priori Knowledge." *Spring 1971: An Annual of Archetypal Psychology.* Zurich: Spring Publications, 1971.

Cox, Patricia. *Biography in Late Antiquity: A Quest for the Holy Man.* Berkeley: Univ. of California Press, 1983.

Crozier, Brian. *Franco: A Biographical History.* London: Eyre and Spottiswoode, 1967.

Cullen, Robert. *The Killer Department: The Eight-Year Hunt for the Most Savage Serial Killer of Modern Times.* New York: Pantheon, 1993.

Dahmer, Lionel. *A Father's Story.* New York: Avon, 1995.

Daniel, Oliver. *Stokowski: A Counterpoint of View.* New York: Dodd, Mead, 1982.

Davis, Bette. *The Lonely Life: An Autobiography.* London: Mac-Donald, 1963.

Day, Sebastian J. *Intuitive Cognition: A Key to the Significance of the Later Scholastics.* St. Bonaventure, N.Y.: Franciscan Institute, 1947.

Deans, Mickey, and Ann Pinchot. *Weep No More, My Lady.* New York: Hawthorne, 1972.

Demos, John. "The Changing Faces of Fatherhood." In *The Child and Other Cultural Inventions,* Frank S. Kessel and Alexander W. Siegel, eds. New York: Praeger, 1983.

Dietrich, B. C. *Death, Fate and the Gods: Development of a Religious Idea in Greek Popular Belief and in Homer.* London: Athlone Press, Univ. of London, 1965.

Dodds, E. R. *The Greeks and the Irrational.* Berkeley: Univ. of California Press, 1951.

———. *Proclus: The Elements of Theology,* 2d ed. Oxford: Oxford Univ. Press, 1963.

Dunbar, Janet. *J. M. Barrie: The Man Behind the Image.* Newton Abbot, England: Readers Union, 1971.

Dunn, Judy, and Robert Plomin. *Separate Lives: Why Siblings Are So Different.* New York: Basic Books, 1990.

Edel, Leon. *Writing Lives—Principia Biographica.* New York: W. W. Norton, 1984.

Eells, George. *The Life That Late He Led: A Biography of Cole Porter.* London: W. H. Allen, 1967.

Eliot, T. S. "Burnt Norton." In *Four Quartets.* London: Faber and Faber, 1944.

————. "The Dry Salvages." In *Four Quartets.* London: Faber and Faber, 1944.

Emerson, Ralph Waldo. "Self-Reliance." In *Essays: First Series,* vol. 1. New York: Harper and Bros., n.d.

English, Horace B., and Ava C. English. *A Comprehensive Dictionary of Psychological and Psychoanalytical Terms.* New York: David McKay, 1958.

Epstein, William H. *Recognizing Biography.* Philadelphia: Univ. of Pennsylvania Press, 1987.

Eyer, Diane E. *Mother-Infant Bonding: A Scientific Fiction.* New Haven: Yale Univ. Press, 1992.

Fest, Joachim. *Hitler.* Trans. Clara Winston. New York: Harcourt, Brace and Company, 1974.

Fisher, Helen E. *Anatomy of Love: The Natural History of Monogamy, Adultery, and Divorce.* New York: W. W. Norton, 1992.

Flexner, James Thomas. *The Young Hamilton: A Biography.* Boston: Little, Brown, 1978.

Flood, Charles Bracelen. *Hitler: The Path to Power.* Boston: Houghton Mifflin, 1989.

Forrest, D. W. *Francis Galton: The Life and Work of a Victorian Genius.* London: Paul Elek, 1974.

Frady, Marshall. *Billy Graham: A Parable of American Righteousness.* Boston: Little, Brown, 1979.

Franey, Pierre. *A Chef's Tale: A Memoir of Food, France, and America.* New York: Alfred A. Knopf, 1994.

Freeman, Kathleen. *Ancilla to the Pre-Socratic Philosophers: A Complete Translation of the Fragments in Diels, Fragmente der Vorsokratier.* Oxford: Blackwell, 1948.

Friedländer, Paul. *Plato,* vol. 1, Bollingen Series 59. New York: Pantheon, 1958.

Friedman, Maurice. *Encounter on the Narrow Ridge: A Life of Martin Buber.* New York: Paragon House, 1991.

Gantner, Joseph. "L'Immagine del Cuor." In *Eranos-Yearbook,* 35–1966. Zurich: Rhein Verlag, 1967.

Gilmore, Mikal. "Family Album." *Granta* 37 (Autumn 1991): 11–52.

Gleick, James. *Genius: The Life and Science of Richard Feynman.* New York: Vintage Books, 1993.

Goertzel, Victor, and Mildred G. Goertzel. *Cradles of Eminence.* Boston: Little, Brown, 1962.

Goldman, Albert. *The Lives of John Lennon: A Biography.* New York: William Morrow, 1988.

Gombrich, E. H. *Art and Illusion: A Study in the Psychology of Pictorial Representation,* Bollingen Series 35. Princeton: Princeton Univ. Press, 1961.

Grant, James. *Bernard M. Baruch: The Adventures of a Wall Street Legend.* New York: Simon and Schuster, 1983.

Graver, Neil A. *Remember Laughter: A Life of James Thurber.* Lincoln: Univ. of Nebraska Press, 1994.

Graves, Robert. *The White Goddess: A Historical Grammar of Poetic Myth.* London: Faber and Faber, 1948.

Greene, William Chase. *Moira: Fate, Good, and Evil in Greek Thought.* New York: Harper Torchbooks, 1963.

Grimm, Jacob. *Teutonic Mythology.* Trans. from 4th ed. by James S. Stallybrass. London: George Bell, 1882–1888.

Gubernatis, Angelo de. *La Mythologie des plantes,* vol. 2. Paris: C. Reinwald, 1878.

Guggenbühl-Craig, Adolf. *The Emptied Soul: The Psychopath in Everyone's Life.* Woodstock, Conn.: Spring Publications, 1996.

Guthrie, W.K.C. *A History of Greek Philosophy,* vol. 1. Cambridge, England: Cambridge Univ. Press, 1962.

Hadamard, Jacques. *The Psychology of Invention in the Mathematical Field.* Princeton: Princeton Univ. Press, 1945.

Hanson, Elisabeth. *My Poor Arthur: A Biography of Arthur Rimbaud.* New York: Henry Holt, 1960.

Harding, Rosamond E. M. *An Anatomy of Inspiration.* 2d ed. Cambridge, Mass.: Heffer and Sons, 1942.

Haule, John R. *Divine Madness: Archetypes of Romantic Love.* Boston: Shambhala, 1990.

Heilbrun, Carolyn G. *Writing a Woman's Life.* New York: W. W. Norton, 1988.

Hendrick, Susan S., and Clyde Hendrick. *Romantic Love.* Newbury Park, Calif.: Sage Publications, 1992.

Herakleitos and Diogenes. Trans. Guy Davenport. San Francisco: Grey Fox Press, 1979.

Herrnstein, Richard J., and Charles Murray. *The Bell Curve: Intelligence and Class Structure in American Life.* New York: Free Press, 1994.

Herzog, Edgar. *Psyche and Death: Death-Demons in Folklore, Myths and Modern Dreams.* Dallas: Spring Publications, 1983.

Highfield, Roger, and Paul Carter. *The Private Lives of Albert Einstein.* New York: St. Martin's Press, 1993.

Hillary, Sir Edmund. *Nothing Venture, Nothing Win.* New York: Coward, McCann and Geoghegan, 1975.

Hillman, James. "Archetypal Psychology: Monotheistic or Polytheistic?" In *Spring 1971: An Annual of Archetypal Psychology and Jungian Thought.* Zurich: Spring Publications, 1971.

———. *The Dream and the Underworld.* New York: Harper and Row, 1979.

———. *Egalitarian Typologies Versus the Perception of the Unique.* Eranos Lecture Series. Dallas: Spring Publications, 1986.

———. "Oedipus Revisited." In *Oedipus Variations: Studies in Literature and Psychoanalysis.* Dallas: Spring Publications, 1991.

———. "What Does the Soul Want—Adler's Imagination of Inferiority." In *Healing Fiction.* Dallas: Spring Publications, 1994.

———, ed. *Puer Papers.* Dallas: Spring Publications, 1980.

Holmes, Richard. *Coleridge—Early Visions.* London: Hodder and Stoughton, 1989.

Holroyd, Michael. "Literary and Historical Biography." In *New Directions in Biography,* A. M. Friedson, ed. Manoa: Univ. of Hawaii Press, 1981.

Hultkrantz, Åke. *Conceptions of the Soul Among North American Indians.* Stockholm: Statens Etnografiska Museum, 1953.

Irving, David. *The Trail of the Fox.* New York: E. P. Dutton, 1977.

Isaacson, Walter. *Kissinger: A Biography.* New York: Simon and Schuster, 1992.

Jaeger, Werner. *Paideia: The Ideals of Greek Culture,* vol. 1. Trans. Gilbert Highet. Oxford: Oxford Univ. Press, 1965.

James, William. "On a Certain Blindness in Human Beings." *Talks to Teachers on Psychology: And to Students on Some of Life's Ideals.* London: Longman's, Green, 1911.

Jayakar, Pupul. *Krishnamurti: A Biography.* New York: Harper and Row, 1988.

Jones, Evan. *Epicurean Delight: The Life and Times of James Beard.* New York: Alfred A. Knopf, 1990.

Jung, C. G. *Psychological Types.* London: Routledge and Kegan Paul, 1923.

Jung, Emma. *Animus and Anima.* Dallas: Spring Publications, 1979.

Kagan, Jerome. *Galen's Prophecy: Temperament in Human Nature.* New York: Basic Books, 1994.

Katz, Jack. *Seductions of Crime: Moral and Sensual Attractions of Doing Evil.* New York: Basic Books, 1988.

Katz, Robert. *Love Is Colder Than Death: Life and Times of Rainer Werner Fassbinder.* London: Jonathan Cape, 1987.

Kazan, Elia. *Elia Kazan: A Life.* New York: Doubleday Anchor, 1989.

Keller, Evelyn Fox, and W. H. Freeman. *A Feeling for the Organism: The Life and Work of Barbara McClintock.* New York: W. H. Freeman, 1983.

Kirk, G. S., and J. E. Raven. *The Presocratic Philosophers: A Critical History with a Selection of Texts.* Cambridge, England: Cambridge Univ. Press, 1957.

Kittel, Gerhard, ed. *Theological Dictionary of the New Testament,* 3d ed., vol. 3. Grand Rapids, Mich.: Eerdmans, 1968.

Kobler, John. *Capone: The Life and World of Al Capone.* New York: Putnam, 1971.

Koenig, Josef. *Der Begriff der Intuition.* Halle, Germany: Max Niemeyer, 1926.

Koestler, Arthur. *The Ghost in the Machine.* New York: Viking Penguin, 1990.

Kovecses, Zoltan. "A Linguist's Quest for Love." *Journal of Social and Personal Relationships* 8(1) (1991): 77–97.

Krafft-Ebing, Richard von. *Psychopathia Sexualis: A Medico-Forensic Study.* New York: Pioneer Publications, 1946.

Kunkel, Thomas. *Genius in Disguise: Harold Ross of* The New Yorker. New York: Random House, 1995.

Kurth, Peter. *American Cassandra: The Life of Dorothy Thompson.* Boston: Little, Brown, 1990.

Lacey, Robert. *Ford: The Men and the Machine.* Boston: Little, Brown, 1986.

Lax, Eric. *Woody Allen.* New York: Alfred A. Knopf, 1991.

Leamer, Laurence. *As Time Goes By: The Life of Ingrid Bergman.* London: Hamish Hamilton, 1986.

Leeming, David. *James Baldwin: A Biography.* New York: Alfred A. Knopf, 1994.

Levinson, Daniel J. *The Seasons of a Man's Life.* New York: Alfred A. Knopf, 1978.

Liddell, Henry George, and Robert Scott. *A Greek-English Lexicon,* 7th ed. Oxford: Clarendon Press, 1890.

Lindeman, Bard. *The Twins Who Found Each Other.* New York: William Morrow, 1969.

Lombroso, Cesare. *The Man of Genius.* London: Walter Scott, 1891.

Lykken, D. T., M. McGue, A. Tellegen, and T. J. Bouchard. "Emergenesis: Genetic Traits That May Not Run In Families." *American Psychologist* 47(12) (December 1992): 1565–1566.

Marcovich, M. *Heraclitus: Editio Maior.* Merida, Venezuela: Los Andes Univ., 1967.

Marek, George R. *Toscanini.* New York: Atheneum, 1975.

Maser, Werner. *Hitler: Legend, Myth and Reality.* Trans. Peter and Betty Ross. New York: Harper and Row, 1973.

Masters, Brian. *Killing for Company: The Story of a Man Addicted to Murder.* New York: Random House, 1993.

McCullough, David. *Truman.* New York: Simon and Schuster, 1992.

Meir, Golda. *My Life.* New York: Putnam, 1975.

Menuhin, Yehudi. *Unfinished Journey.* New York: Alfred A. Knopf, 1976.

Meyers, Kate. "Tarantino's Shop Class." *Entertainment Weekly* (October 14, 1994): 35.

Miller, Alice. *For Your Own Good: Hidden Cruelty in Child-rearing and the Roots of Violence.* New York: Farrar, Straus and Giroux, 1983.

Miller, David L. *Hells and Holy Ghosts: A Theopoetics of Christian Belief.* Nashville: Abingdon Press, 1989.

Monson, Karen. *Alban Berg.* London: MacDonald General Books, 1980.

Mullan, Bob. *Mad To Be Normal—Conversations with R. D. Laing.* London: Free Associations Books, 1995.

Naifeh, Steven, and Gregory W. Smith. *Jackson Pollock: An American Saga.* New York: Clarkson Potter, 1989.

Neubauer, Peter B., and Alexander Neubauer. *Nature's Thumbprint: The Role of Genetics in Human Development.* Reading, Mass.: Addison-Wesley, 1990.

The New Oxford English Dictionary, corrected ed., Leslie Brown, ed. Oxford: Clarendon Press, 1993.

Nitzsche, Jane Chance. *The Genius Figure in Antiquity and the Middle Ages.* New York: Columbia Univ. Press, 1975.

Norris, Joel. *Serial Killers: The Causes of a Growing Menace.* New York: Doubleday, 1988.

Ortega y Gasset, José. *On Love: Aspects of a Single Theme.* London: Victor Gollancz, 1959.

Oxford Latin Dictionary. P.G.W. Glare, ed. Oxford: Clarendon Press, 1982.

Pagels, Elaine. *The Origin of Satan.* New York: Random House, 1995.

Pangle, Thomas L. *The Laws of Plato.* New York: Basic Books, 1980.

Parke, H. W. *The Oracles of Zeus: Dodona, Olympia, Ammon.* Oxford: Basil Blackwell, 1967.

Payne, Robert. *The Life and Death of Mahatma Gandhi.* New York: Dutton, 1969.

Peck, M. Scott. *People of the Lie: The Hope for Healing Human Evil.* New York: Simon and Schuster, 1983.

Penrose, Roland. *Picasso: His Life and Work,* 3d ed. Berkeley: Univ. of California Press, 1981.

Perlman, Michael. *The Power of Trees: The Reforesting of the Soul.* Dallas: Spring Publications, 1994.

Petrova, Ada, and Peter Watson. *The Death of Hitler: The Full Story with New Evidence from Secret Russian Archives.* New York: W. W. Norton, 1995.

Peyser, Joan. *Leonard Bernstein.* London: Bantam, 1987.

Plato. *Phaedrus.* Trans. R. Hackforth. In *Plato: The Collected Dialogues,* Edith Hamilton and Huntington Cairns, eds., Bollingen Series 71. New York: Pantheon, 1963.

——. *Republic.* Trans. Paul Shorey. In *Plato: The Collected Dialogues,* Edith Hamilton and Huntington Cairns, eds., Bollingen Series 71. New York: Pantheon, 1963.

Plomin, Robert. "Environment and Genes." *American Psychologist* 44(2) (1989): 105–111.

Plomin, Robert, J. C. De Fries, and G. E. McClearn. *Behavioral Genetics: A Primer.* New York: W. H. Freeman, 1990.

Plotinus. *Enneads.* Trans. A. H. Armstrong. Loeb ed. Cambridge, Mass.: Harvard Univ. Press, 1967.

Pokorny, Julius. *Indogermanisches etymologisches Wörterbuch.* Bern: Francke Verlag, 1959.

Ponce, Charles. *Kabbalah.* San Francisco: Straight Arrow Books, 1973.

Porteous, Alexander. *Forest Folklore, Mythology, and Romance.* London: George Allen and Unwin, 1928.

Radin, Paul. *Monotheism Among Primitive Peoples.* Basel: Ethnographic Museum, Bollingen Foundation, Special Publ. 4, 1954.

Rauschning, Hermann. *The Voice of Destruction.* New York: Putnam, 1940.

Raymond, John. *Simenon in Court.* New York: Harcourt, Brace and World, 1968.

Reich, Howard. *Van Cliburn: A Biography.* Nashville: Thomas Nelson, 1993.

Reiss, David, Robert Plomin, and E. Mavis Hetherington. "Genetics and Psychiatry: An Unheralded Window on the Environment," *American Journal of Psychiatry* 148(3) (1991): 283–291.

Rilke, Rainer Maria. *Selected Poems of Rainer Maria Rilke.* Trans. Robert Bly. New York: Harper and Row, 1981.

Rodríguez, Andrés. *The Book of the Heart: The Poetics, Letters and Life of John Keats.* Hudson, N.Y.: Lindisfarne Press, 1993.

Roiphe, Anne. In *An American Family.* Ron Goulart, ed. New York: Warner Books, 1973.

Roosevelt, Eleanor. *You Learn by Living.* New York: Harper and Bros., 1960.

Rothenberg, Albert. *Creativity and Madness: New Findings and Old Stereotypes.* Baltimore: Johns Hopkins Univ. Press, 1990.

Rowe, David C. *The Limits of Family Influence: Genes, Experience and Behavior.* New York: Guilford, 1993.

Sardello, Robert, ed. *The Angels.* Dallas: Dallas Institute of Humanities and Culture, 1994.

Sawyer-Laucanno, Christopher. *An Invisible Spectator: A Biography of Paul Bowles.* London: Bloomsbury, 1989.

Schilpp, Paul Arthur. *The Philosophy of Alfred North Whitehead.* New York: Tudor, 1951.

Scholem, Gershom, ed. *Zohar—The Book of Splendor: Basic Readings from the Kabbalah.* New York: Schocken Books, 1963.

Schreckenberg, Heinz. *Ananke.* Munich: C. H. Beck, 1964.

Secrest, Meryle. *Frank Lloyd Wright.* New York: Alfred A. Knopf, 1992.

Sereny, Gitta. *The Case of Mary Bell.* New York: McGraw-Hill, 1973.

Seroff, Victor. *The Real Isadora.* New York: Dial Press, 1971.

Shakespeare, William. *The Tempest.* In *The Complete Works of William Shakespeare,* W. J. Craig, ed. London: Oxford University Press, 1952.

Shipman, David. *Judy Garland: The Secret Life of an American Legend.* New York: Hyperion, 1993.

Smith, Richard Norton. *Thomas E. Dewey and His Times.* New York: Simon and Schuster, 1982.

Stevens, Wallace. "Notes Toward a Supreme Fiction." In *The Collected Poems of Wallace Stevens.* New York: Alfred A. Knopf, 1978.

Sweeney, Camille. "Portrait of the American Child." *The New York Times Magazine,* October 8, 1995.

Szulc, Tad. *Fidel: A Critical Portrait.* New York: William Morrow, 1986.

Toland, John. *Adolf Hitler.* New York: Doubleday, 1976.

Turnbull, Andrew. *Thomas Wolfe.* New York: Scribners, 1967.

Turner, Tina, and Kurt Loder. *I, Tina: My Life Story.* New York: William Morrow, 1986.

Tylor, Edward B. *Primitive Culture,* vol. 1. London: 1871.

Ventura, Michael, and James Hillman. *We've Had a Hundred Years of Psychotherapy—And the World's Getting Worse.* San Francisco: Harper, 1993.

Waite, Robert G. *The Psychopathic God: Adolf Hitler.* New York: Basic Books, 1977.

Walker, Margaret. *Richard Wright: Daemonic Genius.* New York: Amistad, 1988.

Waller, Niels G., and Phillip R. Shaver. "The Importance of Nongenetic Influences on Romantic Love Styles: A Twin-Family Study." *Psychological Science* 5(5) (1994): 268–274.

Ward, Maisie. *Robert Browning and His World: The Private Face (1812–1861).* London: Cassell, 1968.

Warren, Howard C., ed. *Dictionary of Psychology.* Boston: Houghton Mifflin, 1934.

Watkins, Mary. *Invisible Guests: The Development of Imaginal Dialogues.* Hillsdale, N.J.: Analytic Press, 1986.

Weinstein, Edwin A. *Woodrow Wilson: A Medical and Psychological Biography.* Princeton: Princeton Univ. Press, 1981.

Westcott, Malcolm R. *Toward a Contemporary Psychology of Intuition: A Historical, Theoretical, and Empirical Inquiry.* New York: Holt, Rinehart and Winston, 1968.

Wheelwright, Philip. *Heraclitus.* New York: Atheneum, 1968.

Wild, K. W. *Intuition.* Cambridge, England: Cambridge Univ. Press, 1938.

Wilson, James Q., and Richard J. Herrnstein. *Crime and Human Nature.* New York: Simon and Schuster, 1985.

Wilson-Smith, Timothy. *Delacroix—A Life.* London: Constable, 1992.

Wind, Edgar. *Pagan Mysteries in the Renaissance.* Harmondsworth, England: Penguin, 1967.

Wordsworth, William. "The Prelude." In *The Poems of William Wordsworth.* London: Oxford Univ. Press, 1926.

The World Almanac and Book of Facts. New York: Pharos Books, 1991.

Woroszylski, Wiktor. *The Life of Mayakovsky.* London: Victor Gollancz, 1972.

Wright, Lawrence. "Double Mystery." *The New Yorker* (August 7, 1995): 52.

Wylie, Mary Sykes. "Diagnosing for Dollars?" *The Family Therapy Networker* 19(3) (1995): 23–69.

Young, Desmond. *Rommel: The Desert Fox.* New York: Harper and Bros., 1950.

Young-Bruehl, Elisabeth. *Hannah Arendt: For Love of the World.* New Haven: Yale Univ. Press, 1982.

Zeldin, Theodore. *An Intimate History of Humanity.* New York: HarperCollins, 1994.

Zolotow, Maurice. *Shooting Star: A Biography of John Wayne.* New York: Simon and Schuster, 1974.

INDEX

accidents, 8, 203–8
acorn theory, 3–40, 49–50, 64, 67, 70, 96, 97, 102, 228
as methodology, 275–86
see also calling; daimon
Adler, Alfred, 23–24
Adolf Hitler: A Family Perspective (Stierlin), 229
aha Erlebnis, 98
Ajax, 44, 252
Allen, Woody, 106
All's Well That Ends Well (Shakespeare), 253
Amann, Max, 220
American Family, An, 166–68
anality, 219–20
Ananke, see Necessity
ancestors, 83–91, 257, 276
Anderson, Marian, 251–52
anima and animus, 93, 141–42, 143, 199
Anthony, Susan B., 103
apeiron, 47
Aphrodite, 95, 142
Aquinas, Thomas, 38
Arbus, Diane, 72, 74, 103–4, 164
Arendt, Hannah, 73
Aristotle, 12, 129, 134, 196, 201, 206, 280
Arnold, Matthew, 175

Astaire, Fred, 50
astrology, 42, 43, 108, 133
Atalanta, 44, 281
Atropos, 45
attention deficit disorder, 107, 126
Auden, W. H., 175, 176
Augustine, Saint, 278

Bad Seed, see Hitler, Adolf; psychopathy, criminal
Baker, Josephine, 57–62, 172, 243
Baldwin, James, 104, 120–21
Barbie, Klaus, 230
Bardot, Brigitte, 61, 263
Barnes, Michael, 265
Barrie, James M., 68, 159, 205, 207
Bartsch, Jürgen, 236–37
Baruch, Bernard, 106
Beard, James, 204–5
beauty, 35–40, 95, 100, 246
Beethoven, Ludwig van, 24
Bell, Mary, 228–30, 235, 242
Bella Coolas, 188
Bennett, William, 158, 270
Bentham, Jeremy, 232
Berg, Alban, 119, 122
Bergman, Ingmar, 197–202, 260, 269–70
Bergman, Ingrid, 162, 252

Bergman, Justus, 162
Bergson, Henri, 96, 99
Berkeley, George, 126–27
Bernstein, Leonard, 173, 189, 243, 252
Bible, 31, 34, 44, 47, 79, 90, 129, 233, 242
biographies, 3, 4–5, 8, 31, 32, 33–34, 37, 38, 64, 87, 88, 100, 128, 132, 135, 161, 209, 254
    disguise in, 175–80, 183, 184–90
    mentors in, 113–27
    mothers in, 68–70, 71–74, 125
    of ordinary lives, 254
    schooldays in, 101–8, 209, 243
Bloom, Allan, 158, 270
body symbolism, 42
bonding, mother-infant, 75–76, 78
Borgnine, Ernest, 252
Bormann, Martin, 220
Bowlby, John, 77, 78, 79
Bowles, Paul, 102, 107
Bradley, Omar, 105–6, 219, 251
Branagh, Kenneth, 101–2, 107
Braun, Eva, 220
Brazelton, T. Berry, 78
Breggin, Peter and Ginger, 30
Browning, Robert, 102, 107
Bruckner, Anton, 24
Buber, Martin, 125
Buck, Pearl, 103
Buddha, 42–43

Caliban, 229–30
calling, 3–40, 83, 133, 134, 135, 162, 199, 249
    in adolescence, 135
    childhood manifestation of, 3, 7, 8, 13–27, 29, 49, 104–5, 135, 251–52

democratic equality and, 273
demonic, 234–38, 239; see also psychopathy, criminal
efforts of attachment required by, 52–53
as incommensurable with life, 48, 239–42
innate image and, 4–5, 6, 7, 11–12, 30, 49, 51, 203
mediocrity as, 249, 253–55
mystery of, 10–11
Platonic concept of, 7–9
psychology vs., see psychology
recovered sense of, 4
romantic love and, 144–45
terms for, 9, 10
see also daimon
Camará, José Flores, 113–14, 120, 122, 243
Camus, Albert, 55
Canetti, Elias, 27–29, 33, 40, 243, 260
Capone, Al, 232
Capote, Truman, 104, 116, 117–18, 120, 121, 124, 215, 241
Casals, Pablo, 69, 74, 251
case histories, 31, 33, 88, 240, 252–53
Castro, Fidel, 173
Cather, Willa, 103, 175
Cézanne, Paul, 103
Chamberlain, Houston, 222
Chanel, Coco, 206, 207, 208
chaos theory, 139–40, 209
Chaplin, Charlie, 222
character, 4, 6, 7, 10, 13, 128, 133, 135, 251–53, 254–71
    American, 261–71
    in psychopathy, 234, 241, 244
character disorders, 260–61
"Character is fate," 253, 256–59
Chekhov, Anton, 104, 166

Chikatilo, Andrei, 216, 237–38, 239, 242
Child Care and the Growth of Love (Bowlby), 77
childhood, 184
  abuse in, 3, 27, 227
  calling manifested in, 3, 7, 8, 13–27, 29, 49, 104–5, 135, 251–52
  genetic factors in, 132, 134–35
  loneliness in, 53–54
  psychopathy manifested in, 224, 228–29, 237, 238–39, 246–47
  traumas of, 3–4, 24, 207, 227–28, 229, 230, 237
children, 29–31, 42, 179, 246–47
  American neglect of, 84
  drug treatment of, 30, 125, 247
  dysfunctional symptoms in, 13–14, 29, 30–31, 33, 34–35, 85, 107–8, 125–26, 247
  happiness of, 83
  hope perceived by, 76, 79
  imaginations of, 87, 170, 279
  IQ in, 134–35
  multiple influences on, 74–76, 78, 86
  prodigies, 16, 29
  suicide rate among, 79, 84
  World War II and, 78–80
  see also fathers; mothers
choice mechanism, 232–33, 244
Christianity, 9, 31, 41, 43, 100, 109–11, 133, 157, 219, 234, 236, 244
Churchill, Winston, 103, 107, 205, 207, 208
Cliburn, Van, 69–70, 163–64
Clock, The, 51
Cobb, Edith, 87, 158
Cohn, Roy, 72–73

coldness, emotional, 217, 223, 230, 237, 239
Coleridge, Samuel Taylor, 160
Coles, Robert, 76
Colette, 18–20, 35
Collingwood, R. G., 14–15, 16, 19–20
compensation theory, 22–27
concreteness, 240–42
  misplaced, 85, 90
coprophilia, 219, 220
cosmologies, 43–47, 93
  contemporary, 47
  mythical parents in, 85–86, 88, 90, 276
Crane, Stephen, 103
creation myths, 43–47, 62
creativity, 27, 32, 38, 99, 132–33, 134, 234
Crick, Francis, 130
Croce, Benedetto, 99
Crosby, Bing, 50
Curie, Marie, 104

Dahmer, Jeffrey, 215, 216, 234, 237
Dahmer, Lionel, 237
daimon, 5, 8–11, 14–22, 29, 32, 37, 38, 45, 54, 57, 60, 62, 68, 96, 139, 165, 191, 193, 212
  of animals, 75
  dignity of, 26–27
  in disguise, 181, 183, 187–90
  evil, *see* Hitler, Adolf; psychopathy, criminal
  of father, 82–85
  fire associated with, 217–18
  full recognition of, 243–45, 246
  functions of, 8, 9, 12–13, 39, 48, 238, 258–59
  happiness of, 83, 260
  individuality and, 148, 149–50
  intuition of, 107

daimon (cont'd)
    mediocrity and, 249, 250, 252,
        255, 256–60, 269–70, 271
    mentors and, 119, 120
    of mother, 68, 69–70
    Native American terms for, 257
    nature of, 40, 194, 195–96,
        197–203, 206, 258
    parents selected by, 8, 49–50,
        64–66, 70, 74, 157, 162
    prescience of, 39–40
    romantic love and, 144–46
    snake as symbol of, 59
    timelessness of, 216, 225–26
    as transcendent, 224–26,
        235–38, 239, 244
    see also calling; soul
Daniel, Oliver, 186
Dante Alighieri, 217, 242, 244
Darwin, Charles, 41, 64, 116, 120
Davis, Bette, 203
death, 184, 217, 223–24, 281
    Necessity of, 212–13
    psychopathy and, 217, 218, 219,
        223–24, 228–29, 230, 246
    romantic love and, 146
    of Socrates, 42, 43, 203
Declaration of Independence, 272,
    273
Delacroix, Eugène, 172
Della Santa, Roland, 163
democratic equality, 271–74
demonism, see Hitler, Adolf; psy-
    chopathy, criminal
denial, 50, 167, 177, 234, 239,
    247–48, 267
Descartes, René, 88, 129
deus absconditus, 285
Dewey, Thomas E., 261–71
Dickens, Charles, 120, 121, 175
disguise, 172–90
    in autobiography, 172–74, 176,
        178, 189
    in biography, 175–80, 183,
        184–90
    censorship in, 172
    daimon in, 181, 183, 187–90
    doppelgänger in, 179–80, 181,
        183
    in names and nicknames, 173,
        180–84
Dodona, oracle of, 277
doppelgänger, 179–80, 181, 183
drug treatment, 21, 30, 125,
    150–51, 168, 231, 247, 270
Druids, 277
Duncan, Isadora, 103, 173, 178
Dunn, Judy, 132
Durkheim, Émile, 130

Ecology of Imagination in Childhood,
    The (Cobb), 158
Edel, Leon, 175
Edison, Thomas, 103, 151
Egyptians, ancient, 9, 85, 242
Ehrlich, Paul, 104
Eichmann, Adolf, 230, 250
Einstein, Albert, 103, 104, 243
Eisenhower, Dwight D., 71, 105,
    181, 251, 265–66
Electra complex, 22
Eliot, George, 175
Eliot, T. S., 154, 175, 210
Ellis, Havelock, 159, 160
emergenesis, 137–38
Emerson, Ralph Waldo, 31, 97,
    100–101
Enneads (Plotinus), 242
environmental factors, 6, 67, 88,
    128–30, 131–33, 141, 142,
    223, 272
    all-inclusive, 152–54
    in psychopathy, 231–32
    shared vs. unshared, 131–32,
        137–38, 147–50
    see also parental fallacy

epistasis, 138–39
Eskimos (Inuits), 9, 108, 180,
    183–84, 188
ethics, 259–60
eudaimonia, 83, 260
exceptional people, 14–29, 31–35,
    64, 136, 161
    individuality of, 132
    inspirations of, 25–26, 134,
        269
    IQ scores of, 136
    mediocrity vs., 247, 249,
        250–51, 253, 254, 256,
        268–71
    pathology linked to, 29, 31, 134
    see also biographies
exile, sense of, 54, 56–57
existentialism, 55
Eyer, Diane, 75–76, 78, 79

factitious disorders, 179
Fadiman, Clifton, 51–52
family, 48, 62, 63–64, 78, 80, 132,
    148–49, 231
    changing patterns of, 68, 74,
        80, 81
    extended, 169
    fictional, 166
    Loud, documentary on, 166–68
    see also parental fallacy
family romance, 86
family system, 21, 82
family systems therapy, 64
"family values," 63–64, 81, 96,
    268
fantasy, 155–71, 209
    disciplined education vs.,
        155–59
    extraordinary personages and,
        160–61, 169–70
    in love map, 143
    in obsessions, 161, 162, 170–71
    of omnipotence, 17, 22

of omniscience, 224–26
parental, *see* parental fantasy
in pulp fiction, 159–60, 162
withdrawal into, 20–22
Fassbinder, Rainer Werner, 102
fatalism, 191–94, 196, 204, 207,
    258
fate, 3, 5, 6, 7, 8, 10, 11, 12, 29,
    37, 44, 139, 191–213, 224,
    277
    accidents as, 203–8
    analysis of, 195
    nature of, 193–95
    teleology as, 196–203, 204, 207
    see also calling; daimon; Necessity
Fates (Moirai), 45, 193, 208, 213
fathers, 21, 22, 49, 68, 125, 157,
    161, 162, 163, 227, 228, 237,
    276, 279
    absence of, 64, 80–85, 88
    child as daimon of, 83–85
    conventional image of, 81, 82
    daimon of, 82–85
Faulkner, William, 103, 116
Feynman, Richard, 101
fire, 217–18, 239
Fitzgerald, Ella, 10–11, 139, 209
Fitzgerald, F. Scott, 103
Flaubert, Gustave, 144
fontanel, 42
Ford, Henry, 150, 151, 173–74,
    176, 189, 250
Ford, Margaret, 174, 176
Fortuna, 139, 224, 244
Franco, Francisco, 22–23, 26–27,
    29
Franey, Pierre, 204, 205
Frazer, Sir James George, 284
freaks, 220–21, 255
Freud, Anna, 79
Freud, Sigmund, 20, 22, 24–25,
    86, 142, 165, 175, 189,
    202–3, 240, 241, 260

Friedländer, Paul, 95
Froebel, Friedrich, 87, 157

Gall, Franz Josef, 152
Galois, Évariste, 243
Galton, Francis, 156, 157
Gandhi, Mohandas K., 23, 26, 36,
    101
Garland, Judy, 48–57, 59–60, 62,
    241, 252
genetic factors, 6, 11, 49, 67,
    128–54, 223, 272
  chaos theory and, 139–40, 209
  in childhood, 132, 134–35
  in creativity, 132–33
  emergenesis in, 137–38
  epistasis in, 138–39
  in individuality, 128, 132–33,
    134–35, 136–40
  in IQ, 134–36
  in psychiatric disorders, 150–52
  in psychopathy, 229–30, 231,
    246–47
  in romantic love, 128, 140–47
  in traditionalism, 132, 133–34
  see also environmental factors;
    twins
genius, 9, 257, 282
  see also daimon
Gibson, J. J., 86
Gilmore, Gary, 164, 239, 242
Gilmore, Gaylen, 242–43
Glasgow, Ellen, 103
Goebbels, Joseph, 220
Göring, Hermann, 217
Graham, Billy, 106–7, 261–71
grandiosity, 17, 32, 36, 222
Graves, Robert, 277
Greeks, ancient, 7–9, 34, 41, 96,
    112, 193, 195, 241, 244, 246,
    257, 258, 283
Grieg, Edvard, 103
Grimm, Jacob, 278–79

group mores, 231–32
growing down, 41–62, 77, 85, 87,
    206, 222, 225, 226, 243–44,
    245, 260
  ascensionist model vs., 41–42
  in astrology, 42, 43
  body symbolism of, 42
  in creation myths, 43–47, 62
  by Josephine Baker, 57–62
  by Judy Garland, 48–57, 59–60,
    62
  in Kabbalistic Tree, 43–44, 47
  loneliness of, 53–57
  sense of exile in, 54, 56–57
  in soul's descent, 43–47, 62
Guggenbuhl-Craig, Adolf, 234

Hamilton, Alexander, 114–15,
    120, 281
Hamilton, William Rowan,
    155–56, 157
Hardy, G. H., 66
Harrelson, Woody, 227
Hauptmann, Gerhart, 223
Hearst, William Randolph, 104
Heidegger, Martin, 55, 73
Heilbrun, Carolyn, 175–76
hell, 217
Hendrick, Susan and Clyde, 144
Heraclitus, 190, 253, 256–59
heroic mentality, 6, 12, 16, 77,
    192, 207
Herrnstein, Richard, 232, 244
Hess, Rudolf, 220
Hickcock, Dick, 244
Hillary, Sir Edmund, 159–60
Hitler, Adolf, 26, 70, 157, 214–48
  absolute certainty of, 223–24,
    239
  anality of, 219–20
  architectural construction by, 242
  charmed life of, 223–24
  childhood of, 224, 229, 238–39

cold heart of, 217, 223, 230, 239
compelling eyes of, 222–23, 239
daimon of, 215, 216, 218, 224,
 245–46
direct demonic intrusion on,
 226, 227, 238
freaks in entourage of, 220–21
hellfire and, 217–18, 239
humorlessness of, 221–22, 239
karma of, 233
omniscience fantasies of, 224–26
powerlessness feared by, 239–42
rigidity of, 217, 219
sexuality of, 219, 220
shadow projected by, 234, 239
suicides of women involved
 with, 220
supposed monorchidism of,
 239–40
time and, 225–26, 239
wolf motif favored by, 218–19,
 239
Holroyd, Michael, 187
Homer, 277, 280
Houdini, Harry, 211–12
Hudson, W. H., 97
Hughes, Charles Evans, 104
Huldra, myth of, 92–93, 95, 112
Hultkrantz, Åke, 9
humorlessness, 221–22, 239
Husserl, Edmund, 99

Iago, 235
individuality, 11–12, 129–30,
 147–50
 of exceptional people, 132
 genetic factors in, 128, 132–33,
 134–35, 136–40
 mediocrity vs., 250, 252–53,
 254, 272–74
 romantic love and, 144–46
 in twins, 130–32, 140–41, 142,
 143–44

innate image, 4–5, 6, 7, 11–12,
 30, 49, 51, 203
intuition, 97–108, 225
 characteristics of, 98–99
 definition of, 97–98
 fallibility of, 99–100
 tuition vs., 100–108
Inuits (Eskimos), 9, 108, 180,
 183–84, 188
invisibles, 47, 85, 91, 92–112, 144,
 149, 184, 217, 237, 255, 260,
 268, 274
 bridges to, 94–95, 100, 108,
 110–12
 of everyday life, 95–96
 mythical thinking and, 93–97,
 98
 in solids, 96–97
 visible vs., 94–95, 111
 see also intuition
IQ, 134–36
Isaacson, Walter, 177
Izambard, 119–20, 243

James, Henry, 126, 175
James, William, 97, 115–16, 124
Japan, 42, 74–75, 234
Jesus Christ, 110–11, 281
Johnson, Lyndon, 71, 114, 120,
 121, 161, 173, 175, 176, 189,
 265
Johnson, Sam Houston, 173, 176
Judaism, 43–44, 46, 157, 195, 236
Judgment at Nuremberg, 51
Julius Caesar (Shakespeare), 258
Jung, C. G., 24, 99, 108, 116,
 141–42, 143, 172, 181, 188,
 209

Kabbalah, Tree of, 43–44, 47
Kagan, Jerome, 133
Kant, Immanuel, 14–15, 100,
 209–10

karma, 55, 142, 233
Katz, Jack, 236
Kazan, Elia, 50, 116–17, 122
Keats, John, 9, 121, 124, 127, 281
Kelly, Gene, 50
Kelly, Grace, 61
Kierkegaard, Søren, 110, 165
King Lear (Shakespeare), 258
Kissinger, Henry, 174, 177–78,
    265
Kissinger, Paula, 177
Klein, Melanie, 79
Klotho, 45
Korsakoff's syndrome, 179
Krishnamurti, 69
Kubizek, August, 222, 243

Lachesis, 45
lacuna, 234
La Farge, John, 104
Laing, R. D., 164–65
Lanz, Georg, 222–23
Lawrence, D. H., 188–89
LeMond, Greg, 163
Lennon, John, 102, 158, 160, 164
Lethe, 46
Levinson, Daniel J., 164
Ley, Robert, 220
Limbaugh, Rush, 106, 107
Lincoln, Abraham, 164
lip, upper, 46
Lives (North), 254
Lombroso, Cesare, 134
loneliness, 53–57, 227
loners, 241–42
lot in life, 8, 39, 44–46, 49–50,
    138, 139, 162, 191, 193, 205,
    208–9, 252
Loud family, 166–68
love, 166, 245, 247
    styles of, 128, 140–47, 199, 228
love maps, 141–45
Lukács, George, 71–72, 74

MacArthur, Douglas, 164
McClellan, George, 164
McClintock, Barbara, 17, 19–20,
    29, 73, 74, 105–6, 182–83,
    209
Mahler, Gustav, 252
Malcolm, Janet, 187
Mann, Thomas, 101
Manolete, Manuel, 14, 15–16, 18,
    19, 26, 33, 35, 113–14, 120,
    122, 123, 212, 241, 243,
    269–70
Manson, Charles, 215, 227, 242
Marty, 252
Marx, Karl, 130, 133, 165
Mason, James, 53
Masters, Brian, 236
Matisse, Henri, 104
Mayakovsky, Vladimir, 119
mediocrity, 189, 249–74
    American character and,
        261–71
    beliefs in, 262, 263–68
    as calling, 249, 253–55
    character and, 251–53, 254–71
    and "Character is fate," 256–59
    and democratic equality, 271–74
    ethics and, 259–60
    exceptionality vs., 247, 249,
        250–51, 253, 254, 256,
        268–71
    individuality vs., 250, 252–53,
        254, 272–74
    of job vs. performance, 250,
        252, 258
    snobbish prejudices against,
        249–50, 270
    of soul, 250, 256, 273–74
    style vs., 250, 260–61
    talent and, 250–51
megalomania, 240–42
Mein Kampf (Hitler), 224, 239
Meir, Golda, 20, 118–19

Melanchthon, Philipp, 157
Mencken, H. L., 157
Mengele, Josef, 242
mentors, 113–27, 163–65, 209,
    222, 243, 246
  books as, 164–65
  breakups with, 164
  imaginary, 164
  parents vs., 163–64
Menuhin, Yehudi, 17–18, 19–20,
    29, 36, 139, 197, 243, 250
Michelangelo, 9, 146
Mill, John Stuart, 155, 157
Millay, Edna St. Vincent, 73, 74
Miller, Alice, 87, 227, 229, 237
Miller, David, 109
Miller, Orilla, 120–21
Minnelli, Liza, 53
misplaced concreteness, 83, 90
Moirai (Fates), 45, 193, 208, 213
Montessori, Maria, 157
Moore, Thomas, 83
moral theology, 54–55
Morgan, J. P., 164
mothers, 42, 49, 66–74, 83, 93,
    118–19, 148, 162–63, 164,
    205, 274
  in biography, 68–70, 71–74, 125
  of charismatic leaders, 70–71
  child's daimon and, 69–71
  child's opposition to, 71–72
  conventional, 71–73
  daimon of, 68, 69–71
  disparate children produced by,
    72–73
  infant bonding with, 75–76, 78
  myth of, 66–68, 71, 74, 77, 79,
    161
  neglectful, 73–74, 161
  in psychological theories, 64,
    75–76, 77–80, 88, 161
  psychopathy and, 227, 228, 229
motivation theory, 27–29

Mozart, Wolfgang Amadeus, 16,
    24, 29, 49, 100, 252, 281
Munchausen's syndrome, 179
mysticism, 43–44, 94
  radical, 236
myth, 5, 6, 39, 50, 100, 109,
    181–82, 281–82
  cosmic parents in, 85–86, 88,
    90, 276
  creation, 43–47, 62
  of Huldra, 92–93, 95, 112
  modern apocalyptic, 79–80
  of Mother, 66–68, 71, 74, 77,
    79, 161
  oak tree in, 276–79
  origin of, 93–94
  timelessness of, 46, 99
mythical thinking, 93–97, 98, 99,
    100
Myth of Er, 7–9, 39, 44–46, 47,
    62, 67, 135, 138, 139, 193,
    208–9, 224, 252, 274

Nabokov, Vladimir, 175
names and nicknames, 173,
    180–84, 211–12, 275
Nasser, Gamal Abdel, 70
Native Americans, 257, 269
Natural Born Killers, 227–28
Nazis, 78, 174, 177, 231
  see also Hitler, Adolf
Necessity (Ananke), 45, 46, 139,
    192, 193, 208–13, 214
  of death, 212–13
  derivation of term, 209
  escape from, 211–12
  nature of, 208–11
Neoplatonists, 9, 95
Nietzsche, Friedrich, 110, 165
nihilism, existential, 55
Nilsen, Dennis, 234, 236, 239
Nixon, Richard M., 71, 205–6,
    208, 251, 265–66, 267

Nkrumah, Kwame, 70
North, Oliver, 261–71
North, Roger, 254

oak tree, 276–79
obsessions, 7, 161, 162, 170–71,
    202–3, 246
omnipotence, fantasies of, 17, 22
omniscience, fantasies of, 224–26
"On a Certain Blindness in
    Human Beings" (James), 97
O'Neill, Eugene, 103
oracles, ancient, 276–79
Origin of Satan, The (Pagels), 247
Original Sin, 54–55
Ortega y Gasset, José, 124, 145
Othello (Shakespeare), 235

Pagels, Elaine, 247
paradeigma, 9, 45–46, 98, 135, 138
parental fallacy, 20, 22, 49, 63–91,
    125, 161, 162, 195, 227
    act of conception and, 64
    ancestors and, 83–91
    love styles and, 142–43
    psychopathy and, 227–28, 229,
        230, 237
    reactive causality in, 67
    vertical causality in, 74–77
    see also fathers; mothers
parental fantasy, 160, 161–71
    absence of, 165–68
    in collective social code, 168
    rebellion against, 168
parentalism, 87, 227
parents, 62
    deconstruction of, 74–80
    goal of, 83
    mentors vs., 163–64
    misallied, 64–66
    mythical, 85–86, 88, 90, 276
    as selected by daimon, 8, 49–50,
        64–66, 70, 74, 157, 162

Parry, Sir Charles Hubert, 185
patriarchy, 80–81, 133
Patton, George S., 103
Paul, Saint, 109, 240
Peary, Robert, 23, 26
Peck, M. Scott, 244–45
perception, imaginative, 113–27,
    163
    see also mentors
perfection, goal of, 48
Persinger, Louis, 17
personal ads, 121–22
phrenology, 152
Picasso, Pablo, 7
Plato, 12, 95, 109, 142, 157, 158,
    162, 211, 279
    democratic equality vs., 271–74
    Myth of Er related by, 7–9, 39,
        44–46, 47, 62, 67, 135, 138,
        139, 193, 208–9, 224, 252,
        274
Plomin, Robert, 132, 151
Plotinus, 8, 12, 46, 110, 139, 191,
    214, 242
Plutarch, 31
Poincaré, Henri, 100
Pollock, Jackson, 24–26, 35, 39,
    102
Ponce, Charles, 44
Porter, Cole, 68, 159, 160
powerlessness, fear of, 239–42
prodigies, child, 16, 29
projection, 88, 141–42, 234,
    239
Proust, Marcel, 103
providence, 13, 153
pseudologia fantastica, 179
psychology, 3–40, 111, 243, 254
    anxiety raised by, 38, 161
    beauty neglected by, 35–40
    calling vs., *see* calling
    case histories of, 31, 33, 88,
        240, 252–53

childhood traumas emphasized
in, 3–4, 24, 207, 227–28,
229, 230, 237
children and, 13–14, 29–31, 33,
34–35
compensation theory in, 22–27
concretistic theories of, 240
contemporary language of, 37
deadening effect of, 36
developmental frameworks of,
5, 7, 30, 77, 207
deviations feared by, 30, 270
diagnosis in, 30–31, 32, 125,
244–45
drug treatment in, 21, 30, 125,
150–51, 168, 231, 247, 270
exceptional people and, 31–35
father in theories of, 227
French rationalism in, 151–52
imaginative perception vs., 122,
125–26
interpretations in, 22, 24–25,
36, 93
intuition in, 97–98
methods of, 11, 38, 92, 145
mother-based theories of, 64,
75–76, 77–80, 88, 161
motivation theory in, 27–29
polarities in, 128–29
soul ignored by, 10, 92
statistical emphasis in, 5, 11,
30–31
time and, 5, 6–7, 34
victim mentality engendered by,
6, 54, 77
withdrawal into fantasy and,
20–22
see also environmental factors;
genetic factors; parental fallacy; symptoms, dysfunctional
psychopathy, criminal, 9, 27,
214–48, 260–61
character traits in, 234, 241, 244

childhood manifestation of,
224, 228–29, 237, 238–39,
246–47
childhood trauma in, 227–28,
229, 230, 237
choice mechanism in, 232–33,
244
concreteness of, 240–42
conventional explanations of,
227–38, 244–45
cultural attainments present in,
242–43
death and, 217, 218, 219,
223–24, 228–29, 230, 246
demonic call in, 234–38, 239
derangement of senses in,
236–38
emotional coldness in, 217, 223,
230, 237, 239
fear of powerlessness in, 239–42
general characteristics of,
222–38
genetic factors in, 229–30, 231,
246–47
group mores in, 231–32
information vs. knowledge in,
224–25
karma in, 233
malicious pleasure experienced
in, 235
parental fallacy and, 227–28,
229, 230, 237
prevention of, 238–48
rituals and, 242–48
sexual component of, 219, 220,
234, 235, 239–41
shadow in, 233–34, 239
society affected by, 215–16, 225,
239, 246–48
see also Hitler, Adolf
Puccini, Giacomo, 104
puer eternus, 281–83, 285
pulp fiction, 159–60, 162

Quispel, Gilles, 271–72, 274

Radin, Paul, 133
Raubal, Geli, 220
Rauschning, Hermann, 218
Reiter, Mimi, 220
religion, 11, 90, 91, 94, 126–27, 247
monotheism, 133
Republic (Plato), 7, 44, 273
Revelation of St. John, 79
rhesus monkeys, 74–75
Ricoeur, Paul, 236
Rilke, Rainer Maria, 81–82, 110
Rimbaud, Arthur, 119–20, 243, 281
Rime of the Ancient Mariner, The (Coleridge), 160
Roiphe, Anne, 167
Romans, 9, 46, 96, 139, 242, 259, 279
Romanticism, 5, 9, 17, 29, 32, 39, 97, 122, 145, 157, 158
romantic love, 128, 140–47, 199, 228
Rommel, Erwin, 23, 26, 39
Roosevelt, Eleanor, 20–22, 27, 40, 156
Roosevelt, Franklin D., 71, 74, 114, 120, 121, 161, 265
Roosevelt, Sara Delano, 71
Roth, Philip, 186
Rothenberg, Albert, 27
Rousseau, Jean-Jacques, 87, 157, 158
Rowe, David, 75, 78
Rowe, James H., 114, 121
Royce, Josiah, 97

Sackville-West, Edward, 175
Sade, Marquis de, 219
Salinger, J. D., 175
Sallust, 46

Saroyan, William, 102–3
Schelling, Friedrich, 99
schizophrenia, 131–32
schooldays, 101–8, 209, 243
"self," 144, 257–58
Self-Consciousness (Updike), 184
Sereny, Gitta, 228–29
Seroff, Victor, 178
shadow, 233–34, 239, 266–67, 268
Shakespeare, William, 229–30, 235, 253, 258
shamanism, 9, 93, 274
Shank, Anna B., 117, 122, 243
Shaw, George Bernard, 187
sibling rivalry, 23, 25, 148, 201
Simenon, Georges, 60, 173
snake, symbolism of, 59
Socrates, 42, 43, 121, 181, 203, 258, 284
Somé, Malidoma, 277
soul, 8–10, 11, 42, 60, 92, 96, 153, 159, 203, 206–7, 260
conceptualization of, 9
descent of, 43–47, 62
lack of, 214, 223, 250
location of, 46, 129
lot chosen by, 8, 39, 44–46, 49–50, 138, 139, 162, 191, 193, 205, 208–9, 252
mediocrity of, 250, 256, 273–74
postnatal forgetting by, 8, 46, 57
spirit-, 180, 257, 269
see also daimon
soul trees, 276–77
Speer, Albert, 221
spermatikoi logoi, 278
Spinoza, Baruch, 99, 126
Spitz, René, 79
Spock, Benjamin, 125
Stefansson, Vilhjalmur, 23, 26, 36

Stein, Gertrude, 104, 115–16, 123
Steiner, Rudolf, 157, 158
Stevens, Wallace, 39
Stevenson, Robert Louis, 97
Stierlin, Helm, 229
Stokowski, Leopold, 184–86, 189
Stone, Oliver, 227
Stravinsky, Igor, 72, 74, 186
sublimation, 24–25, 162, 241
Suetonius, 31
Sweden, 92–93, 162
Symbolism of Evil (Ricoeur), 236
symptoms, dysfunctional, 43, 202
    in children, 13–14, 29, 30–31, 33, 34–35, 85, 107–8, 125–26, 247
    as compromise formation, 53

Tagore, Rabindranath, 101
Tarantino, Quentin, 160, 227
Tarnas, Richard, 129
Tchaikovsky, Peter Ilyich, 252
teleology, 196–203, 204, 207
Teller, Edward, 69, 125, 250
telos, 196–97, 202–3
Tempest, The (Shakespeare), 229–30
Terkel, Studs, 252
Teutonic Mythology (Grimm), 278–79
Thackeray, William Makepeace, 175
Thompson, Dorothy, 156–57
"throwness," 55
Thurber, James, 125, 205, 207
time, 6–7, 34, 39, 46, 47, 95, 99, 139, 225–26, 239
Tolstoy, Leo, 97
traditionalism, 132, 133–34
traumas, childhood, 3–4, 24, 207, 227–28, 229, 230, 237
Truman, Harry, 71, 161, 164, 251, 267

Turnbull, Andrew, 64
Turner, Tina, 73–74, 182
Twain, Mark, 172, 177, 179
twins, 128, 130–36
    doppelgänger and, 179–80
    individuality in, 130–32, 140–41, 142, 143–44
    shared vs. unshared environments of, 131–32, 137–38, 147–50
    sibling rivalry in, 148
Tylor, E. B., 9

Ulysses, 44–45, 252, 279
unconscious mind, 12, 25, 152–53
Undset, Sigrid, 101, 118, 121
Updike, John, 184

Van Fleet, James, 105
Vasari, Giorgio, 31
Ventura, Michael, 84
Verdi, Giuseppe, 252
victim mentality, 6, 54, 77
Voltaire, 193

Waite, R.G.L., 217
War Against Children, The (Breggin), 30
Washington, George, 114–15, 120, 164
Watkins, Mary, 79, 170
Watson, James, 130
Watznauer, Hermann, 119, 122
Wayne, John, 172–73, 192
Wells, H. G., 104
Welty, Eudora, 175–76
West, Rebecca, 157
Whitehead, Alfred North, 83, 91, 99
Whitman, Walt, 97
Wilson, James Q., 232
Wilson, Woodrow, 71, 125
Wind, Edgar, 33

Wings of Desire, 255
Winnicott, D. W., 79, 88
Wizard of Oz, The, 51
Wolfe, Thomas, 64–66
wolf motif, 218–19, 239
Wood, Catherine, 118, 120, 121
Woollcott, Alexander, 157
Wordsworth, William, 96–97

World War II, 78–80, 107, 215–22
   see also Hitler, Adolf
Wright, Frank Lloyd, 68, 74, 159
Wright, Richard, 159

Zeitgeist, 233, 235
Zohar, 43–44
Zola, Emile, 103

ABOUT THE AUTHOR

JAMES HILLMAN is a psychologist, scholar, international lecturer, and the author of some twenty-odd books including *Re-Visioning Psychology, Healing Fiction, The Dream and the Underworld, Inter Views,* and *Suicide and the Soul.* A Jungian analyst and originator of post-Jungian "archetypal psychology," he has held teaching positions at Yale University, Syracuse University, the University of Chicago, and the University of Dallas (where he cofounded the Dallas Institute for the Humanities and Culture). After thirty years of residence in Europe, he now lives in Connecticut.

ABOUT THE TYPE

This book was set in Bembo, a typeface based on an old-style Roman face that was used for Cardinal Bembo's tract *De Actua* in 1495. Bembo was cut by Francisco Griffo in the early sixteenth century. The Lanston Monotype Machine Company of Philadelphia brought the well-proportioned letter forms of Bembo to the United States in the 1930s.

PERMISSIONS